Hermaphrodite Logic

Hermaphrodite Logic

A History of Intersex Liberation

Juliana Gleeson

V

VERSO

London • New York

First published by Verso 2025
© Juliana Gleeson 2025

The manufacturer's authorized representative in the
EU for product safety (GPSR) is LOGOS EUROPE,
9 rue Nicolas Poussin, 17000, La Rochelle, France
contact@logoseurope.eu

1 3 5 7 9 10 8 6 4 2

Verso
UK: 6 Meard Street, London W1F 0EG
US: 207 East 32nd Street, New York, NY 10016
versobooks.com

Verso is the imprint of New Left Books

ISBN-13: 978-1-83976-093-8
ISBN-13: 978-1-83976-094-5 (UK EBK)
ISBN-13: 978-1-83976-095-2 (US EBK)

British Library Cataloguing in Publication Data
A catalogue record for this book is available
from the British Library

Library of Congress Cataloging-in-Publication Data
A catalog record for this book is available
from the Library of Congress

Typeset in Sabon by Biblichor Ltd, Scotland
Printed and bound by CPI Group (UK) Ltd, Croydon CR0 4YY

Contents

Preface

As I was preparing the final drafts of this book, two new controversies brought the question of irregular sex into the spotlight. First, hostile responses erupted around the victory of Algerian boxer and Olympian Imane Khelif in a strikingly one-sided welterweight match at the Paris 2024 Summer Olympics. Her competitor, the Italian Angela Carini, was so outmatched that the bout lasted only forty-six seconds. A former policewoman, Carini broke convention by refusing to shake Khelif's hand after their fight. While there was no evidence that Khelif had been either assigned or raised male, her victory was invalidated after her Olympics performance brought to wider attention an earlier internal ruling by the International Boxing Association to exclude her. (The IBA is not recognised by the International Olympic Committee, which oversees the Summer Games and which cleared Khelif to compete in their own ruling.) Rumours spread that Khelif's blood work was unusually rich in androgens, and that her chromosomes were 'male'.

Intersex advocacy group interACT released a statement supporting Khelif, while noting that she had not been confirmed as having any variation (despite much lurid speculation).[1] For the rest of that summer, many who had never previously passed public comment on intersex affairs issued statements either backing or denouncing Khelif. Many argued the treatment of the North African boxer by her defeated white Italian opponent drew from obvious colonial legacies. Months later, Republican Donald Trump's campaign for presidency repeatedly turned on Khelif, attacking the boxer in both stump speeches and crude social media posts. As election day neared, the campaign issued an official statement: 'There will be no men playing in women's sports when we're elected.' While it's unclear what authority the US president enjoys over the IOC, this rhetoric resonated with American voters – Trump enjoyed a blowout electoral win over Kamala Harris (winning all seven swing states).

Later that year, the Zambian footballer Barbra Banda was voted the BBC's 2024 'sportswoman of the year'. As well as captaining the Zambian national team, Banda had been the highest-scoring Olympian across Africa, establishing her ranking among the best football players in the world. Banda's victory attracted the ire of J. K. Rowling – a renowned children's novelist turned monomaniac social media agitator. Implying Banda's appearance revealed her to be a male, Rowling declared that the BBC had decided to 'spit directly in women's faces' with their decision (despite the winner being decided by a popular vote).

Both cases featured photos of the athletes shared suggestively by critics, with no clear sense of where the limit for ruggedness would be for a female boxer or footballer. Both Banda and Khelif are African athletes, with those hounding them drawing on centuries of 'racial scientific' association of black women with manliness and excessive vigour. These appeals to the athletes' appearance had a shared intent: they were outside the natural order – not merely sportswomen, but not women at all. And while no firm evidence was presented to prove this – a look would suffice.

These controversies followed from the sex scrutiny faced by South African track runner Caster Semenya (whose career chapter 4 of this book follows). Similar to reporting on Khelif, early coverage of Semenya included heavily repeated footage of a weeping white opponent. But since the worst of the accusations Semenya resisted so resolutely, a powerful 'anti-gender' movement had arisen – which proved equally anti-intersex. For those who style themselves as opposing 'gender ideology', sex is held to be a straightforward matter: all can be sorted decisively either male or female. Rather than being up for discussion, determining sex is the preserve of objective clinical science. Medical professionals are best placed to diagnose those with sex developmental 'disorders' (out of the natural order expected from mortal women, and into the preternatural order of Olympians). Yet this view quickly gave way, as fantasy novelists, sports pundits, and political candidates supplanted doctors in determining 'true sex'; as soon as male and female could be set scientifically apart, the crudest eyeballing tests were quickly validated.

The savage pillorying of these African athletes is another case not of objective disagreement, but an evident *anxiety* around sex. This anxiety is widespread, but most readily exploited by the political right. Rather than drawing a firm red line, the anti-gender tendency picks distractedly at a scab. Sex is an immutable constant, yet its boundaries have to be strictly protected. Sex can be judged at a glance, yet boys could easily be raised as girls. Is sex more complex than that? Undoubtedly. Genetics, anatomy and hormonal flows, appearance and identification – these can never map onto two neatly divided buckets – much as Trump and Rowling might like them to. Many intersex people are obliged to live in the fuzzy boundaries between whatever 'common sense' partitions happen to be drawn.

But this book is not simply a celebration of complexity. Intersex people were first brought into full public view not by a biology seminar, but a political movement. In the 1990s, even social scientists working on intersex topics as part of their academic careers quickly found themselves drawn into a budding human rights movement. (And what else could these feminists have done?) Intersex liberation worked not just *educationally*, but *politically*. Politics is the art of pressing the uncommitted to pick a side. And making things simple enough to be widely understood is often the practical business of liberation. To that end, the intersex movement brought to light injuries routinely done to those born with irregular sex traits. These violations were typically performed by doctors who worked with minimal oversight, and without meaningful follow-up. Intersex children's parents were then instructed to conceal their variations from them – a convention that hid intersex people away from others, and from themselves. But from 1996, those subject to these non-consensual treatments began speaking up publicly. At first, a tiny number of people began to openly share accounts of horrors done to them in cold, clinical contexts. But their numbers swelled: today intersex liberation is a worldwide movement, bringing together advocates from across continents. Understanding the birth of this movement in the '90s is necessary to grasp what sex will become in the rest of the twenty-first century. Intersex people are not just the victims of the worst sexism – their advocacy challenged our established shared understanding of sex. It highlights how male/female only ever appears as a simple split through contrivance: scar tissue, hormonal injections, and hidden records.

With that in mind, whose side are you on? Many readers will already have found themselves intuitively siding with Khelif and Banda, against their often-racist critics. More generally, many have some vague sense that intersex people have been mistreated. Far fewer appreciate how this understanding was the consequence of a hard-won struggle. The aim of this book is to fill in those blanks – *Hermaphrodite Logic* provides a new history of the political movement that made intersex people widely understood as people at all.

First, let us take a look at what (and who) the old order of sex left hidden away.

Introduction

Sex Is Expressive

What is revealed when we unveil lifelong acts of concealment? How can we shed a disguise that was never our own? Discussions of intersex variations usually begin with a scrupulous definition of the physiological traits in question: their morphology and origin, the normal sex division and then deviations from it sketched out, accompanied, perhaps, with a list of examples. Intersex variations are usually described as posing a 'challenge' to social mores around sexual difference (i.e., that male and female be held apart, immutably and insuperably split physically, while complementary culturally). But much of this upset is engendered not by bodies themselves, but through spirited arguments intersex people have launched for themselves.

So let's try again.

In the 1990s, a small circle of intersex people came to know one another. They met face-to-face and connected over the internet, then a novelty. As they shared life experiences, medical records, and perspectives on the injuries and neglect they endured, a consensus quickly arose. They found shared struggles, caused not solely by widespread ignorance of ordinary human variance in reproductive development, but also by the ways they were *known over*.

At worst, this meant surgeries and other treatments carried out with little regard for their consent, then usually concealed from them. Medical jargon and vague euphemisms had been layered along with scar tissue. The truth of their treatments was left impossible for intersex people to reach individually, but was easily recognised when they gathered. Then, they could intuitively grasp the shared wounding and neglect that previously isolated intersex people.

Intersex advocates first focused on dialogue, both internal and external, by raising consciousness at small community meetings and on purpose-made web forums, and developing connections with allies in feminist scholarship and the LGBT movement. Intersex advocacy of this era had an unmistakable imprint of both the feminist and lesbian and gay movements, drawing slogans, strategies, insights, and approaches from earlier twentieth-century counterculture – and merging with the prevailing provocative style of the '90s queer campaigners.

After just three years of underground consciousness-raising organisation, intersex advocacy took to the streets. Advocates began confronting the professionals responsible for the harms done to intersex children, with the hope that future generations could be spared the developmental injuries that so many in the movement had endured.

This new view of intersex variations would come to upset the history of sex. The perceived neutrality of clinical wisdom and guidance would be suddenly put into sharp dispute. As the new century began, doctors struggled to reassert their claim to predict the likely lives of intersex youth. The intersex movement's agitation and self-advocacy had unsettled conventional models of clinical care for those born with innately atypical physiologies (an eccentric and sinister research field, known as sexology). Since the nineteenth century, intersex anatomies had been split between those exhibiting 'spurious hermaphroditism' and 'true hermaphroditism'. By the twentieth century, breakthroughs in understanding of the gonadal tissue meant that most intersex people were declared 'pseudo-hermaphrodites'. Causing ramifications for both legal verdicts and clinical treatment (or mistreatment), doctors held that skilled examination by trained professionals could offer a final verdict of each anatomy. Apparent ambiguity would yield to designations of either male or female.

While medics had styled themselves as the managers of sex, by the twenty-first century their efforts were subverted and sabotaged by their patients. Before the 1990s, an overbearing imperative guided clinicians in their attempt to draw sharp dividing lines between male and female. They followed the belief that causing confusion in either parents or children would disrupt a delicate developmental sense of 'psychosexual identity'. This orthodoxy peaked in 2000, when the American Academy of Pediatrics claimed each obviously intersex infant posed a 'social emergency'.[1]

Through the rise of the intersex movement, a set of resistant communities drew together an understanding that rivalled this pathologising outlook. While focused on the lifelong harms to intersex children done by clinicians, these circles of intersex advocacy also posed a new ethical challenge: they pushed against reducing the whole life and experience of intersex people to clinical terminology. They introduced arguments and appeals to life experience that would never have been gathered by conventional clinical researchers. By the end of the '90s, groups opposing this medical violence were founded in North America, South Africa, Germany, and Uganda.

These challenges focused on prevailing conceptions of intersex variations, and the mistreatment of those with them. Thanks to the limiting imperative that sex be differentiated (by whatever means seemed necessary), harm had become just as standardised as neglect was widespread. Prior to their protests, intersex people had appeared in medical literature from a remove: while reports from physicians examining them would occasionally feature a quote from their testimony, physicians' reports were more likely to include photographs (often taken without clear consent from the person being recorded). These clinical photographs were used for professional training, and often displayed anonymised subjects with blanked-out eyes – reminiscent of classical depictions where hermaphrodites were portrayed as sleeping.

But in the 1990s, an awakening took place. The world was forced to come to terms with intersex people not only as flesh to be managed, but as humans: those who offer reasons, and respond to them. As one early movement video's title had it: '*Hermaphrodites Speak!*' Now the medical profession was forced to encounter intersex people not simply as an educational resource, or patients to manage, but people – who *argued with them openly*.

Sex assignment had previously been a process filled with conceit and secrecy. Now it was dragged into public debate. Many in the medical profession found this development upsetting. Medics had previously taken themselves to be in the business of 'managing' intersex people: they performed surgeries and issued scripts to parents, guiding how disclosure might be tastefully attempted with curious relatives. The birth of intersex advocacy unsettled this management process, calling into question whether it was the business of parents and medical professionals to express their unease through 'correcting' intersex children. In response, the medical professions projected their disturbed emotional state back onto intersex people. Terminology reducing human variation that had once been dubbed 'hermaphroditism' now came to reduce intersex to a set of 'disorders'.

The intersex movement took two phases: From the 1990s, intersex advocates appropriated for their own purposes medical terminology originally intend to 'manage' their childhoods. Then, from the mid-2000s to the present, they refused use of a new clinical idiom that framed their physiologies as defined by 'disorders'. In their attempts to uproot this normalised and devastating order, intersex advocates purposefully refused to limit themselves to sympathetic appeals. As well as relating a unique set of experiences, intersex advocates have provided a distinctive form of *reasoning*. To grasp why the medical profession found itself at a loss to respond to the intersex movement, we have to understand the arguments they presented in their own terms and context.

Given the harsh and standardised abuses done to intersex people, it would be forgivable for advocates to have responded with a formless howl, or to have limited themselves to personal or emotive accounts. Although confessional writing was necessary by the end of the 1990s, intersex advocates were fully integrated in the global intelligentsia. Accordingly, their writings and campaigning were characterised by a playful flair, a sardonic wit, and judicious coldness. With these efforts, intersex advocates achieved not only moments of revelation unearthing previously suppressed experiences – they also sustained a *logical* account that recounted both harms done to them and their baselessness in any justifiable framework of therapeutic care. The advocates' unflinching ambition and determination in the face of adversity have to be acknowledged in order for this movement to be understood.

Intersex advocates' success in challenging the routine harms done to them by the medical profession can be understood in specific context of those struggles. The history of intersex liberation is as much a story about rationality as it is about bodies.

Beginning in the 1990s, previously scattered testimonies began to erupt into public view. This moment saw the formation of *rational* communities: dialogues that could refashion sex distinction in light of the harms done by existing processes for managing sex. In particular, these intersex communities would frustrate the need for finality clearly felt by most medics. Clinical professionals usually assert sex as a natural kind, possible to extract in whatever instance from a series of tests around measurable features. Today, they frame themselves as the arbiters of orderly sex, against its 'disorders'. But in truth, clinicians are *only one* community that deliberates on intersex questions.

The testimony shared by intersex advocates reshaped not only our sense of our own *experiences*, but also what anyone can soundly *infer* about sex. What the intersex movement has presented to the world is not only passion and pathos in the face of obvious injustice, but reasoning too. Intersex advocacy is not only a challenge but a gift: these advocates have advanced rational claims that each of us may listen to, repeat, and adopt for our own ends. To dismiss these revelations is to overlook the true shape of sex.

This book charts the phases of the intersex movement from the 1990s to the present: its emergence in dialogue with feminist scholarship and countercultural consciousness-raising, its rupture around the impasse of either focusing on 'patient advocacy' or defying clinical authority openly, and finally the ascendancy of intersex liberation as it has played out via the language of human rights. Along the way, this movement did not have any one voice. Intersex liberation spoke out through a cacophony of experiences, converging around moments of shared harm and glimpses of 'eros' not yet freed. This book will allow these divisions within the movement to play out.

Existing studies of intersex history have often satisfied themselves with focusing primarily on the development of *clinical concepts*. This approach risks mirroring exactly the reduction of intersex variation to a set of developmental problems. It's inevitable that accounts which focus primarily on medical archives and arguments risk relegating the actual life struggles of intersex people to background noise. Instead, the *ethical life* of intersex people needs to be captured just as the 'ethical question' posed by intersex variation demands our acknowledgement. How can a life worth living continue despite the harms and neglect intersex people routinely live through? Some of these habitual harms done to intersex people have required political agitation to overcome, and others do still. The intersex movement arises from that specific ethical impasse and has posed questions we all have to account for when speaking about sex.

This book concerns a breakthrough that's still in motion, and easily misunderstood. The routinised nature of harms done against intersex people has required urgent political organisation. The intersex movement not only pushed to recover from developmental injuries already done, but also to cause a historical rupture that would prevent such harm to future generations. Since the mid-'90s, this movement has urged us all to consider sex anew. That struggle remains far from won. But with care, we can sharpen our view of intersex liberation as it has unfolded so far – specifically the logical breakthrough these groups achieved. The intersex movement is not only a network of political organisations, but also an intellectual breakthrough that has already reshaped the history of science, and sex.

Sex Is Expressive

'Sex' is usually taken to name the immutable, natural, fixed, and unerring, in contrast with the vicissitudes and vagaries of gender. Yet we find ourselves drawn to speak of this obvious truth explicitly. Rather than clarifying easily, our terms and dividing lines appear to vary. This leads quickly arguments over its limits. We even find ourselves denouncing those who disagree with our conclusions as defying the obvious, undeniable contours of nature herself.

What the intersex movement has shown us is that sex is altogether more varied, less predictable, and more flexible than many would prefer to assume. Rather than splitting the world tidily into male and female, sex is an enfolded complex involving genetics and epigenetics, hormone levels and receptors, anatomical features and physiological processes, juridical classifications and emergent phenotypes, each found in alignment or apparent conflict differently by differing observers.

Even the three simplest categories of sex become complex and overlapping when examined, namely sex as *legal* status (how state documents record sex and confer rights); sex as *apprehended* (how sex characteristics are interpreted and perceived); and sex as *reproductive capacity* (what kind of role an individual can play conceiving children – if any).

We can see that indeterminacy between divergent senses of 'sex' is unavoidable. Attempts to simplify sex tend to produce still denser tangles. And worse still for those hoping for some unified concept of sex to serve us as a sturdy foundation, still more confusion results from any attempt to 'tighten up' even *one* sense of the word. Reduce sex to the idea that 'anyone with a Y chromosome is male', and some 'males' will give birth. Sex makes a fool of those who wish to treat it *strictly*. It's this potential for *dissonance* that twentieth-century medics attempted to manage.

Whatever alignment of the several senses of sex is pursued through professional means, whatever arts or technical skills are deployed to solve this problem, *indeterminacy* will remain sex's overarching feature. While many hope to split sex neatly into two, at least three sets of problems are always in play for the purposes people have in mind (legal, apprehension, reproduction). Individual markers that are seen as reliable are grasped on to (whether a passport says 'M' or 'F', whether a full karyotype test would return with a 'Y' or without), even if these may not match any disputed point in question.

So sex exists scattered across each means of assessment, while those discussing sex usually crave decisive answers. Rather than smoothing over the partition of sex between male and female, medics gave away more of their own subjective involvement in these matters than they probably ever intended to. Expressiveness cannot be smoothed over completely: passivity or objectivity can simply be poses adopted.

In an argument that will by this point be fully familiar and follows directly from the rhetoric of the earlier intersex movement, feminist scholar Katrina Karkazis states that 'intersex embodiments are congenital variations that are disabling not so much in that they present functional limitations, but rather in that they ... violate cultural standards'.

More to our point, Karkazis argues that medical replies to these violations convey a broader disdain for irregular anatomy which intersex people are prone to encountering within clinical contexts: 'Whether cast as corrective, reconstructive, or cosmetic, such a surgical reshaping of atypically embodied persons has the effect of limiting human variation and *expressing a disdain* for atypical bodies.'

In their 'management' of intersex variations, the medical profession has focused primarily on eliminating variations that are visible. Clinical care has exceeded the limits of therapeutic treatments, often directly working against them. As Karkazis correctly notes, a discomfort evidenced by clinical interviewees toward unusually large clitorises appeared despite the lack of any corresponding risk to these children's overall health.

At times, doctors have clearly sided with one of these faces of sex over others. For instance, doctors typically encouraged castration for those born with complete androgen insensitivity syndrome (CAIS), given that most people *apprehending* these patients would take them to be girls or women. Yet doctors made no effort to retain sex in the reproductive sense, and often removed gonads perfectly capable of secreting feminising hormones (in the case of CAIS adolescents, testosterone, converted through aromatase), necessitating patients' lifelong reliance on doses of exogenous estrogens. This routinised harm demonstrates the real shape of 'management' in the medical sense: introducing medical problems in the guise of avoiding them.

The very motivation of doctors moving to *stabilise* the consistency of sex demonstrates its complexity. Far from sex establishing itself through a wholly natural unfolding, particular human variations appear to inspire predictable bouts of panic, or at least unease. These result in active remedies that are therapeutic first and foremost to the shaken cultural expectations and delicate psyches of those overseeing them.

This complexity does not mean that sex is infinitely malleable, or impossible to draw together into any coherence. And it certainly doesn't suggest that sex is a 'realm of freedom' for any given person, however well trained or informed. The tidings of the intersex movement are clearly not altogether hopeful ones – what is clear from this liberation struggle is that sex is far more expressive than *self*-expressive.

While sex is not fixed in place, its mutability appears to differing degrees at different moments. Our bodies do not operate as we want them to, and they do not reflect only our own will. Those who wish to impose on us have often found ways and means to reshape our anatomy, posture, resonance, and how we are seen. The expressiveness of sex resides not just in our self-realisation, but also in moments of coercive direction. Domination can play out permanently, or can be undone only at a cost. Those around us express through us, we encounter orders that have their way with us.

Clinicians and parents too often find themselves imposing an *overwriting* that cannot then be easily lived through. Far from bringing intersex people in line with the ordinary, aggressive interventions and prevailing clinical neglect create unique needs. But denouncing the current state of medicalism is not the limit of intersex liberation. The intersex movement has attempted to overturn governance of the atypical by harmful and narrow norms while also celebrating the ethical exuberance which exists *despite* the ingrained, everyday expressions of contempt towards intersex variations.

Sex's expressiveness appears as a double entendre: First, sex is the interplay between hormones and genetics. And equally, sex is the need to *explicitly address* this chaotic process in ways that seem to make sense of it, draw firm lines in tidal sands, and establish arbitrary conceptual cut-offs. For that reason, sex is expressive but not *self*-expressive: it is asserted by ourselves, about ourselves, but it's also a set of limits overseen by lawyers, medics, priests, fathers, mothers, parliaments.

The revelation provided by intersex struggle shakes the social foundations of clinical and household authority. But in return, it provides us with a new style of thinking: a sarcastic calm in the face of truisms veiling indignity and atrocity. Listen to the unbearable message delivered in deadpan, the uncertain audience drawing a sharp intake of breath. A dark laugh follows at harms done by a brutal twofold split, opening a stranger shape for life beyond it.

Intersex struggles reveal the *lability* of sex itself, as well as the damage done by attempts to reduce the full scope of human variation into terms suitable for clinical oversight (the management of atypical bodies). As much as the intersex movement is shaped by variations themselves, it is also shaped around the need to end and reverse routinised harms enacted by those professionally trained to perform (and then justify) them.

The intersex movement has shown the world that the expertise of the medical profession has its limits. These limits are demonstrated by doctors' lack of comprehension of certain modes of knowledge, including the testimonies of those they refuse to listen to. In their continued refusal to acknowledge (never mind respond to) this revelation, medics have only reinforced the salience of the intersex movement. Even in the face of the sophisticated accounts of medicalisation as a psychological palliative for parents presented to them by protesters from 1996 onwards, medics have resisted overhauling treatment of intersex people with curt dismissals. The core sense of clinicians as the 'managers' of atypical sex was never relaxed.

As a group, intersex people are often regarded as a perfect 'case in point' proving the variability of sex. But what's revealed by their political struggle is not the varied natural shape of sex, but how it takes shape through both technical intervention and rational discussion.

Put another way, the story of sex as expressive is the story of the twentieth century. Between the term 'hormonally intersex' being coined in 1915 (by German–Jewish biologist Richard Goldschmidt), and the Boston protest of 1996, eight decades reshaped our grasp of natural human distinction irrevocably, in ways that are still being made sense of.

By the early twentieth century, sex's suspension or procession was found to route through a constellation of glands and receptors known as the endocrine system. What had previously been considered a set of natural forms (which could be reduced through gelding) became understood as constituted across time through the body's cyclical regulation.

The pre-eminence of endocrinology followed on from later nineteenth-century investigations of thermoregulation, which had discovered the body's most basic sex hormones through sometimes brutal animal experimentation. These breakthroughs began with the identification of stress hormones, via the removal of adrenal glands from dogs. By the later 1940s, the first stress hormone treatments would appear, along with commercial production of cortisone (first used for reducing inflammation caused by rheumatoid arthritis). But crude injections of androgens extracted from animal gonads began decades prior: the pioneering theorist of thermoregulation, Charles-Édouard Brown-Séquard, gave his name to the Brown-Séquard Elixir (drawn from dog and guinea pig gonads), extolling its rejuvenating properties despite many of his peers denouncing his recklessness.

By the early twentieth century, isolation and categorisation of sex hormones was in full flow. Estrogens, progesterone, and androgens were extracted and isolated, and by the mid-twentieth century came to be mass fabricated in bioidentical forms through plant extraction. At this point, medical experimentation with the reproductive anatomy (and replacing it) developed at a rapid pace. Some experiments were attempted on consenting adults (for instance the partial vasectomy operations performed across the 1920s–30s by Austrian endocrinologist Eugen Steinach and his followers, who attracted celebrity clients seeking 'rejuvenation'). Other experiments blended with the history of eugenics.

The merger of animals and humans appeared throughout this process: one of the earliest commercially available estrogens, Premarin, was drawn from the urine of pregnant horses. Experimental surgeries also attempted to merge animals and humans. One of the most popular examples was the 'xenotransplantation' of monkey glands into humans, performed in interwar France by the fraudster Serge Voronoff. While seen as eccentric even for this emboldened era of biochemical experiments, Voronoff enticed the elite men of Paris, and later teams of English football-ers, to receive grafts of animal gonads, supposedly to provoke virilisation. Voronoff's poorly sourced claims were so well known as to inspire a cocktail, the Monkey Gland.

While a rich opportunity for scam artists, this process of com-parative understanding allowed both for new forms of domination of animals by humans, and a fresh grasp of their relative com-monalities. True to this context, the term 'intersex' came to be understood originally through a paper by biologist Richard Goldschmidt. Goldschmidt's reference to 'hormonally intersex' humans appeared in passing, with the paper more focused on the prospect of androgens accounting for the bull-like behaviour and appearance of freemartins. Similarly, understanding of human chromosomes followed on from studies of fruit flies, which like humans were found to have XO and XXY chromosomes. A flurry of studies of fruit flies across the 1920s led to speculation that sex determination resided in the second X or first Y chromo-some.[2] This culminated in Canadian researcher Murray Barr publishing a study where he and his co-author claimed to have developed a staining technique suitable for determining the sex of a cat through treatment of their neurons.[3]

Through pseudo-bulls, fruit flies, and cats, human sex was always grasped in comparison to other animal species, with responsive speculations linking humans into the rest of the nat-ural world. At every turn, breakthroughs in understanding animals opened new horizons for grasping (and correcting) our own sex.

The chemical components that were discovered across the early twentieth century revealed a newly manipulable and muta-ble face of sex. But each of these discoveries also allowed more detail and texture to be added to accounts that cast sexual dif-ference as only 'natural'. While these discoveries sketched out the lability of sex, at each turn more conservative voices could redeploy any measurable difference as evidence for the immuta-bility of social division. This ambivalence was pronounced by the mid-twentieth century, with the mass availability of hormonal contraceptive treatments causing a set of controversies around fertility and autonomy that continue to rage into the twenty-first century. At once the mutability of human sex became undeniable, and insistent voices presented sex as not unsettled, but decisively demonstrated by science.

At this point, apparent 'fixes' to intersex variations were available, and because the medical community treated variations as an emergency, these 'fixes' were considered justifiable even when patients were still too young to have any say in the desired outcome. Intersex variations were taken to be a human iteration of the same indeterminacy that was found in rich variety throughout other species. Yet this new view did not lead to ready acceptance. Instead, the finer understanding of sex seemed to suggest surgical solutions to whatever social problems intersex people faced. If visible from birth, these 'conditions' were best treated by being tucked and stitched out of view.

From the 1990s onwards, it fell to the intersex movement (aided primarily by feminist and LGBT allies) to show the limits of these attempts to 'correct' sex. Intersex advocates emphasised the failure of medics both by any humane standard and on clinical science's own terms. While sex *is* responsive to human alteration, a limit was clearly apparent in the form of scar tissue: lacking the full elasticity of typical skin, reduced in responsiveness to the touch, and beyond the ordinary that doctors had pursued. As intersex advocates emphasised, the very procedures intended to eradicate intersex physiques from view often served to emphasise them, while treatments framed as therapeutic caused ailments from infertility to lifelong trauma. What afflicted intersex people was less their so-called conditions, and more their 'management'. Interventions against intersex people were not applied in context of the historic transformation of sex that was underway, but much more narrowly. Attempts to reform these treatments usually refined existing techniques, rather than questioning basic assumptions. Equally, external efforts to curb the inhuman aspects of clinical sex interventions were reduced to 'bioethics': honing and improving clinical decision-making referencing moral considerations, rather than calling into question whether such deliberations should be performed at all.

The intersex liberation movement's character was set by its moment in history. Intersex consciousness emerged at a moment uniquely hostile towards internationalist politics (the 1990s). Nevertheless, by the 2020s the movement had expanded, with worldwide campaigns against the harms done to intersex people (chiefly focusing on abolishing routine clinical violence).

While focused on the needs of a small minority, the intersex movement has presented a range of arguments of universal concern. Anyone fighting for liberation can learn from both the campaign's victories and the limits of the approach taken by the intersex movement. Some hostile clinicians have been quick to cast the intersex movement as group of excessively passionate and extremism-driven 'zealots', but the movement tends to show a more sardonic and conciliatory face. Intersex liberation writings include everything from gallows-humour cartoons to exhaustive reports for NGOs. Both registers strive for a kind of coldness that belies the passionate involvement of these advocates. Instead of relying on pathos, intersex movement writings have tended towards quieting obvious reactions and sublimating traumas into displays of wit, meticulousness, and sang-froid.

In this way, the intersex movement is a child of its time: by the end of the twentieth century, bodies of knowledge that were once firmly professionalised became distributed in new and unlikely ways by the boom of information technology. Encyclopaedias dissolved into memes, and autodidacts on a mission came to challenge the claims of authorities who had once buttressed the medical profession (using their own terms). Who could claim to be an 'expert' on intersex matters shifted from a foregone conclusion to an open question. This book follows what the intersex movement made of this opportunity.

Making sense of the intersex movement's *political* history requires an expanded vision. The movement has cast up material across forms, from medical journals to memoirs, archived websites to philosophical essays, and scans of movement VHS tapes to medical records, pastiches, poems, and polemics. All this and more allows the full shape of sex to come into view.

In other words, today the history of sex is as much as anything a *movement* history, one that demands taking the *intellectual breakthroughs* of intersex people themselves just as seriously as any concept devised to manage them. As quickly as the harms done to intersex people were shared between them, whether this really *was* their inevitable fate became unclear. Organisation between intersex people and the feminist movement not only upset the order of sex, but allowed us to picture another world, and a new science. The harms done to intersex people are not akin to polishing a mirror (to see the true, twofold reflection of sex), but rather an *active expression* of prejudices that cannot be justified. If distinguishing sex is a process, it's one we can set into a new form. If sex is expressive, we can choose new songs to sing.

While the harms of 'normalising' intersex people have been made routine, they are the work of history: they can be known, and ended.

1

The Boston Revelation

Unknown to those inside, demonstrators appeared outside the 1996 annual meeting of the American Academy of Pediatrics (AAP) in Boston, Massachusetts. As one of the protestors would later recall, it was 'a glorious fall day, the like of which you can only find in New England, under a crackling, cloudless sky'. A clearinghouse for US healthcare professionals (including nurses and social workers) observed by more than seventy-five reporters, the AAP's gathering was intended to allow physicians to network and keep abreast with the state-of-the-art practices in children's healthcare.[1] But two intersex speakers leading the protest held a less conventional set of intentions for the event.

The protest's two ringleaders came dressed for dystopian sci-fi, or a hardcore show: both had short hair and glasses; one was dressed in a black bomber jacket over denim, the other in a dark green ankle-length trench coat.

After some confusion about whether they would be given an opportunity to participate in the event itself, the demonstrators improvised by picketing the enormous Boston Convention Center's front approach. Flanked by members of Boston's local transfeminist group, Transexual Menace, and their allies from across Massachusetts, the group provided a spectacle quite unlike typical proceedings for a paediatricians' conference. They unfurled a banner reading 'HERMAPHRODITES WITH ATTITUDE' and picketed the event for the rest of the day. Many paediatricians brushed them off, but the sense of spectacle was unmistakable. The pair conversed with the minority of passing professionals who'd stop to speak with them, sharing both their personal stories and statistics collected from interviewing other intersex people. They delivered talks to press cameras, fielded questions from intrigued reporters, and held aloft placards with slogans including 'SILENCE=DEATH' and 'KEEP YOUR SCALPELS OFF INTERSEXED KIDS!!!'.[2]

As they explained, both of the protest's leaders had themselves sustained harms from the same wing of the medical profession that gathered there to discuss their own clinical 'best practices'. This made their appearance picketing the event's threshold both strategically obvious, and personally demanding.

Who was this strange pair? And who were the 'intersexuals' of North America, whom they claimed to speak for? Certainly, some of the clinicians who encountered them could be forgiven for being at a loss as to their origins. For others, their presence would serve as an entirely unwelcome reminder of an ongoing professional struggle that was now entering a new era.

The two advocates, Max Beck and Morgan Holmes, were both members of the Intersex Society of North America (ISNA). This advocacy group had been founded three years prior, originally as a discrete underground organisation (organising through emails and newsletters, with members often publishing under pseudonyms). Their AAP picket was the group's first appearance on the streets. Yet even in these early days, the arguments they offered were both clear and sophisticated. Drawing on accounts of the aftermath of medical treatments on many intersex people (including Beck and Holmes themselves), the protesters charged the US medical establishment with routinising devastating procedures. Genital-damaging surgeries and gonadectomies targeted those too young to offer meaningful consent – often with unclear therapeutic aim. While framed as emergency treatments to correct pressing congenital defects, intersex procedures aimed to sooth cultural anxieties (on the part of both clinicians and parents). Rather than preventing harm, they caused lifelong numbness. Rather than improving aesthetics, they imposed scarring and permanently delimited any future options.

So how had this set of hard-hitting arguments (still so unfamiliar to their targets in the medical profession) been developed? Why did a group advocating for reforms intended to shape a more humane clinical practice draw on a mythological allusion mixed with a hip-hop reference to declare themselves 'Hermaphrodites with Attitude'?

The origin story of the Intersex Society of North America is a strange one. Announced in 1993 through a letter to the editor of academic journal *Sciences*, the group really began three years before, with a dialogue between intersex advocates and sympathetic academics. The story of intersex advocacy's earliest history is inextricable from the history of feminist scholarship, and especially critical readings of scientific approaches to sex. By the 1990s both the *conceptual* and *ethical* bases of clinical practice towards those deemed abnormal had been called into question. Publications attempting to form a clinical understanding of *hermaphroditism in humans* had been extensive throughout the twentieth century, but from the post-war period this conceptual understanding had come to converge around a narrow set of precepts. Rather than demonstrating the unavoidable diversity of human formation around reproduction, intersex variations came to appear as a crisis awaiting a sequence of technical *solutions*. Terms that otherwise became associated with feminists ('socialisation', 'assignment') here were deployed to support a stiflingly conservative set of prognoses and corresponding surgical treatments of newborn bodily forms. Feminist scholars dissatisfied by appeals to the 'normal' now targeted what had previously been a lockstep medical orthodoxy.

In other words, the 1990s saw a narrow set of professional standards brought to light and unsettled. The previously homogeneous attitudes of these medics came under new scrutiny by feminist readers of the medical and biological sciences. And it would be these clinical orthodoxies that would be disturbed in the century's last decade, as critical feminist perspectives on the sciences began to reach new audiences. One community which these viewpoints swiftly reached was intersex people themselves.

The upsetting of medical consensus around intersex by feminism began in 1990, when a psychology professor, Suzanne Kessler, published her essay, 'The Medical Construction of Gender: Case Management of Intersexed Infants'. As well as consulting the manuals and textbooks used by paediatricians, Kessler interviewed six medical professionals (three men and three women) who specialised in the 'management' of intersex infancy and childhood.

What Kessler's interviews revealed was a lockstep orthodoxy around a basic set of principles, intended to align the embodied state of children with a coherent sense of self, variously known as 'psychosexual orientation' or 'gender role/identity'. Doctors saw it as their task to gauge the 'optimum gender of rearing' (OGR), taking measures to ensure that the assignment stuck in place through means that could shock outsiders: intersex infants were routinely scheduled for surgical castrations, partial clitorectomies, or extensive suturing and remodelling of the penile shaft.

Doctors overseeing this 'assignment' process sometimes voiced unease around whether the barrage of testing (chromosomes through karyotypes, hormone levels, anatomical measurements . . .) truly guided their determinations. Far from being founded in decisive clinical science, these decisions were based more on crude assumptions, and eyeballing genitals. Medics would base surgical decisions on speculations concerning intersex children's potential integration in locker rooms or performance in marital bedrooms.

The relationship between clinicians and parents was a deliberately lopsided one. As Kessler observed, medics seemed to prevaricate between second-guessing the attitudes of parents and selectively drip-feeding them information. Their manipulative control of knowledge would shrewdly direct outcomes toward surgeries that legally required parents to sign off. Their explanations of intersex variations to parents would swing between vague euphemisms and unfamiliar clinical terms. Doctors used this sleight of hand anxiously: behind the scenes, they'd admit freely to the lack of sound empirical basis for evaluating the ramifications of intersex procedures. To Kessler, many physicians specifically voiced discomfort with the lack of follow-up studies. While follow-up was required to fully grasp the lasting impact of procedures on delicate tissues and the highly subjective functions under consideration, few doctors would keep in contact with intersex children as they became adults. So both medics and parents would be left balancing unknown harms done against sexist fantasies. Rather than citing rigorous studies or the testimony of living intersex adults, doctors would describe fraught moments that might be encountered in 'the locker room' (or much later in life, the marital bed). Under pressure, clinical science was narrowed to fragments of fantasy.

Despite these doctors' admissions of practical ignorance, none interviewed broke from a monocultural set of attitudes towards the acceptable shape of sex. Kessler noted that these physicians shared as their operative assumptions a consensus unusual in the history of science. The orthodoxy installed by the end of the twentieth century ran as roughly as follows: 'Gender and children are malleable; psychology and medicine are the tools used to transform them. This theory is so strongly endorsed that it has taken on the character of gospel.'

In particular, these physicians seemed guided by concerns that ambivalence across time would cause 'confusion' for children, and that certain surgeries (especially partial clitorectomies) would prevent difficult interactions around male/female sex between parents and their young children. Put simply, they feared those left raising a boy without what was undeniably a penis might struggle, and experience either subtle or obvious breakdowns. An accompanying phobia of childhood transition ensured that these doctors felt highly pressured to issue a definitive guess, and that it stood permanently (without active input required from the intersex child).

In other words, as one doctor interviewed by Kessler had it, surgeries removing gonads and erogenous tissue were framed as easily justified on the grounds that parents 'need to go home and do their job as child rearers with it very clear whether it's a boy or a girl'. Answering relatives, friends, or strangers who inquired, 'Is it a boy or a girl?' was taken to be the first order of business for any parent. Kessler's introduction of intersex surgical norms continued: 'In the face of apparently incontrovertible evidence – infants born with some combination of "female" and "male" reproductive and sexual features – physicians hold an incorrigible belief in and insistence upon female and male as the only "natural" options.'

In other words, physicians had taken on the duty not only of comprehensively understanding breaches of sex's natural order, but also, when necessary, serving as its enforcers.

Even infants and children whom doctors perceived as clearly male or female could receive surgical fixes to dubiously defined problems. For instance, hypospadias urethral formations (where the slit appears along the underside of the shaft, rather than the tip of the glans) were 'corrected' on the assumption that boys should be able to urinate standing. In the worst cases, these hypospadias reroutes would trigger a succession of procedures that would attempt to correct the damage done by previous ones, generating an accumulation of scar tissue and urinary dysfunction that would need further procedures to mitigate, causing further scarring. Doctors dubbed these patients 'hypospadias cripples'. In this way, even a variation medics would classify as relatively minor and 'unambiguous' could trigger a procession of interventions that attempted to set sex into place (while by any practical assessment, only further undoing it).

What kind of a challenge could feminism pose to this process of attempting to both classify and correct the natural shape of sex?

While sharing psychological training with the most influential figures in sexology (chiefly John Money), Kessler was an outsider to this field of clinical practice, and chose a feminist journal, *Signs*, to publish her write-up. This meant that her research extracted the norms of clinical treatment (and mistreatment) of intersex children from their expected context. Pulling this sexological 'orthodoxy' into broader view would be crucial to undermining its claim to providing neutral 'management' of intersex. For the rest of the 1990s, the clinic would continue to lose its assumed authority. As the workings of medics came into wider comprehension by those outside the profession, evaluations of their achievements and atrocities came to follow a more fragmented standard.

After the publication of Kessler's research, the clinical abuse of intersex children came to broader attention among feminist scholars. But her *Signs* essay was not only read by potential allies to the intersex movement. Although she wasn't present in person at the Boston protest, the early history of the intersex movement can't be easily understood without the figure of Bo Laurent. An MIT graduate, Laurent had spent her early adult life as a tech worker, graphic designer, and Japanese translator at Hiroshima University – before suffering a breakdown in her mid-thirties. Having experienced lifelong genital numbness and scarring, she finally confronted her family. Her mother informed Laurent that for the first year of her life she'd been raised as a boy. Then at eighteen months, Laurent's doctors had advised her parents to authorise a partial clitorectomy, to enable raising her as a girl. Her mother informed her that the surgery had been successful, before admitting Laurent had been left mute for the next six months. Remarkably, the doctors even suggested Laurent's parents move to a new town so that their child could simply be introduced as female, rather than reintroduced (they obliged).

Not yet out publicly, Laurent focused on private letters, adopting the movement moniker Cheryl Chase for her published work and appearances. While coming to terms with her own history, and beginning to connect with those who shared it,

Laurent also approached an array of researchers re-examining the 'management' of intersex. Early into this process of networking, Laurent wrote to Kessler, sharing her own experiences and offering to further contextualise the psychologist's research. At this point, Kessler had not interviewed intersex people subjected to surgeries – but she proved eager to correct this. By 1996, Kessler had become a key institutional ally for ISNA: she helped Beck, Holmes, and Laurent hijack a surgeon's colloquium run by the Mount Sinai Health System in NYC, and filmed their intervention denouncing harms done by 'corrective' operations. In 1998, Kessler published her first book, *Lessons from the Intersexed*, which balanced the stated intentions of surgeons with testimonies from intersex people who'd directly endured their handiwork.

Through this interplay of the earliest intersex organising and feminist scholarship, a new challenge to clinical reason percolated. ISNA's foundation was officially announced when Laurent wrote a letter to the journal *Sciences* replying to feminist biologist Anne Fausto-Sterling's provocative essay 'The Five Sexes'. A skilful and sardonic contribution to feminist approaches to science, Fausto-Sterling's essay drew on the existing body of sexological conceptualisations to propose that sex was now widely understood as divided between five categories: male and female (as before); ferms and merms (those with reproductive capacity that appeared incongruent with their broader phenotypic appearance or hormonal regulation – what clinicians then referred to as 'pseudo-hermaphrodites'); and herms (those with mixed reproductive systems, such as ovotestes or streak gonads). While this fivefold configuration was quite obvious (Fausto-Sterling argued) and a matter of medical consensus, it had been wilfully obscured because so few intersex children had escaped surgical traducement into one of the 'Platonically' acceptable shapes (male or female). Science had come to a more sophisticated understanding of sex, only to immediately attempt elimination of three known forms.

Fausto-Sterling's breezy style and conceptual radicalism still confounds readers today (especially those unaccustomed to women delivering darkly humorous monologues). While according with the emerging scholarship exposing intersex treatments as a pressing moral concern, 'The Five Sexes' presented its case with a satirical bite: readers were offered a tongue-in-cheek taxonomy all too easy to take at face value. This style subverted the typical contrivance of authorial objectivity: only by acknowledging Fausto-Sterling's *wit* could one reveal her true point.

Laurent wrote both private and public responses to Fausto-Sterling's 'Five Sexes'. Laurent's letter to the editor of *Sciences* introduced two arguments that were repeated across early intersex advocacy. First, that intersex variations were persisting features of those born with them which had defied surgical 'correction', and second, that clinicians were abandoning a responsibility to collect comprehensive longitudinal studies on their work's direct consequences:

> Surgical and hormonal treatment allows parents and doctors to imagine that they have eliminated the child's intersexuality. Unfortunately the surgery is immensely destructive of sexual sensation and of the sense of bodily integrity . . . Follow-up of adults to ascertain the long term outcome of intervention is conspicuously absent.

Laurent continued to charge the medical profession with deploying gender to justify dehumanising treatments. These surgeries aimed not to provide therapeutic support, but to fit human variety into a cruel bifurcation: 'Intersex specialists are busily snipping and trimming infant genitals to fit the Procrustean bed that is our cultural definition of gender.'

In classical mythology, Procrustes was a bandit who stretched and chopped his captives apart to fit across an iron bed – lending his name to the application of arbitrary standards to which precise conformity is forced, at whatever cost.

But the letter was not only critical of clinicians. Replying substantively to the original 'Five Sexes' essay, Laurent challenged Fausto-Sterling's assertion that intersex people who escaped surgery were vanishingly unusual (Laurent by this point had met several). She implicitly linked Fausto-Sterling's notion of merms and ferms with a 'gonadal determinism'. Strikingly, Fausto-Sterling's reflection on the essay's history in 2000 conceded that its provocation came at the cost of retaining gonad-centrism.[3]

But beyond these public disagreements, what did this point of contact amount to?

Closing her reply to Fausto-Sterling, Laurent invited 'intersexuals' to join her new group, aiming both to provide support and set about 'documenting our lives'. The newly founded Intersex Society of North America nominally drew together intersex people from across the United States and Canada. But de facto much of the group's work became based online (making them much farther reaching). Retreats were hosted at Laurent's farm in Northern California (home of so much twentieth-century counterculture), drawing newly out intersex people from across the world.

Kessler's earlier breakthrough had been published by a dedicated feminist journal, while Fausto-Sterling's 'The Five Sexes' appeared in a mainstream science journal. That provided a broader audience for her snarkily delivered insights, and extended a platform to Laurent. Another consequence of this intervention into the 'mainstream' of scientific discussion was that Fausto-Sterling quickly drew hostile replies from the defenders of sexology's orthodoxy – including from John Money himself. Forty years after his epochal essays 'An Examination of Some Basic Sexual Concepts: The Evidence of Human Hermaphroditism' and 'Hermaphroditism: Recommendations concerning Assignment of Sex, Change of Sex and Psychologic Management', John Money's last book, *Gender Maps*, attempted to address the challenges posed by feminist science scholars to the previously dominating system of intersex 'management' he had been widely credited as installing.[4] The eccentric field of 'sexology' would continue to find itself in a rearguard position for the rest of the decade. A direct confluence between a new school of critical feminist readings of science and the new networks of shared experiences and solidarity between intersex people had started to rewrite our understanding of sex. This began openly in 1993.

For her part, Fausto-Sterling quickly became immersed in intersex advocacy, which further fuelled her conceptual radicalism. As well as public debate with Kessler (who took objection to the 'five sexes' model's retention of the genitals as the crux of correctly sexing humans), Fausto-Sterling's arguments were honed through extensive dialogue with early intersex activists. References to ISNA appear throughout her 2000 book *Sexing the Body: Gender Politics and the Construction of Sexuality*, which features both direct testimonies from intersex people and accounts of their organising to end widespread mistreatments.

For their part, intersex advocates echoed the arguments made by feminist researchers like Kessler and Fausto-Sterling: sex was asserted through a process shaped by the narrow, heterosexist demands of the clinical gaze. Feminist research extracted the work of sexologists from its original context (into journals, websites, and other publications not directly controlled by clinicians). This left room for political challenges to the legitimacy of those deemed experts of sex. Regarding both the procedures and core concepts of the medical profession, researchers found themselves horrified by the treatment of intersex patients (even before having knowingly met any). As intersex advocates and academics entered into dialogue, the standardised horrors intersex children faced were brought to light.

Internally, between 1993 and 1996 the Intersex Society of North America focused on consciousness-raising. At this point, an organisation which included all intersex variations was still a novelty. After meetings with older groups focused on advocacy for specific intersex variations, Bo Laurent had concluded that

ISNA should be an organisation with a broader remit, drawing together all those subjected to clinical 'management'. The hope for the new group was to challenge the overall system that treated atypical sex formation as an emergency or developmental mishap – an unwelcome anomaly best resolved through surgeries, accompanied with shamed silence.

To recruit members, the group set up an email list (advising members how to join this still-novel technology in their newsletter) and advertised in the personals of San Francisco's gay press. They soon became known across the United States and beyond through word of mouth and internet searches. In ISNA's video *Hermaphrodites Speak!*, one attendee recounts being sent a photocopy of the group's newsletter by a thoughtful friend. Reading through *Hermaphrodites with Attitude* (*HWA*) was a life-changing experience for them, 'ending the isolation' that had defined their life up to that point.[5] Many who contacted the group conveyed a sense of relief and surprise to connect with others who'd shared obviously overlapping experiences that had previously left them feeling 'freakish'. One can picture hundreds of such stories fuelling the group's earliest years of operation. This rapid expansion took advantage of newly popularised communication technologies and developing ideas following on from those already published by Kessler, Fausto-Sterling, and Laurent.

The intersex movement now adopted consciousness-raising circles, which had been a mainstay of earlier twentieth-century counterculture, to probe the basic order of medical harms and neglect done to them. The feminist movement in particular had used small, intentional meetings to pursue in-depth discussion of oppressive experiences between women. Feminist consciousness-raising had led to the collective recognition of ubiquitously experienced – yet previously unnamed – phenomena such as sexual harassment. Now intersex consciousness-raising drew together those whose treatment had previously consigned them to silence and solitude. The earliest intersex liberation movement focused on gathering, and breaking that silence. Many of the difficulties faced by those born intersex came to be understood as damage done by clinical violence, lifelong neglect, and isolation of those with atypical physiologies. Just as feminist organising had conjured the vision of a society beyond patriarchy, intersex self-organisation called immediately into question whether the harms intersex people shared between each other could ever be justified or permitted to continue.

From these intense, small-scale gatherings ISNA's early material drew a mordant and often sarcastic style. This material made heavy use of 'gallows humour', with accounts of experiences outsiders would probably find startling introduced dryly, or even with self-deprecation. Playful identification with medical terminology was commonplace, alongside personal reflections on stigma and trauma enacted by twentieth-century clinics and parenting. These early intersex movement writings bristled with the technical vocabulary that had restricted their understanding of their bodies and subtly led them towards self-perceptions of *irregularity* as *dysfunction*.

In this respect, intersex liberation was born very much of its time: the 1990s had seen a revival of the more hard line advocacy found in early GayLib. The 1990s saw the foundation of the first explicitly queer groups. Groups such as Queer Nation and the Lesbian Avengers would use slurs freely to hone their understanding of oppression, exhibiting a confrontational and vivid style. These groups were ambivalent about asserting and undermining shared claims to identity, making it clear that being queer was as much a question of political commitment as happenstance of birth. This confrontational tendency was inspired by the ongoing crisis of HIV/AIDS, as well as the continued prevalence of phobic street violence. The most relevant example for our purposes is Transexual Menace, whose Boston chapter directly supported ISNA in their picketing of the American Academy of Pediatrics. That group referred to themselves as a 'menace' in response to earlier mainstream feminist leaders' contempt for lesbians as the 'lavender menace'.

Each of these organisations favoured small-scale dedicated memberships over the broader (blander) coalitions necessary for lobbying via the Democratic Party or civil society NGOs. This seemed like an obvious organisational model for intersex liberation at a time when only a handful of people would publicly disclose their variation. The first two intersex protesters took measures to ensure their overlaps in strategy and style were unmistakable: one wore a 'Transexual Menace' T-shirt, the other held an ACT UP sign. When it emerged in the 1990s, ISNA was unmistakably stitched from the same fabric as the rest of later twentieth-century counterculture (in-jokes and all).

Even before their first demonstration, the cutting edge of '90s spirit was found in ISNA's ready use of slurs: their in-house publication was titled *Hermaphrodites with Attitude*, and their first VHS tape was called *Hermaphrodites Speak!* While Laurent had opposed Fausto-Sterling's use of the term 'hermaphroditism' in their exchange in *Sciences*, across the rest of the '90s the group clearly settled into a defiant and playful use of the word. (The name of the group's newsletter was a hip-hop reference to the pioneering Compton act N.W.A.). The question of slur reclamation remains a lively one both in intersex and LGBT circles – this book's title is an obvious example. But fluent use of slurs didn't exhaust ISNA's edginess. The inaugural issue of ISNA's newsletter (published December 1994) was a masterclass in edgy '90s herm counterculture. Beginning by apologising for the delays typical of self-publication, the newsletter continues, saying the group's mailing list 'now reaches intersexuals in five countries and in 14 of the United States'.

Celebrating Christmas in a brutal style, the front page also features a comic, which I usually refer to as the 'Mutilated Rudolph' (see Figures 1 and 2). The caption of the comic reports a 'disfiguring hypertrophy of the nose' (mimicking typical language actual doctors would use to discuss 'clitoromegaly'). The caption continues: 'an excellent cosmetic result was achieved', contrasting a picture

■ Intersex Society of North America ■

Hermaphrodites with Attitudes

Volume 1, Number 1, Winter 1994

$3

© 1994 ISNA
Free to copy and distribute

Welcome, readers!

Long promised, long delayed, but here it is. ISNA now has its own newsletter. I hope that many of you will contribute short articles, stories, poetry, and illustrations so that the next issue can be even more of a collaborative effort.

Who are we? In the 16 months since ISNA was founded, we have responded to hundreds of inquiries from intersexuals, therapists, educators, parents, physicians, academics, and journalists. The Intersex Society mailing list now reaches intersexuals in five countries and in 14 of the United States.

(continued page 6)

Case report
Will B. Dunn, M.D., FACS

The patient was a 2 year old reindeer (*Rangifer tarandus*) who was brought to the clinic by guardians for diagnosis of a disfiguringly prominent nose. Some even said it glowed. (fig. 1, left) Although no objective standards have been published for proboscal length in reindeer, it is a simple matter for the surgeon to judge.

Under general anesthetic, the offending tissue was excised and sent for frozen section microscopy. While awaiting the (continued page 6)

The Awakening
Kira Triea

I really awakened about a year ago, though I realize that my awakening has had many stages. Some time before the onset of memory, I awakened to the knowledge that I was different; when I was thirteen I learned that I was not "a boy"... I was actually "a girl." Now I know that I am an intersexed person.

Before this last year I rarely thought about sex, gender or relationships. My "hermaphroditism" was completely off limits as a topic for introspection, except in vague despondent moments when I would reflect to myself that "people like me" were just not able to become involved in relationships or have sex. I absolutely never entertained the notion that I would talk about my biological status with anyone... it was too dark a secret even for me to contemplate for very long. When I was thirteen I chose my sex in a game of binary roulette at Johns Hopkins and with that choice I accepted the implied vow of silence: "Don't ask, don't tell."

On February 28, 1993 something happened and I awoke, I don't know why. I experienced what I can only describe as a *constructive breakdown*. The intense awareness of my life and the implications of being intersexed ripped through my existence and the implosion hurt. I couldn't continue in school with my math and computer science degree; I was too busy crying and wondering and hurt-
(continued page 6)

Figure 1 (*A, left*) Note disfiguring hypertrophy of nose. (*B, above*) Post-surgical aspect. An excellent cosmetic result was achieved.

■

Figure 1.

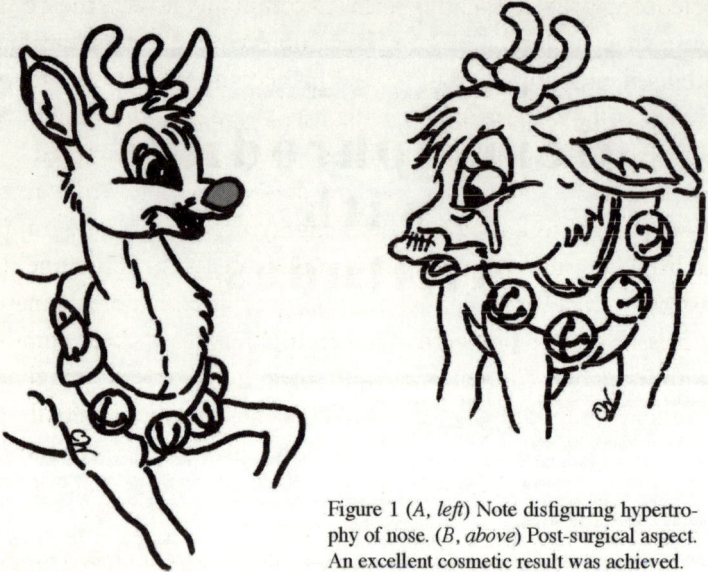

Figure 1 (*A, left*) Note disfiguring hypertrophy of nose. (*B, above*) Post-surgical aspect. An excellent cosmetic result was achieved.

Figure 2.

of a weeping and stitch-scarred reindeer with a picture of the bounding, smiling reindeer in its pre-surgical state.

The Mutilated Rudolph embodies a rhetorical strategy used by the earliest intersex advocates: sardonic mastery through appropriated medical terminology. This jargon was placed in a new context that directly undermined its original authority. We can call *HWA*'s appropriation of the technical terms and dry style of medical institutions "90s Edgy'.

Playing off the desiccating bedside manner of medics, this comic extends well beyond crude shock tactics and was one way the intersex movement developed self-consciousness. An external observer may be horrified to witness the treatment routinely meted out to intersex humans alluded to here; perhaps all the more so because the subject is a cutesy cartoon animal. But for an intersex reader, the image could open a moment of familiarity. These depictions allowed intersex people to counterpose their position against those who dominated them (parents, medics, societies at large). Repeating terms of command, now in their own voice, they undermined how faux 'objective' presentation had stabilised violations against them. This account of harms sketched a vision of how these offences against intersex children might be repeated across coming generations – or forcefully disrupted.

The work of early intersex advocates was avant-garde: arguments that would appear in dry, lengthy academic monographs published decades later appeared in punchier form sometimes in passing, with a sardonic shrug. At other points, arguments made by Kessler in her pioneering research paper reappeared unmistakably in a bleak, comedic guise. In the reindeer comic, imagined commentary by a physician highlights the arbitrary 'eyeballing' tests clinicians typically resort to: 'Although no objective standards have been published for proboscal length in reindeer, it is a simple matter for the surgeon to judge.'

Coldness of the kind displayed in *Hermaphrodites with Attitude* provided a high-stakes parody: while the professed 'objectivity' of medical examinations and reports was meant to solidify authoritative posturing, these advocates parodied the dehumanising treatment they had been subject to with the very terms used to justify it. Nineties edgy rhetoric sharpened its satirical bite by cladding itself in the idiom of management. Allowing for the cynical mockery of those relatively empowered, as well as a tacit denigration of their claim to command, this style was so ubiquitous in early intersex advocacy that those deploying it may have done so by reflex. Advocates used this edginess to cool their rage at ingrained incompetence and inane justifications for lifelong harms done to them.

The cynical humour and transformative insights birthed from intersex liberation's consciousness-raising circles were recorded in *Hermaphrodites Speak!* (1997), a short documentary filmed with technical support from trans historian Susan Stryker. This footage captured the first international gathering of intersex people at North Californian counter-cultural retreat Isis Oasis ('A Retreat Center and Animal Sanctuary guided by the Divine

Feminine'). The fledgling intersex advocates met in summer 1996, several months before ISNA's street debut. In *Hermaphrodites Speak!* we see Bo Laurent take the role of interviewer, calmly teasing responses from those attending. The 'hermaphrodites' voice powerful and mixed emotions at overcoming a lifetime of isolation, now surrounded by other intersex people:

> 'Are you a hermaphrodite with attitude?'
> 'I'm a hermaphrodite with major attitude!'
> (*Cheers*)

As the video continues, an advocate remarks that the meeting (and those like it) had assuaged a previous sense of seclusion: 'Before, what I felt was an identity of isolation, mainly. So changing that to being mirrored by people.' Another remarks on an adult encounter with a doctor who was horrified they'd escaped surgery, and clearly had no interest in providing emotional support, but instead 'wanted to fix what she saw as a technical abnormality'.

Another member of the group reports being told by their parents that their ovaries did not develop. (In reality they had been diagnosed as a 'male pseudo-hermaphrodite' with under-developed testes.) They summarise: 'Basically they encouraged me to believe the doctors had lied to me.'

Laurent quickly replies: 'Doctors lied, to you?' The exchange later continues, each taking their turn to adopt a facetious obliviousness or quote the doctors responsible for their medical harms:

> 'I remember them removing my penis, when I was five . . .'
> 'They *removed your penis*?'
> 'Oh I'm sorry, I mean it was an "overly large clitoris"!'
> 'They *removed your clitoris*?'
> 'Well, they reduced it in size to "more closely approximate a normal female appearance".'
> 'Does it approximate a normal female sensation?'
> 'No.'

The sarcastic rhetorical charge of 'A doctor lied, to you?' provides both a moment of humorous bonding for all present and a tacit *clarification* of concealment between medics (or parents) and their injured patient. The same mock obliviousness reappears when Laurent asks the group whether their ill-treatment was based on their physician's lack of prior experience, or whether experienced specialists shared a similar sensibility. (Predictably, it was the latter.)

Self-consciousness formed as harms that had previously been experienced in isolation now came to stitch together newfound communities. This process was a delicate but powerful one, founded in commonality of harm across context and recognition of a shared position among those with human variations that were previously reduced to individual dysfunction and tucked out of view.

Hermaphrodites Speak! playfully derided the categories that the medical profession had developed to classify intersex people. One of the attendees claims that being born with a hypospadias (a urethral opening beginning along the underside of the penis, rather than the tip) makes him 'a *real* hermaphrodite, not like all you other fake hermaphrodites!', to raucous laughter. Across the '90s, this diligent and playful community-building achieved a form of reasoning that was resistant to the clinical logic which dominated the social condition of intersex people. This level of intersex advocacy began with revelations that played out between advocates before being brought to light for the rest of the world. The necessary precondition for 'taking to the streets' was a much longer process of networking and mutual support, which had continued for around three years prior to ISNA surfacing into full public view. From the outset, the Intersex Society of North America had been well connected with academics, from the biological sciences to history to bioethics. These ties quickly blended the careers of intersex scholars and their key allies: Anne Fausto-Sterling was on the committee of Morgan Holmes's MA defence, where Holmes and Bo Laurent also met in person for the first time.[6]

Morgan Holmes and Max Beck – the two ISNA advocates who took to the streets of Boston – were both part of the intelligentsia, if quite different parts of it: Holmes was a Canadian sociology researcher; Beck, a technical manager at a factory. Tellingly, Beck introduces his education level as measly, outlining his extended struggle to complete a university degree. That Beck felt bashful for 'only' having a bachelor's degree in natural science demonstrates that many participants in early intersex liberation were highly educated. (The highly educated have continued to be over-represented in the movement ever since.) It should not be surprising that early intersex liberation attracted the highly educated, given the fluency in medical terminology we've seen in early intersex movement writings and agitation. This social context influenced the strategy taken by the Boston protesters: Holmes explains that the reason the protesters took to the streets, rather than risking arrest by intruding into the meeting venue itself, was the threat of permanent deportation. (Being barred from US institutions could have derailed the Canadian academic's career).

Together, Holmes and Beck had previously been involved in a session with the Mount Sinai Health System surgeons. This draining outreach session had won unexpected support from medics, including an official statement calling for an end to non-consensual childhood surgeries by the Gay and Lesbian Medical Association. Holmes notes that several of the event's attendees who stopped to converse with them were familiar with that statement (perhaps tacitly outing themselves to protestors in turn by mentioning it).

But ISNA's campaigning had also recently experienced a major setback: in 1996, the United States introduced federal legislation banning 'female genital mutilation'. This was the result of long-standing lobbying by the US feminist movement, which had increasingly concerned itself with 'global' affairs. Despite ISNA's best efforts, explicit provisions permitting the genital cutting of intersex infants and children appeared in the bill, in contrast to the total ban of cutting endosex (non-intersex) girls. Legal protections against clitorectomies applied to relatively few US residents otherwise likely to perform *ritualised* cutting (almost exclusively migrant families from already marginalised minority groups such as Somalian Americans), and did nothing to prevent *routinised* harms performed as standard practice by America's medical professionals.

ISNA's failure to prevent explicit exemptions of intersex genital cutting from this federal bill demonstrated the limitations of behind-the-scenes lobbying for a new group still trying to break through to widespread public recognition. The step change after the Boston picket went some way to correcting that. It advanced a more open discussion of sexual difference, which had previously occurred mainly among 'intersexuals', away from public view (in closed web discussions and dedicated retreats).

So what arguments did these self-declared 'Hermaphrodites with Attitude' offer to expectant TV cameras? What interruption did they offer to the mass of physicians who passed their picket with bemusement or faux indifference? The speech that Beck delivered to media cameras pressed the decade's feminist insights home, posing a direct challenge to clinical authority. Beck compared the work of healthcare professionals to the collective knowledge shared between those with intersex variations:

> We understand intersexuality, not because we have studied the medical literature – although many of us have – not because we have performed surgeries, but because we have been grappling with intersexuality every day of our lives.
>
> We're here to say that those who would have us believe that intersexuality is rare cloud the issue by breaking us and separating us into narrow etiological categories which have little meaning in terms of our actual, lived experience.

With these words, Beck counterposed professional training (the raison d'être for the AAP's annual meeting in Boston) with the *practical wisdom* required of those who grappled with the visions that clinicians and parents had imposed on them. In simpler terms, Beck told the press and physicians what it was like to be intersex, and *known over*.

Beck's speech voiced a resistance to the division of intersex people into 'etiological categories' (splits intended to bring into view the *origin* of a disease). Intersex advocacy in the 1990s was first and foremost directed towards undermining the idea that intersex variations were a set of maladies that doctors would do their best to cure. Max Beck made this case by drawing on a term used by medical researchers:

> Intersexuality is assumed to be a birth defect which can be corrected, outgrown and forgotten. The experiences dredged to light by intersex support groups indicate that intersexuality cannot be fixed; an intersex infant grows up to be an intersex adult. This hasn't been explored, because intersex patients are almost invariably 'lost to follow-up' . . . Part of the problem is that we were lost to follow-up, and there were reasons for that. But we're here today to say we're back, we're no longer lost, and we'd like to offer some feedback.

For their part, the American Academy of Pediatrics made a hurried statement defending their best practices regarding clitoral cutting and castrations, where necessary, to firm up male/female designations. This was then sent out via fax to Holmes by a friendly journalist. While outraged in the moment, Holmes and Beck tactically benefitted from the opportunity to rebut the AAP's reply, point by point, and in front of media cameras.

Resist for a moment the urge to class this exchange of words (ISNA versus the AAP) as a conflict between activists and clinical scientists, or even between wounded victims and self-justifying perpetrators. What happens if we take this encounter as an exchange between different modes of reason? The hijacked host organisation's tone attempted to strike a note of sympathy and a certain resigned resolve: 'The Academy is deeply concerned about the emotional, cognitive, and body image development of intersexuals, and believes that successful early genital surgery minimizes these issues.' While it is touching that they were 'deeply concerned', such patrician sentiments are surely outside the remit of fastidious objectivity! Let's consider the *justification* offered to intersex advocates (and the watching world) by the AAP in 1996:

> Research on children with ambiguous genitalia has shown that a person's sexual body image is largely a function of socialization, and children whose genetic sexes are not clearly reflected in external genitalia can be raised successfully as members of either sexes if the process begins before 2 1/2 years . . . From the viewpoint of emotional development, 6 weeks to 15 months seems the optimal period for genital surgery.

While written as a defence of the AAP's best practice, this press statement was a confession note. Just as Suzanne Kessler had found in her 1985 interviews with medics, they 'considered a treatable condition of the genitals, one that needs to be resolved expeditiously'. Clearly by the mid-1990s, nothing much had changed.

The phrasing of the AAP's response to the opening salvo of intersex agitation contains some terminology which requires introduction: 'sexual body image' had apparently come to serve as a stand-in for the earlier sexological term 'gender identity'. By this point, talk of gender had already become something of a conceptual quagmire, now a central concern for feminist thinking and queer cultural production. 'Gender identity' itself had replaced 'gender role/identity', which had in turn been a development of the earlier 'psychosexual orientation'. What each of these terms revealed was the *inner sense* of attachment that physicians would reluctantly turn to when measurements deemed more 'objective' began to falter. While today associated with the feminist movement, the origin of the term 'socialization' in this sense lay in the so-called sexological practices of John Money.

John Money was a white New Zealander who'd migrated to the US to complete a doctorate as a clinical psychologist, dissertating on the treatment of 'hermaphroditism in humans' – a topic which preoccupied his career. While never trained as a surgeon, Money came to head deliberative teams that would decide the fates of intersex infants and children. Breakthroughs in paediatric endocrinology left much work to be done for enterprising medics overseeing the rearing and 'treatment' of atypical infants and children. The first of these outposts was the Psychohormonal Research Unit at Johns Hopkins University in Baltimore. Money's best-known works were collaborations: he co-authored a treatment protocol for human 'hermaphroditism' with the married couple Joan and John Hampson. Subsequently he developed his notion of gender role/identity with his successor at UCLA, Robert Stoller. Nevertheless, the uniform bedrock position of focusing on genitals (and especially imagined scenarios of parents and school peers observing them) came to be synonymous with Money.

Money's approach to intersex downplayed the importance of either chromosomes or gonads alone, and attempted to establish an analytic view of sex as reducible to five or six clinically observable characteristics. Money settled upon the notion of 'gender role/ identity' as a failsafe for this measurement of physical characteristics or measurable physiological process.[7] If the sex of a child could not be decisively measured, clinicians should make recourse to examining their behaviour, manner, and self-understanding. Informed closely by the cybernetics craze that then gripped the United States' post-war intelligentsia, Money spun out his work as an interactive model.[8] In this context, Money and his collaborators stressed the importance of early childhood 'socialisation'. The goal was to achieve a skilled technical harmonisation of cultural expectation and the wilder variance of human morphology. Concern specifically came to focus on how child-hood caregivers may respond to any apparent mismatch between the *assignment* of children as boys or girls, and their outwardly visible genitals.

What did this protocol, born from the unique historical con-ditions of the mid-1950s university hospital system, have to do with the AAP's defence of itself in the 1990s? *Everything.* It was Money's eccentric orthodoxy that the American Academy of Pediatrics still appeared to be fully wedded to in 1996. They would only further double down four years later in a 2000 statement that declared intersex births an 'emergency'. But what the AAP's first response to ISNA lacked in terms of sub-stantial rebuttal, it compensated for with direct admission that intersex advocates had correctly diagnosed the medical estab-lishment's normative commitments. While Morgan Holmes and Max Beck addressed the routinised harms inflicted on them and others like them, physicians fretted more over children's disordered 'body image'. Having started off as a fix for the failure of any one measurable marker to help sort the sex of patients, here gender reappeared as key for twofold sexed map-ping. (The body could be destroyed to save the image.) This faux sophistication came to serve as an ongoing justification for perpetuating the clinical harms intersex advocates agitated to end.

The appeal to surgeries as requisite for the 'emotional devel-opment' of intersex people may appear absurd on its face, given the obvious risk of traumatising children with genital surgeries, lifelong scarring, and loss of erogenous tissues. Yet, the doctors' confidence in their existing best practice would always appeal to earlier, more primitive, eras – bad and bygone days which they had surely moved well beyond: 'Management and understanding of intersex conditions has significantly improved, particularly over the last several decades.' The legitimacy of 'management' was clearly not in question as far as the AAP was concerned, only the quality. The vaguely asserted timeframe of 'the last several

decades' should also give us pause, given that systematic protocols of intervention for intersex children and infants had only
emerged in the United States in the 1950s. This 'narrative of progress' is one that medics, in defending their practices, stick to
closely up to this day.

In this light, Holmes's account highlights ISNA's relatively
young leadership at the time. For these advocates, who had been
born between 1950 and 1970, the AAP's claim that treatments
had been greatly improved by recent innovations seemed empty –
especially since it lacked detailed cases of procedures and treatments
that had been discarded as unnecessary. This puncturing of vague
assertions of 'progress' with concrete reference to continuity
(conceptual or practical) is fairly typical for academic work in
the history of science. But the protest forcefully introduced this
argument to a much wider audience.

With the conceptual foundations of their treatment protocols coming under close scrutiny, the challenge posed by Beck
and Holmes's protest was one that medics could only concede
to on their own terms, by calling for more data (i.e., more
funded research) while setting aside the criticisms of their
standard procedure as presented by the demonstrators. This
was strikingly non-responsive, given that the protestors argued
not only that they'd been 'lost to follow-up' but also that
research featuring intersex children had previously been harmful to them.

This book is entitled *Hermaphrodite Logic*, as this protest
cast a shadow over the idea of sex as experienced by those who
spoke out. It provided a lasting challenge to what any of us can
infer about sexual difference. When brought to the fore, this
moment in Boston is not only what it initially appears to be: a
struggle within the history of medicine (self-advocacy in the face
of flawed professional practice, rowdy activists challenging the
regular business of sex clinics). Beyond this kind of 'patient
advocacy', I see this dispute as one episode in the history of
rationality. One type of reasoning came to struggle against

another: clinical expertise was confronted with a form of testimonial authority which had somehow become alien to it. Rather than having their 'objectivity' undercut by passionate, impulsive activists, clinical professionals came into contact with another kind of coldness. Dragged into public debate, wrong-footed by their authority being unceremoniously stripped, these hapless medics took their turn to play victim. Their terms of art were mocked, as their psyches were suddenly and unexpectedly dredged into clear view.

So what type of logical argument did these advocates express? Most notable to my mind is a logic of *reversal* as used by Max Beck to account for the true work of medicalising intersex physiologies:

> When an intersex child is born, parents and caregivers are faced with what seems to be a terrible dilemma: here is an infant who does not fit what our society deems normal. Immediate medical intervention seems indicated, in order to spare the parents and the child the inevitable stigmatization associated with being different. Yet the infant is not facing a medical emergency; intersexuality is rarely if ever life-threatening. Rather, the psychosocial crisis of the parents and caregivers is medicalized.[9]

Here, Max Beck argues that intersex treatment ran through a *reversal* of appearances: while the AAP's official statement stressed the need to protect 'emotional, cognitive and body image development' – suggesting a delicate psychic need for radical treatments to avoid botched identification – Beck relocates the crux of surgical imperatives in the concern eased by surgical procedures.

This reversal argument was spelled out in Foucault-inflected style across the theoretical work of Bo Laurent's essay on intersex surgeries (published under the nom de plume Cheryl Chase), which closed a collection mostly focused on female genital cutting: 'Cutting intersex genitals becomes yet another hidden mechanism for imposing normalcy upon unruly flesh, a means of containing the potential anarchy of desires and identifications within oppressive heteronormative structures.'[10]

In this turn of phrase we can see equally the origin of intersex advocacy in the critical views of feminist thinkers, who following Kessler would come to understand intersex 'management' procedures in terms of heterosexism, and also the medical profession's perception of intersex advocates as 'unruly' extremists. While Laurent had been able to secure sterling allies for the nascent movement through extensive intellectual networking, she found that many others simply refused to provide a fair hearing. Many within the medical profession and beyond were simply unwilling to expand their basic conceptualisation of sex, spurning the insights revealed for them by those who'd never found themselves at home in a twofold split. The pathologisation of intersex people was not simply a pseudo-technical understanding of their physiologies, but a *legitimation* of parental unease indulged by medical professionals. This argument must have hit all the harder coming from someone wearing a 'Transexual Menace' T-shirt. Beck was open about his experience as an 'intersexual' and his transition: he appeared in the 1999 documentary *Gendernauts* alongside his wife, with the two discussing their personal trajectory from a lesbian relationship to an unlikely marriage. In 1996, coalitions between intersex advocates and other queer groups appeared not as a strategy to be argued for, but quite intuitively.

While the 1996 AAP annual meeting picket likely remains the ISNA's best-known action, it was also the proximate cause for a split in the group. A 2015 personal reflection by Holmes for an intersex movement website, titled 'When Max Beck and Morgan Holmes Went to Boston', includes a little-known aside detailing her departure (never publicly announced) from the Intersex Society of North America. Despite Holmes's version of the dispute never having received a public reply from Laurent, it can help us grasp the extent to which intersex advocacy is a contribution to the sciences *and* to reason. Although trans-national in aspiration, in reality ISNA was primarily based in the US and remained there until its closure in 2008.

While Bo Laurent had planned the action, she was conspicuously not present at the protest itself. Holmes attributes this absence to the fact that Laurent was not out as intersex at this time. (She was still using the pseudonym Cheryl for publications and the *Hermaphrodites Speak!* video.) Further, Holmes recounts how on the day of the protest she shared with Laurent her fears that (given the nature of the targeted event) she might run into the very surgeon responsible for her partial clitorectomy. As AAP attendees streamed past Holmes, she found herself scanning conference name tags for the name 'Jeff' (but thankfully didn't encounter him). After sharing these anxieties with her absent activist friend, Laurent, Holmes discovered a fabricated account had been shared with ISNA supporters over email. Although Holmes casts some doubt over the email's authorship, whoever wrote it claimed that the encounter with her surgeon that Holmes feared truly *had* taken place, leaving the activist sprawled in tears on the venue's entrance steps. After reading this falsehood about her own participation, Holmes writes that she dropped out of any further involvement with ISNA, without announcement. Explaining why this distortion of her testimony caused her to leave the group, Holmes makes the case for a colder approach to advocacy, which refuses pathos as a fuel: 'In the years since, I have not seen sympathy as a useful emotion to try to evoke, but rather prevail upon people's sense of logic, fairness and principles of human rights and autonomy.'

The '90s edgy style of early intersex advocacy was surely intended to cause a stir, and to cast doubt on the standing of the powerful to arbitrate social questions 'objectively'. But equally, Holmes's method was *not* to reduce these questions to the emotive. Once ISNA had the attention of the press and the powerful, they didn't speak through raw passions. They presented medics with perverse reversals of their conventional truisms, bolstered by both provisional statistics and harrowing anecdotes harvested from community interviews.

That Holmes split with the group following an embellished email shows the prominent role the internet had played facilitating community-building for those with intersex variations. As with most things during the 1990s, the group's claim to represent 'intersexuals' across North America was grounded on the new ease of transnational communication that the decade had brought. Writings from '90s intersex advocates make it equally clear that many of these connections were made online. Even following the moment of ISNA's in-person emergence in 1996, Max Beck's description of sharing a train ride with Morgan Holmes tacitly highlights the normalcy of web and telecommunications for the group:

> There's no describing the thrill, though, of all that work, all those phone calls, all those miles. Riding a clattering subway on a Saturday morning, seated beside another living, breathing, laughing, swearing intersexual, hugging near-strangers at unfamiliar airports, then riding back, together, defiant, determined, organized, to the heart of so much of our pain, so much of our anger, so much of our need.[11]

These references to breath, laughter, hugs, and swearing underscore that the typical form of intersex advocacy was remote. At first, intersex people congregated through purpose-printed movement publications and internet outposts. Online circles and friendships around variations were enabled by early search engines, chat rooms, and forums, which allowed intersex people to come to terms with their shared treatment in relative anonymity, before (sometimes) developing a broader perspective they could share openly. As one advocate put it during *Hermaphrodites Speak!* atypical sex was harder to raise in face-to-face conversations than in correspondence. Contrastingly, as an information-sharing protocol, the internet would distribute these experiences much more readily, puncturing the isolation which concealed treatment had imposed.

But as well as permitting *contact* across great distances (and especially over national borders), information technology breakthroughs permitted advocates to develop a formidable familiarity with clinical terminology and standard practices, despite physicians often working purposefully to obscure the nature of their treatments. Online resources allowed for dissemination of technical terms and basic definitions that had previously been more successfully hoarded through professional training. Jargon that had allowed medics the upper hand in exchanges with parents and patients became easily understood, and deflated. (In particular, the medical professions had long relied on use of clinical Greek and Latin to clad identifiable symptoms in a mysterious lexical veneer that reinforced their mastery.)

In other words, intersex advocates built up a familiarity with idioms originally intended to subordinate them. The movement converged around resistant concepts that quickly gained traction across a heterogeneous array of national contexts. But the '90s edgy style had obvious limits. Whatever the therapeutic value of black humour, this era of intersex advocacy provided no clear means *out* of a growing despair. It could show up the pretensions of clinicians, but emerged decades after the more ambitious moments of the New Left (such as anti-psychiatry) had fully receded.

Nevertheless, the intellectual legacy of intersex advocacy speaks not only to the decay of professional authority, but to the fact that passion-rousing wasn't the only goal of advocacy, even for the individuals who pioneered methods of foregrounding marginalised experiences. Rather than confine themselves to evoking pity, the advocates who made it to the streets sought a more thoroughgoing transformation in clinical practice.

So what does intersex advocacy's origins suggest to us today? Rather than the emergence of a discrete identity (the 'intersexual'), the earliest intersex advocacy was a moment birthed *from* a counter-cultural coalition. The case made by intersex advocates was a *distinctive* one: that intersex people had seen their lives 'managed' in destructive ways that had to be exposed and undermined. Yet it was also a *convergent* struggle, shared with other groups who also pressured the medical establishment by familiarising themselves with its terms of art and institutional workings (AIDS activists, gays and lesbians, transsexuals, many feminists). The overlaps between Beck and Holmes's picket and the more radical wing of AIDS advocacy were addressed directly by the slogan 'SILENCE=DEATH' found on their placards. This slogan had originally been used by the gay agitprop group ACT UP. By 1996, the group's struggles to improve research and treatments for those surviving HIV/AIDS had not yet won the mass roll-out of antiretroviral treatments. (That began the following year.) In Boston, the slogan 'SILENCE=DEATH' was repurposed to address the stigma and silence that prevailed around intersex childhood treatments.

Later in ISNA's history it would prove ironic that their key Boston slogan was drawn from the HIV campaigning group ACT UP. By the mid-2000s, intersex advocacy would run aground in a way that was remarkably similar to the splits which arose across the 1990s in AIDS advocacy. In the case of ACT UP, disagreements over presentation style and acceptable scope of interactions with the biomedical research establishment arose, and a group calling themselves the Treatment Action Group (TAG) split from the better-known ACT UP. Abandoning the original group's agitprop tactics, TAG presented a more moderated and professionalised face, locking into dialogue with conventional health experts.[12] By a similar token, intersex advocacy would become divided over whether to prioritise 'patient advocacy' (between intersex groups and the medical profession), or hold true to their earlier harder-line push for depathologisation (the stance the Organisation Intersex International would be founded around).

So from the outset, intersex advocacy was in full dialogue with conceptual critics of the existing social order and advocacy groups involved in related struggles. For this reason, it's misleading to speak of the exchange between ISNA and the AAP as the birth of an intersex 'identity': even those present pressed home other overlapping identifications. (For instance, Max Beck presented himself as a 'Transexual Menace', as much as he was an intersexual.) Since the mid-1990s, intersex advocacy has become strikingly more global in scope – a necessary shift given the imposition of Western, especially American, clinical models through colonial avenues in the post-war twentieth century. This has only heightened the need for advocacy which presses across contexts and draws together adjacent social positions.

Yet it is necessary to bring the 1990s clearly into view in order to understand how intersex liberation first began reshaping the history of sex, introducing much-needed chaos to an orthodoxy that had long since failed to keep track of its own workings.

Through newsletters, dedicated gatherings, dialogues with like-minded researchers, and eventually open protest, the intersex movement *shattered* the existing order of treatment and clinical commands. The end of the twentieth century marked the beginning of the end for this order of 'concealed treatment'. Not because doctors gathered and agreed to put an end to all falsehood and parental scripting, but because by the close of the twentieth century, new forms of knowledge and fresh communities flourished through the greatly accelerated pace of correspondence. It became not only obviously unethical to lie to children, but increasingly untenable.

The direct aims of the protestors were not swiftly achieved: physicians responded by feigning obliviousness while doubling down on the *fragmentation* of intersex, against which Max Beck (on one fine autumn day in New England) spoke out. Intersex liberation's base in a nascent sliver of the intelligentsia left them with a tendency towards internal divisiveness that, even during these early days, had already been showcased through Morgan Holmes's quiet but clearly acrimonious departure from the group.

Nevertheless, within a few short years the shape of 'sex' had found itself reset. Silencing regimes were being overturned. Doctors had found the limit of the *plasticity* of sex: through intersex advocacy, they encountered both the limits of flexibility they had tried to work with, and the explosive potential of their meddling. Intersex variations had been treated as deformations from one of two forms. Surgeries and other clinical remedies aimed to make these manifold variations snap back into their expected shape. Now clinicians were swamped with 'feedback' that was spilling from contexts they could hardly hope to understand, and that was stitched together by the shared acknowledgment of injuries sustained by intersex people.

The Boston protesters openly presented an epistemic challenge to the medical profession: they counterposed what intersex people *knew* against the ways that they were *known*. Fundamentally, the argument made by these two advocates who arrived in person to picket a stronghold of professionalised knowledge, which presumed to manage their bodies, was that these clinicians *did not know what they were doing*.

Despite having used a classical flourish in their labelling of 'pseudo-hermaphroditism', the medical profession was now at a loss when encountering a movement birthed from the Hermes of feminism and the Aphrodite of the gay movement. With the wisdom of consciousness-raising and barbed insights of '90s queer agitprop, the intersex movement left the clinical establishment repeating its mantras, even as it unravelled. One party had been forced to understand the other's terms all too well, and their wit was merciless.

The experience of this encounter left doctors disoriented as they witnessed the shaking of the foundations of sex and the refusal of the 'socialisation' model they had peddled. For their part, the intersex movement had reflected not only on their own sufferings, but the origins of these harms in the fearful psyches of those empowered over them. As one participant in *Hermaphrodites Speak!* put it, 'What's been taken is a very specific eroticism, a hermaphroditic eroticism that must really scare people, and really cause a great deal of anxiety.'

Throughout the twentieth century, the divide between male and female had been shored up through sacrifice by those who had never volunteered. And from the 1990s to the present, those subjected to this sacrifice would speak back in force.

2

The Clinic Strikes Back

In 2001, a pair of endocrinologists based at two US children's hospitals published a paper that responded to the now-controversial treatment of intersex patients. This short essay set out the rhetorical ploy medics seeking to justify continuing aggressive treatments of intersex children would largely adopt across the rest of the decade. They proposed curbing the cruel excesses of their outdated protocols (established by the now-disgraced and senescent John Money), while equally resisting the perils of 'activism' dethroning expert deliberation:

> The traditionalist practices no longer conform to modern legal or ethical standards of care. The position of some intersex activists ignores the potential for psychosocial harm to intersex children and our society's general and strong deference to parental discretion in decisions for and about their child.

Subtly, the authors placed themselves at a remove from much of clinical sexology, while the bugbear of 'psychosocial harm' had been invoked as a key risk following the birth of an intersex child. Key to this 'moderate' positioning was the way medics had framed themselves as sex's modernisers, balanced between the extremes of the old school and the movement position opposing all non-consensual intersex surgeries (therefore equating intersex advocates with the sexologists who'd so harmed them, labelling them as twin extremes).

This conceptual centrism was to be a main order of business for medics in the 2000s. By the start of the twenty-first century, the intersex movement had destabilised the pathological approach the medical profession had previously applied without challenge. The first decade of the new century would see the medical profession riposte by retrenching clinical authority both conceptually and organisationally.

The intersex community arose when the growth of the tech industry allowed people who were once isolated to begin communicating and forming communities. Intersex people came to a new understanding of their circumstances, revealing to each other the continuous deception their medical treatments and upbringings had impressed upon them. These revelations were then shared with the wider world. Their movement's challenge was a new form of knowledge. But the clinical profession's reply would take a similar shape: supported by some feminist scholars (previously prominent allies of the intersex movement), medics now advanced a vision of each variation as a separate entry in the rare diseases database. Facing down 'Hermaphrodites with Attitude', medics would disrupt their political movement by trying to disaggregate the concept of 'intersex'. 'Human hermaphroditism' was to be disaggregated into a bundle of 'disorders'. Previously, the medical profession had posited an authoritative model of what they called the likely psychosexual or psychohormonal development of intersex children. Yet after intense campaigning, the medical profession retreated to a strategy of *displacement*. Specifically, it was argued that whatever the ethics and science of human development, *parental expectations* for children raised neatly as girls or boys demanded interventions that doctors would be expected to provide.

While parents are granted a relatively extensive set of legal controls over their children in the United States, this argument was not exclusively appealing in the US context: in Germany, one parental advocacy group proposed that any restrictions on authorising intersex surgeries would be a matter of 'family privacy'. This appeal to privacy as the limit point for personal autonomy (the capacity of families to offer 'private laws' internally) would be adopted by medics and parental advocacy groups alike.

Since the 1990s, the intersex movement had pressed for a transformation based on the 'feedback' that they introduced both forcefully and sardonically. The reply from clinicians was that intersex variations were not really freakish, but unexceptional: the 'strong deference' to families that appeared elsewhere should hold here, too. Given how the law privileged parental authority in all other matters, why should atypical sex be protected? Could a weighty matter like sex assignment be left to mere amateurs? It was in these terms that medics would argue for their continued competence as arbiters of true sex. Towards this, intersex variations would be recast as a cluster of developmental dysfunctions, which still cried out for technically skilled evaluation and clarifying interventions. The reassignment of intersex variations as 'disorders' rearranged the organisational form for evaluating intersex, without allowing any relaxation of the basic sense that the clinic was the fitting site for ethical management and professional guesswork.

Sexology's Twenty-First-Century Crisis

Having played its role setting the post-war order of sex in place, sexology entered the new century in a state of crisis. A succession of research papers written by critical intersex scholars presented a challenge, and the arbiters of true sex had no substantive reply.

By the 2000s, it was not only pressure from intersex advocates which called into question the canonical work of post-war sexology. The figurehead of post-war intersex treatment, John Money, would be disgraced by the turn of the twenty-first century. Following a BBC investigation, Money had been found to have falsified his famous account of the David Reimer case. Reimer was an identical twin whose penis was severely injured during a botched circumcision. On Money's instructions, Reimer was subsequently castrated, then raised as a girl. Under the moniker John/Joan, this case had been widely touted as proving Money's hypothesis that 'socialisation' across the first two years of life set sex identification in stone. Yet far from serving as a demonstrative success story for Money's notions, Reimer had experienced lifelong distress and dysphoria. Money further stood accused of sexual molestation by one of the siblings involved, who charged that the sexologist had coerced them into incestuous erotic exercises. This affair caused a scandal in the United States after a 1996 report by John Colapinto, followed by his book *As Nature Made Him: The Boy Who Was Raised as a Girl*, which outlined the allegations against Money in detail. By the time of its publication, Reimer had resumed living as a male. Within a few years of the exposé against Money, both David Reimer and his brother, Brian, were dead (David from suicide, Brian from a drug overdose).

While Money refused to respond publicly to this affair, his decades of deception caused a public outcry. While not directly concerning an intersex child, the scandal drew intensified attention to clinical treatment of all children with atypical sex. Since Money had been a ubiquitous presence in post-war sexology (from peer-reviewed journals to talk shows), this obvious tarnishing of his reputation provided an opportune moment to replace the protocols he had written. (With convenient timing, Money himself died in 2006.)

The intersex movement had charged post-war sexology with instituting a set of routinised harms. But voices against this approach had already long existed within clinical sciences: Money's longstanding critic Milton Diamond, a researcher of reproductive anatomy based at the University of Hawaii, had also played a decisive role in his exposure. Diamond had long questioned Money's protocols' emphasis on 'socialisation', instead arguing that hormonal evidence demonstrated sex attachment was more of a preset neurological affair. Whatever the merits of this argument, it motivated Diamond to advocate for more humane treatment for intersex people. Yet the medical profession proved stubborn: Diamond's argument that intersex physiologies could be understood simply as 'variations' was rejected by medics. Clinicians moved to *double down* on their pathological understanding of human variation across the earliest years of the twenty-first century. This managerial ethos would receive a new cladding ('pseudo-hermaphroditism' replaced seamlessly by 'disorders of sex development'). This much was immediately obvious to the intersex movement.

It was not an innovation to refer to intersex variations as 'disorders of sex development': publications by medics using this term interchangeably with 'intersex' and 'hermaphroditism' dated back to the 1940s at least. The term appeared in one chapter of the 1951 training textbook *The Urology of Childhood* ('Hermaphroditism and Disorders of Sexual Development'), by Great Ormond Street children's hospital physician David Innes Williams.[1] This was a strange choice for an attempted replacement of the terms 'pseudo-hermaphrodite' and 'intersex'. Yet in the 2000s, this term would be reintroduced as a new order, supposedly intended to replace both diagnoses.

In 2005, a meeting was held in Chicago, in collaboration between the US medical establishment (in the form of the Lawson Wilkins Pediatric Endocrine Society) and the European Society for Paediatric Endocrinology. This was reflected in the national affiliations of the clinicians present (largely US American and British, with several from the Netherlands, Germany, and a few other EU nations). Bo Laurent and a German advocate (Barbara Thomas) were invited to attend. The reframing of intersex as a 'disorder' was officially inaugurated at this meeting, which would develop what came to be referred to as the 'Chicago Consensus'. Attendees of the Chicago gathering were primarily physicians and geneticists, with 'consensus' referring to agreements between these two professional fields.[2]

While ostensibly replacing the 'optimum gender of rearing' model, the 'disorders of sex development' model retained the sense that professionalised guesswork on the part of medics would remain key to avoiding disaster.[3] As philosopher Catherine Clune-Taylor has it, just like 'optimum gender of rearing' as a managerial framework, 'DSD aims at securing a cisgendered future for the intersex patient, referring to a normalized trajectory of development across the lifespan in which multiple sexed, gendered, and sexual characteristics remain in "coherent" alignment.'

Their apparently modest gesture of ceding responsibility to families concealed an underlying continuity in the medics' aims. From the 2000s, the guiding priority would be to establish an outcome that prevented genital ambiguity where possible and averted later transition between male and female. Medical authority would thus undergo an ostensible modernisation, without any basic principle being abandoned.

Medics' focus on treating *hermaphroditism in humans* had previously been explicitly admitted behind closed doors, on medical records, and across decades of in-house publications. This admission now had to be suppressed. Yet the new order would still frame each 'disorder' as a breakdown of either female or male reproductive anatomy. Through this newly reclad governing concept, the medical establishment's old 'pseudo-hermaphrodite' would be buried, and yet live on. The three newly acknowledged sexes were: male, female, and chaos.

The Birth of Disorders

The Chicago gathering was to strike the terms 'pseudo-hermaphroditism' and 'sex reversal' from the record, seeking even to dispose of the term 'intersex' altogether. Although two members of the intersex movement were included, their involvement was arranged to preclude their input in discussions of surgical reforms. The two intersex people present were described as representatives of 'support groups', rather than patient advocates. According to Barbara Thomas, the subgroup focusing on intersex surgeries did not include an intersex advocate.[4] (In contrast with previous such meetings, there were no attempts by uninvited members of the intersex movement to gatecrash.) So the 'consensus' claimed by name was nothing of the kind: inspired by an obvious political challenge, this update of medical terminology would open a still-greater rift between the intersex movement and clinical professionals.

The meeting decided to make a few precise changes to clinical practice. For instance, on the Prader scale of virilisation (clitoral growth deemed excessive), only those children born with congenital adrenal hyperplasia (CAH) exhibiting Prader III or IV should receive cosmetic procedures (Prader I as the base level, II as mild 'excess' growth). However most changes made were institutional: multidisciplinary teams such as those which had been run on an experimental basis since the 1990s would be rolled out as standard through 'centres of excellence'. Each 'disorder of sex development' would be given a designated code, so that it could be found in rare diseases databases.

The previous prevailing system, 'optimum gender of rearing', had been officially instituted by John Money. The 'multidisciplinary teams' would dethrone psychologists and psychiatrists, who would instead provide support to patients after their surgeries. While justified as part of a shift towards 'patient-centred care', the establishment of multidisciplinary teams was really a move towards the abnegation of clinical authority to commands issued by parents. As one study into the emergence of these teams concluded, 'responsibility for the continuation of surgery is increasingly shifted to parents'.[5] In interviews, physicians often reported themselves being pressed by parents to operate even on variations they deemed 'mild'.

These specialist interdisciplinary centres would expand rather than replace the authority of the clinic. And although intersex advocacy had focused on ending non-consensual surgeries, the new regime was not hesitant to perform cosmetic procedures. As the 2006 'consensus' document put it: 'It is generally felt that surgery that is carried out for cosmetic reasons in the first year of life relieves parental distress and improves attachment between the child and the parents.'

The manual's instructions on intersex surgeries spelled out the expected institutional continuity: surgeons were expected to carry out much the same set of operations they'd been originally trained to. The advice continued: 'Only surgeons with expertise in the care of children and specific training in the surgery of DSD should undertake these procedures.'

The proceedings of the event were published twice over, in the specialist journals *Pediatrics – Official Journal of the American Academy of Pediatrics* and *Archives of Disease in Childhood*. The accord would not last long: although the matter was presented as a 'consensus', letters to these journals from intersex advocates rejected the term unequivocally. This immediately contested any sense that sex disorder terms were widely accepted.

The published version of the Chicago Consensus featured tables comparing old terms and classifications to new, retaining most intersex variations as before (for instance chromosomal anomalies and hypospadias urethral formations) while failing to expand the definition of 'disorders of sex development' into the clearly more capacious sense of reproductive anatomical irregularities. So the meeting's ambitions appeared to have been limited to introducing a new categorisation for intersex, and instructing medical professionals in how to conceal its features during briefings to parents. As a critical reader of the consensus statement found, the document assumed that:

> there are elements, such as the reference to the karyotype, which, while important from a conceptual and theoretical point of view, should be avoided in the context of the doctor–patient relationship, probably to avoid the supposed 'confusion' that this information can create for patients and their families.[6]

Although stressing the complexity of sex differentiation and the need for humane and 'patient centred', as before, the DSD clinical guidelines offered provisions for medical professions determining the correct assignment of infants. Intersex variations would remain framed as developmental dysfunction, these physiques framed as born 'unfinished' and often requiring skilled correction.

Necessarily, this enshrined continuity between surgeons accustomed to the previous set of management manuals, and Chicago's new order. The shift towards referring to intersex in terms of 'disorders' was a modernisation in two senses: both the phrase 'optimum gender of rearing' and the term 'hermaphrodite' were closely associated with the figure of John Money. Besides being an obvious moral disgrace, the elderly Money was at this point relatively easy to present as an archaic element to cast aside while clearing house.[7] A subsequent rash of 'brain organisation' studies were used to undermine the salience of 'socialisation'. But Money's *managerial* ethos would survive: physicians continued to feel the need to safeguard 'psychosocial' development of those born with atypical sex traits. Although it lacked the grandiose vision of the senescent sexologist John Money, this new school retained his core mission.

More implicitly, use of the term 'personality disorders' had become ubiquitous in clinical psychology, replacing much of the quasi-Freudian terminology of Money's era. This meant a kind of consistency between medical fields was achieved (a point rarely dwelt on by medics).

While the medical professions disavowed earlier practices enacted against the intersex, they were more resistant to abandoning a pathologising stance towards these variations. Locked into a repetition of management thinking, they could only rearticulate hermaphroditism in this new containing form. The male/female split was left undisturbed: doctors still believed in a true sex that only their professional scrutiny could reveal.

The terminological change was affirmed in the following terms by the so-called consensus document:

Terms such as intersex, pseudohermaphroditism, hermaphroditism, sex reversal, and gender based diagnostic labels are particularly controversial. These terms are perceived as potentially pejorative by patients, and can be confusing to practitioners and parents alike. The term 'disorders of sex development' (DSD) is proposed, as defined by congenital conditions in which development of chromosomal, gonadal, or anatomical sex is atypical.[8]

As even the account of an intersex advocate relatively sympathetic towards the terminology change makes clear, this event was run by medics. Discussion unfolded without space for any sincere dialogue between doctors and patient advocates. As one ISNA activist recounted, the two intersex people present were sidelined and heavily outnumbered by physicians:

> The 2005 meeting brought together 50 professionals working in the field, plus 2 activists (Cheryl and another person from Europe). Then they broke into smaller 'working groups' – forcing the two intersex activists to choose two working groups that they wanted to have influence in the most, and each of the two activists had to face off 5–6 medical professionals alone.[9]

With the intersex movement thus involved only as a token gesture, the meeting would serve as the hook for wholesale *relegitimation* by the medical professions. Parents were now brought explicitly into focus, with extensive efforts to 'manage' their perceptions of their children guided by a new instruction manual for intersex birth.

Previously, the diagnosis of 'pseudo-hermaphrodite' (hatched out of the 1800s distinction between true versus spurious hermaphrodites) was found on the medical records of intersex people, with references to 'pseudo-hermaphroditism' and 'intersex conditions' used interchangeably. But beginning in the 2000s, the teleology of sex development would name its irregular forms only implicitly. Sex development would appear split: two orderly forms (the male and the female, unmistakable and apart), against 'disorders' that merged the two, or left either one partially completed. The dehumanisation of intersex people was reaffirmed conceptually: a terminological conjuring trick sought to disperse any sense of intersex as a category of human at all.

The Myth of Incompletion

The same process through which medical professionals subtly coerced parents into approving surgeries that was first scrutinised by academic feminists from the 1980s would not be abandoned but restructured. This reformed process was later recounted by one paediatric specialist involved, Lih-Mei Liao. Liao had helped establish the NHS's first multidisciplinary team in 1998. Surveying with obvious dismay the harms done by the post-2005 order, she summarised the barrage of experts parents were run through:

> The child is positioned as an emergency patient, which usually implies serious health risks. The child undergoes extensive examining and testing and attracts a vast number of observers. Surgeons are introduced to parents early on. Parents are first overwhelmed by uncertainty and later by esoteric biogenetics. Shame and secrecy isolate them from their support network. Child and family psychologists are more than likely absent because they are either not part of the team or considered irrelevant until medical doctors have finished their work.[10]

Liao's testimony shows that 'DSD' was not only a concept: its introduction served as part of an *organisational* manoeuvre, allowing continuity in mistreatment of intersex people through intensification of clinical management. The 'disorders' framework came accompanied with a trained specialist team, who could more easily alarm and overwhelm parents of young children.

Between these conceptual eras, what persisted was that 'DSD' served as an acronym used as part of in-group fluency (just as the polysyllabic pseudo-hermaphroditism had been). Clinical knowledge was shared selectively, hoarded even as divulged. What DSDs keyed into was the need for doctors to sustain their *professional identity*, through skilled demonstrations of insider knowledge. Just as doctors had used terms such as 'hermaphroditism' much more openly among themselves than with parents and patients, they now swung between using 'differences' openly, and 'disorders' among themselves. The facade of professional objectivity required devices to sort those familiar with what these bundles of letters stood for from those who were not.

Medics typically tend to cut loose behind closed doors, or in publications where they feel unlikely to be read by outsiders. In 'Should CAH in Females Be Classified as DSD?' the authors make quite explicit the elitist contempt obviously latent in the disorder/difference double entendre: 'The term "disorders of sex development" implies that there has been an alteration or deviation (or more politically correctly, a difference) in the normal path of development of the sex organs.'[11]

In her research of this process in motion, Paula Sandrine Machado observed that Brazilian medics similarly pivoted in their language around parents when speaking of 'ambiguity':

> I realized that in the course of their daily practice the medical staff used the term *ambiguous genitalia* amongst themselves when referring to certain conditions considered intersexuality. However, this use was strictly contraindicated in the presence of families and intersex people, in which case they preferred using the expression *incompletely developed genitalia.*[12]

Again, we see the development of a twofold account by physicians: one framing to be presented among peers (and suitable for in-house publication), and another more decisive framing ('incompletion') to be used among parents, to better facilitate the action physicians see fit. Paula Sandrine Machado came to term this interplay of clinical authority and appeals to genetics as a 'sex code': an understanding of sex as taking a true form only know-able by *initiates*.

This pervasive underhandedness was a new iteration of the process of professionalisation which had been unfolding since at least the nineteenth century: medical professionals would adopt varying masks between peers and patients, shifting between an idiom that spelled out their work plainly or occluded it, as required. The shift from 'pseudo-hermaphroditism' to 'DSDs' was a new chapter in a disingenuous history. Arguments among professionals over the exact limits of these brackets were tolerable, as long as the key relation of clinical domination was sustained.

Intersex between Clinical and Subclinical

Any system applying a therapeutic model of healthcare faces an imperative to somehow sort features of life demanding medical care from the merely 'subclinical'. While certain unusual features may be more or less prized or despised, there are clear limits set by the binding expectations of cultural norms. To push the point to absurdity: no man with a large penis would be termed as having a 'variation of sex development'. Variations which end up classified as posing a clinical concern are a narrower and more socially disruptive band of physiological quirks. Intersex variations became classed as such not only because they challenge ordinary expectations of male and female physical forms – but also because they present stress points for the very conventions of assessing and addressing medical ailments. That's why medics' justifications of interventions so quickly stray away from the idea of physiology and towards the imagined psychological ramifications of living a full life with an unusual body.

After the introduction of 'DSDs', as before, clinical practice would be guided by the need to manage parental unease around unusual physiques, as much as any more pressing set of therapeutic needs. Due to this, the medics' overblown fears for children born intersex clearly extend beyond a minimal understanding of their accompanying medical needs. These phobias appear to arise not only from personal conservatism, but also from the demands of professionalisation. Overstating the risk posed by *social* and *psychological* dimensions of anatomical irregularity was not only irrational, but calculating: once management was accepted as a frame, it could be turned to various ends with equal ease. Whatever perceived problem was being solved, though, the risk posed by these variations was played up necessarily. That was because some measure of harm is required for human variation to be perceived as requiring medical attention at all. Returning to 'Should CAH in Females Be Classified as DSD?', we can see this imperative has survived among medical researchers:

> Ambiguity of the external genital organs presents many problems for the affected individual, her or his parents, and the medical team involved. The problems begin at birth when the baby is usually declared to be a boy or a girl and a gender-appropriate name is given and continue for the entire life of the affected individual with physical and psychological repercussions.

A 2004 paper on 'surgical management' of intersex variations in cases of so-called genital virilisation was still more emphatic:

> When a child is born with ambiguous genitalia, it can be catastrophic for the parents, and management requires the expertise of a team that includes a pediatric surgeon or pediatric urologist, endocrinologist, neonatalist, and a psychiatrist. The sex of rearing for these children may be controversial; therefore the final decision should be made by the intersex team and family.[13]

The looming risk of *catastrophic* outcome (for parents) has continued to be conjured by these clinical papers and other material referenced during training. In this context, there is still a pressing need to introduce measures to contest and resist pathological conceptions. But accepting that there were *associated* health needs with atypical sex variations could be achieved without the need for overt pathologisation of all atypical sex variations.

Conceptual Breakdown

The term 'disorders of sex development' has been vehemently rejected by today's intersex community, yet has remained in regular clinical use since the mid-2000s. Why did the medical establishment select such an offensive term to reclassify intersex variations? And how did this doubling down on pathologisation come to be presented as a point of 'consensus'?

Ostensibly, the shift towards 'disorders' has moved clinical deliberation beyond conceptual questions around inclusion (i.e., what does and does not count as 'really' intersex). If we accept this aim at face value, the introduction of 'DSDs' can be considered an unambiguous failure. Rather than closing debate, this designation stirred dissent around which clinically identified variations should constitute a 'disorder'. Chromosomal variations such as Klinefelter's/XXY and Turner syndrome were called into question, being primarily genetic rather than reproductive in their aetiology.[14] The fact that children raised male with XXY chromosomes commonly have atypical scrotal development (such as cryptorchidism) is usually disregarded.

The emergency care required to treat the salt-wasting form of congenital adrenal hyperplasia was regarded as a decisive argument for continued pathologisation by those defensive of the medical profession. Yet many with congenital adrenal hyperplasia, along with their families, vehemently rejected the DSD acronym. One study published in 2015 in the *International Journal of Pediatric Endocrinology*, titled 'Congenital Adrenal Hyperplasia Patient Perception of "Disorders of Sex Development" Nomenclature', found that 71 percent of patients disliked or strongly disliked the term 'DSD', nearly 84 percent stated they did not identify with the term, and 76 percent felt that the term has a negative effect on the CAH community.

In the study's overview of the testimonies submitted, the hostility of those with CAH variations became still clearer, and uniform across those supposedly with 'DSDs' or without:

> Words used by survey participants in response to the term DSD include *horrific, offensive, humiliating, confusing, embarrassing, traumatizing, derogatory, demeaning, alarming,* and *sensationalistic.* The words 'stigma' and 'negative' were used over 100 times in comments by participants. Others remarked that calling CAH a DSD detracts from the more important medical issues related to adrenal insufficiency, especially since the term DSD refers only to females with classical CAH and not to patients with non-classical CAH or males.

Both those classed as having congenital adrenal hyperplasia 'DSDs' and those who weren't rejected the new term in equivalent numbers, many citing the need for community cohesion. This need for unity is understandable when we consider another study written by German clinicians just ten years after the Chicago Consensus. Writing in the specialist journal *Frontiers in Pediatrics*, these self-styled sex experts list a set of 'problems' that clinicians might hope to reduce for CAH patients, including lesbianism:

> Those with greater degrees of prenatal androgen exposure (Prader grades IV and V) raised as females also identify themselves as females but experience more male-like behaviour in childhood, have a greater rate of homosexuality, and have greater difficulty with vaginal penetration and maintaining pregnancies. Improvement in surgical techniques, better endocrinological, psychological, and surgical follow-up may lessen these problems in the future.[15]

Nevertheless, the paper questions whether the 'virilised' genitals of female-raised CAH children suffice to classify them as DSDs.

The authors identify an inconsistency in the fact that hydroceles (fluid growths along the scrotum) and undescended testicles are not included as DSDs, while vaginal agenesis is. They conclude: 'These and other arbitrary choices give the impression that the conditions grouped as DSD were selected with questionable scientific criteria.'

That congenital adrenal hyperplasia might not be classed as a 'disorder of sex development' may seem peculiar, given the paper's own listing of 'male-like' behaviour (including lesbianism . . .). Yet this conceptual exclusion has become typical in the United States, as bills instituting legal protections for intersex children have been targeted by clinical lobbying groups. These medics have been supported by the parent advocacy group the CARES Foundation (which represents parents who authorise clitoral-cutting surgeries on their children). As historian Elizabeth Reis discovered in her revised edition of *Bodies in Doubt: An American History of Intersex*, the CARES Foundation has long refused funding for research which frames congenital adrenal hyperplasia as potentially causing either 'DSDs' or intersex variations.[16] In other words, securing the continued legality of genital-cutting surgery has directly undermined the conceptual coherence of 'DSDs', just as it did 'intersex'. That doctors are willing to collaborate with CARES on the basis of their shared legal aims fully demonstrates that the Chicago Consensus succeeded in shoring up medical authority rather than any kind of conceptual cohesion. The DSD rebranding of intersex was never more than a means to an end.

Variation or Disorder?

Even though it was meant as a compromise between patient advocates and clinicians, most intersex advocates rejected the term 'DSDs'. As Australian theorist Morgan Carpenter put it: 'The shift to DSD never received widespread acceptance by intersex individuals, advocates and organisations; the term is regarded as pathologising and poorly translatable.'[17] Hida Viloria (then head of ISNA's rival, Organisation Intersex International) argued that 'DSDs' should effectively be treated like a slur: 'While some intersex people call themselves "people with intersex conditions" or "people with DSDs", it doesn't mean that it promotes equality to do so. It also isn't reason enough for non-intersex people – especially allies – to describe us that way.'[18]

Some intersex people have adopted the term 'disorders of sex development' for themselves. Conditional deployment of the term can help people navigate clinical contexts where overt resistance could be a disaster. As one reporter recounting her research on an annual US Androgen Insensitivity support group conference put it:

> 'I do embrace it,' she says, 'and it is a part of my identity, but it still feels like a disorder to me in a way.' She pauses as the waiter deposits our curries. She can imagine someone growing up thinking about being intersex as 'a normal part of them, not a thing you had to fix,' she says, but that wasn't her experience. 'I think I feel that it's a disorder because I was raised having my body corrected. At the conference, someone else said, "It is a disorder because it has caused so much disorder in my life," and I would agree with that.'[19]

Yet even this interviewee twins the 'disorder' not so much with how she was born, but with the fact that she was 'corrected' throughout her upbringing. The 'disorder in my life' is implied to be as much a matter of medical scrutiny and subsequent intervention as any hormonal insensitivity itself.

Nothing about Us, without Us

While a few token intersex advocates had been brought into the fold by the early 2000s, advocacy developed confrontational forms of knowledge elsewhere. No longer a member of the Intersex Society of North America, intersex advocate Morgan Holmes remained a prolific writer. Holmes's 2002 paper, 'Rethinking the Meaning and Management of Intersexuality', examines several intersex treatment case studies in detail, arguing that these interventions were clearly neither *enhancements* nor *treatments*.[20] Extending the arguments she'd delivered in person to the AAP in person years before, Holmes asserted that surgeries could not succeed in eliminating intersex. Indeed, these procedures appeared to leave their patients (or rather victims) still *more* intersex. Intersex was therefore social in origin, but not exactly a disability: many of the ways intersex people find themselves physically impaired are a direct *consequence* of surgeries. In his work on hypospadias operations, historian David Andrew Griffiths divides both justifications and surgical purposes between the performative (boys should be able to pee standing up), the psychological (how's he going to feel in the locker room?) and the perfect (the Platonic ideal of a penis). Yet as Iain Morland – an intersex scholar who had multiple such surgeries personally – has argued, these justifications fail not due to their immorality, but also on their own terms. Intersex surgeries often leave children subjected to them *more visibly intersex*. The bodily variations they intend to hide instead become spotlit. The consequences of surgery become both the visual and haptic basis for social differentiation from belonging 'normally' in one sex, or the next. So while the medical profession sought to eliminate intersex, or at least drive it from view, their operations were not truly 'treatments'. Like so much of this writing, Holmes's and Morland's critiques of clinical practice were largely ignored by medics. Needless to say, no reference was made to these writings in the Chicago Consensus declarations.

Yet even if the work of these intersex scholars seemed relatively easy for the medical profession to disregard, a new wave of intersex thinking was emerging through the victories of intersex consciousness-raising. Intersex scholars including Georgiann Davis, Hil Malatino, Sean Saifa Wall, and David Rubin would write books and essays which brought together scrupulous examination of standards of care, pointed reflections on personal experience, and radical social theory. This culminated in Holmes's 2009 collection *Critical Intersex*, featuring scholars from several national contexts who offered a compelling account of intersex without reliance on clinical concepts.

Which Ethics?

By the start of the twenty-first century, advances in prenatal screening of unborn children would make many intersex variations detectable in the womb. The medical establishment quickly moved to institute frameworks of selective abortions to eliminate these births. Specifically in the case of congenital adrenal hyperplasia, the 2000s saw medics pioneer the use of a hormone they touted as a means of preventing 'virilisation' of daughters. This was a process they both prematurely and emphatically declared 'safe for mother and daughter' (dexamethasone). With minimal public discussion, prenatal screening for congenital adrenal hyperplasia would become mandatory across much of the United States.

Far from aiming to offer better support for the unique health needs of intersex people, much of this research exhibited a drive towards their pre-emptive elimination. As if in a mockery of the agitation of intersex advocacy, medics envisioned an end to intersex surgeries and hormonal barrages: medics moved to prevent intersex lives from ever taking place, rather than responding to entreaties from those currently alive.

While bioethics research became preoccupied with intersex surgeries, the movement voiced outspoken criticisms of the field. Emi Koyama's essay 'Why I'm Suspicious of Bioethics' and Morgan Carpenter's more recent 'When Bioethics Fails' both explored how limited the changes achieved by ethics research have proven to be. Doctors never allowed medical protocols against intersex people to be transformed root-and-branch, rather framing them as evolving through an ongoing technical process of trial and error. Bioethicists ostensibly were solely concerned with 'whether' questions, but ultimately this came to look like a tidy division of labour. Koyama describes how bioethicists' readiness to answer *how* not *whether* questions could only be validating for medics, and provide both guidance and cover for clearly dubious practices. Bioethics provided a refinement of management tools, rather than any imperative to set them aside. This discipline came to serve an advisory role in the imposition of clinical norms, rather than digesting insights from the intersex movement. Carpenter argues bioethics provides limited tools to escape the epistemic injustices faced by intersex people (what I've called being *known over*: their oppression through being denied knowledge, being disbelieved, and being known in harmful ways). Here, intersex advocacy plays a role that academic moral inquiry will always fail to.

3

Bringing in the Intersex

In the ISNA protest outside the American Academy of Pediatrics 1996 Annual Meeting, Max Beck had argued against intersex variations being reduced to 'birth defects which can be corrected, outgrown and forgotten'. Superficially, the medical establishment appeared to have brought these criticisms in-house quickly: by 2000, Bo Laurent had accepted an invitation to speak before the Lawson Wilkins Pediatric Endocrine Society, which attracted an audience of specialists in childhood hormonal regulation and development.[1] John Money's direct predecessor, Lawson Wilkins, was credited with saving thousands of lives through his innovative use of stress hormones to regulate intersex infants' metabolisms. Wilkins wrote an earlier, less publicised version of Money's 'optimum gender of rearing' approach to assigning genders to intersex people. Wilkins believed that those 'virilised' in the womb could be raised as boys irrespective of their genetics, an approach he dubbed discerning their 'better sex'.[2] Laurent's appearance addressing a professional gathering of childhood endocrine specialists at the start of a new century was symbolically charged. The era of 'feedback' announced by Max Beck four years before had reached a new phase: demonstrations being replied to with keynote invitations.

During her talk, Laurent outlined the harms done routinely to intersex people, drawing on available studies and her own insights gained through seven years of advocacy and through founding and heading the ISNA. Not all those who attended were convinced by Laurent's lecture: one physician later complained in an interview that the testimonials presented were 'just opinions' with 'no data'.[3]

Laurent's softening of her account to fit the audience could only go so far. However politely delivered, an account of the injustices done to intersex people would implicate the medical profession. Few physicians could stomach a movement whose publications and gatherings made constant jokes at their expense and rendered their jargon as fodder for barbed punchlines. Few will allow themselves to be talked out of a job, and fewer still convinced their professional training readied them for the orderly perpetuation of human rights violations.

Yet for their part, the intersex movement began to adopt a conciliatory stance: by the 2000s the Intersex Society of North America had begun to engage with clinicians directly, and on their own terms. Appeals to 'hermaphroditic eros' and withering sarcasm towards medical professionals gave way to the drier work of back-channel dialogues with medics and geneticists. Laurent's newly moderated advocacy and skilled networking began to transform the group she'd founded. As ISNA restructured itself to become a conventional NGO, it tacitly abandoned depathologisation as an aim, reframing intersex advocacy as *reform* of clinical care. Medics were to be enlightened and updated, not denigrated or mocked. Clinical professionals also came to dominate the organisation: ISNA recruited a medical advisory board that had grown to twenty-three members by 2005. An endosex hospital manager (married to board member Alice Dreger) sat on ISNA's board. This drift inevitably softened the group's stance towards the medical profession. What had been a liberation struggle was reframed as 'patient advocacy'.

But the reality was ISNA was entangled with a *faux* receptiveness from medics, who offered false hope of change. Some medics always appeared ready to discuss honing techniques to provide 'progress' to their authoritative interventions. But this openness was belied by their discussions both privately among themselves, and in their in-house publications. Here, they retained their core concept – 'management'. This was consistent with their refusal to respond sincerely to the charges pressed by the intersex movement, or to accept any binding limits to what they still framed as surgical or hormonal 'corrections' performed upon those with incompletely developed sex. However, intersex advocates delivered their message, medics refused to reflect on the key charge of the intersex movement: that their 'treatments' were really palliatives for their own discomfort with irregular bodies. As such, they found themselves doomed to repeat their original error, in fresh terms.

'I Like to Be Helpful'

Foremost among the advocates for the new 'disorders' framing was historian Alice Domurat Dreger. Dreger was originally recruited into the intersex movement by ISNA's founder, Bo Laurent. While initially reluctant to pursue the issue of intersex as a contemporary political struggle (given her lack of medical training), Dreger was convinced through typical activist persistence:

> Cheryl was unrelenting, and finally, with her encouragement and with the help of my medical-student husband, I began to look at the present-day medical literature . . . I found unproven claims that a girl born with a large clitoris . . . would grow up a tomboy or a lesbian; that a boy born with a very small penis (smaller than 1 inch when stretched at birth) had to be castrated and made into a girl; that in cases of intersex doctors had an ethical duty to withhold personal records and facts from patients and parents (though this would be considered unethical in other contexts) because otherwise the normalizing treatment wouldn't work and the patient might commit suicide.

Laurent had read Dreger's first peer-reviewed publication in a 1995 issue of the academic journal *Victorian Studies*. A self-described historian of anatomy, Dreger had researched the treatment and diagnosis of 'hermaphroditism' in Victorian-era Britain and France for her dissertation, which would later be reworked into her first book, *Hermaphrodites and the Medical Invention of Sex*.

Having been brought into the fold of the early Intersex Society of North America, within a few years Dreger was immersed in the group's '90s edgy style (even referring to herself as a 'hermaphrodite wrangler'). Dreger was troubled by the regime of shamed silence that prevailed in households raising intersex children. Distinctively, this produced a patient advocacy that had to come to terms with having been medicalised in secret. So Dreger's first task for ISNA was to conduct 'facilitated autobiographies', lengthy one-on-ones with ISNA members unfamiliar with recounting their perspectives, before writing the transcripts up as 'I' statement narratives. This technique built off Dreger's historical training, while honing the ability of new advocates to speak in their own terms.

But Dreger soon found herself framed by the media as a 'supposedly objective expert', a more reliable spokeswoman than any intersex person could be (even when advancing typical ISNA talking points). As Dreger remarked in 2018:

> Because I was a non-intersex historian, I was often seen as a 'safe' person to invite to medical groups interested in hearing about intersex, and so it was often easier for me to get into the halls of medicine than intersex people who were feared as 'angry former patients'.[4]

All this meant Dreger enjoyed platforms rarely extended to outspoken intersex advocates. Dreger used her unique access to the medical profession to become personal friends with several of North America's foremost sexologists, facilitating pioneering mergers of clinical theory and activism. For instance, key Money-protocol critic Milton Diamond contributed an essay to *Intersex in the Age of Ethics*, appearing alongside Bo Laurent and other advocates. Intersex people and their 'experts' were suddenly on an even footing.

Beyond the cause, Laurent and Dreger developed what the historian called a 'sibling-like devotion'. Their similar upbringings (liberals from large right-wing Roman Catholic families) and shared background in critical science training honed their outrage at the shoddy treatment of intersex people through clinical care. The pair quickly operated in lockstep through ISNA.

The publication of *Hermaphrodites and the Medical Invention of Sex* would greatly enhance Dreger's reputation by any measure: easily the most popular academic study on intersex, Dreger's account of development of clinical concepts memorably posited sex assignment being redefined by a Victorian 'age of the gonads'. She argued medical investigations by the later nineteenth century vastly overstated the role of gonads (presenting them as key to sex). Since hormonal secretion was only vaguely understood, speculations ran unchecked (fuelling wild animal and human experimentation). The medical subfield of *histology* emerged, which examined the likely history of tissues. When histologists examined gonads in the later nineteenth century (prior to the role of hormones being fully understood), they framed testes and ovaries as sex's *engine*. This theoretical weighting would only fully collapse in the mid-twentieth century, Dreger argued (when John Money linked viable genital tissue, or the external shape of sex, with the healthy development of the psyche through parenting).

While praised as scrupulous and richly documented, *Hermaphrodites ...* began passionately: Dreger denounced these doctors for disregarding the self-understandings of hermaphrodites they treated. Dreger's headlong immersion in the nascent intersex movement reshaped both her scholarship. A contrasting counterpart was *Changing Sex: Transsexualism, Technology, and the Idea of Gender*, by feminist theorist Bernice Hausman. Published in 1995 (the year before ISNA's appearance in Boston) this technocratic account presents intersex physiques as the mute stepping stone for surgical techniques that served as the technical underpinnings for what Hausman calls 'transsexualism'. Hausman's book featured extensive photographs of naked intersex people taken under circumstances their movement would denounce as clinical 'forced stripping'.[5] Dreger and Laurent decided together to compose a send-up of this very practice on the front cover of *Intersex and the Age of Ethics*: Dreger appeared naked with a blackout bar covering her eyes, surrounded by photographs of clothed intersex advocates.

Yet despite these humane and subversive flourishes, Dreger's best-known historical work has since been criticised for limiting its focus to medical concept development. While Dreger was willing to denounce doctors, her account of their thinking continued without clear grounding of these clinical notions within their broader juridical context.[6] Geertje Mak compares Dreger's and Hausman's accounts of sex's origins to reveal a shared limitation:

> Despite Dreger's extended description of the medical practices that established someone's sex, and the confusions and contradictions that resulted, her argument ultimately privileges medical opinion and definitions . . . What is missing from both is the question of authority and competence.

Though it can be helpful to simplify medical language when speaking to a general audience, speaking of medical history in terms of 'eras' and 'ages' inevitably overstates the role of scientific core-notions. Terms of art were used to *dominate others* (in this case patients and their parents), as much as they were used to develop sincere understanding. Mak notes that Dreger's 'age of the gonad' requires her to disregard numerous clinical decisions that do not use gonads as their primary basis for assigning sex. This concept-focused approach to historical change would not only be found in Dreger's writing, but her organising.

By the end of the 1990s, the Intersex Society of North America had become an above-board NGO. Dreger had facilitated that in every way possible: the group was officially registered at her house in Michigan, while both Dreger and Laurent's partners also each served as members of the board. Like Laurent, Dreger was a prolific networker – even claiming to ghost-write peer-reviewed papers repeatedly for friendly physicians. ISNA had expanded their medical board to twenty-three members by 2005, fostering an increasing tendency to see the impact of their earlier 'Hermaphrodites with Attitude' phase as a hindrance for further clinical reform, rather than a historic breakthrough in consciousness.

For their part, ISNA was clearly wowed by Dreger's scholarship. By the 2000s references to her historical ideas and outright adverts for her book proliferated across ISNA's unsigned website posts. But this affection often did not seem mutual. While Dreger's scholarly work was focused on abnormal bodies, she exhibited a surprisingly narrow political vision. Dreger believed the group's '90s edgy, herm-mode advocacy had led doctors to find the term 'intersex' itself awkward, or even unspeakable:

> By this time (2004), the term 'intersex' had become a heavily politicized term allied with the lesbian, gay, bisexual, and trans-gender (LGBT) rights movement. This presented a problem. Pediatricians did not want to ascribe the heavily politicized (essentially queer) identity of 'intersex' to babies, so among themselves they continued to use terms 'true hermaphrodite' and 'pseudo-hermaphrodite'. But the 'hermaphrodite' labels were understood by doctors to be stigmatizing enough that they often would still not tell parents these diagnoses, lest they upset them.

In other words, the regime of concealment which Dreger had discovered in the mid-90s had not been undone at all. Doctors were simply withdrawing more information from parents, giving them less to lie about to their intersex children. It's telling that Dreger sees this as a consequence of the 'politicised' condition of the term, rather than an extension of the heterosexism in treatment that Kessler had identified in the 1980s. In Dreger's liberal accounting, doctors are left constrained by the intemperance of a rowdy movement.

ISNA's Downfall

By the early twenty-first century, ISNA concessions to reforming medical treatment of intersex people had split the worldwide intersex movement. Groups outside the US were typically hostile towards the new terminology for intersex. The shift of ISNA to accepting pathological frameworks could have seemed quite abrupt, from an external view. But really the involvement of ISNA's leadership in the rebranding of intersex had begun years before. The satire and consciousness-raising of the group had given way to a more earnest register, signalling the group's intention to serve as the angel on the shoulder of respectable professionals.

By the early 2000s, Alice Dreger and Bo Laurent were the de facto leaders of the Intersex Society of North America. They shared the basic aim of replacing intersex as a category of person with a variation on 'people focused language' found in the US disability rights movement (where the label 'disabled people' was replaced with 'people with disabilities'). At this point, Alice Dreger had become central to the effort to recast intersex variations as 'disorders': ISNA had secured funding to hire her as editor-in-chief of two new handbooks (one for medics, one for parents). These manuals developed a biomedical framing for intersex, attempting to do away with the term to better enable this. While now a manager of a project that would have global influence over the treatment of intersex people, Dreger still saw her role as operating as a 'smoothing' intermediary between those subject to intersex genital cutting and those who cut them:

> I used drafts produced years earlier by two social workers, Sallie Foley and Christine Feick, and substantially revised them with the help of more than fifty 'consultants' from the three stakeholder

groups: clinicians in the field, intersex adults, and parents of intersex children (young and grown). There were many differences of opinion I had to smooth out in many phone conversations, and a lot of time was spent educating people about why we were saying what we were saying.

But Dreger had apparently come to see her position as less that of an unflinching advocate for intersex people, and more an NGO diplomat balancing the vying needs of doctors, intersex people, and their parents. All these had to be 'educated' by Dreger. Like most actual diplomats, however, she exhibited a dedicated partiality: on various personal and professional levels, she'd become close with several leading sexologists. These self-styled sex experts inherited John Money's determination to achieve decisive and final assessments over atypical sex. When pressed, whatever their disagreements, Dreger would exhibit a fierce loyalty towards these men – both professionally and personally.[7]

Dreger's work for ISNA and the old school sexological establishment would converge at Penn State University, where an academic group named the Network on Psychosexual Differentiation would develop various attempted fixes for the perceived problem of intersex categorisation and clinical care. Across postwar sexology, references to the 'psychosexual' and 'gender identity' were used interchangeably. This preoccupation would direct the handbook's emphasis on the need to correctly assign and manage the sex of intersex children. Old school sexology had been fuelled by a desire to provide final clarification to fraught sexual questions, which the DSD manuals carried over into the twenty-first century. While the intersex movement of the 2000s would often argue that their cause was a matter of addressing medical harms, and not identity, for contemporary sexologists, 'gender' remained a guiding fixation.

The DSD handbooks attempted to provide a more humane update to post-war protocols for supporting and 'managing' intersex infants and children, as well as parental expectations. In an apparent homage to John Money (who'd also provided instructions for parents fielding questions from relatives) the guidance for parents even included a script for various eventualities:

> Our baby was born with a kind of variation that happens more often than you hear about. Our doctors are doing a series of tests to figure out whether our baby is probably going to feel more like a boy or a girl. We expect to have more information from them within [say how long], and then we'll send out a birth announcement with the gender and the name we have chosen. Of course, as is true with any child, the various tests the doctors are doing are not going to tell us for sure who our baby will turn out to be. We're going to go on that journey together. We appreciate your love and support and we're looking forward to introducing you to our little one in person soon.

(It's hard to imagine any parent delivering this monologue in full, to even the most indulgent aunt).

As important as the 'research output' of their guidebooks (and their accompanying website), Dreger would head a DSD Consortium that would set the terms for future research funding. For some years, this would see the term 'disorders of sex development' proliferate in peer-reviewed research from the centre out. Dreger originally proposed the term 'disorders of sexual differentiation', but discovered geneticists and clinicians used 'differentiation' in another sense. (By these professionals at least, 'disorders' was clearly taken to be fine). Similarly, 'sexual' was replaced with 'sex' to eliminate the connotation of orientation. (This fine-tuning simply did not translate to several European languages). With this much deliberation, 'disorders of sex development' was decided upon as a new global term for intersex. The fact that geneticists and not intersex people had a veto seems to reveal the gathering's true purpose.

The introduction of 'DSD' as the ISNA-approved term of art was controversial, to say the least. The work of Dreger and the

DSD consortium came under fire from other groups in the intersex movement immediately. The consortium had prepared a website which featured photographs and personal accounts, but three intersex people profiled rejected the new term. (An update to the website admitted the error). Given that the intersex movement had long protested non-consensual medical photography used in medical education, the misuse of this submitted private photography was unnerving.

Resistance to the introduction of 'DSDs' was organised through the Organisation Intersex International (OII), which had been founded two years earlier in 2003. In particular, the handbooks drew the ire of OII's founder, Curtis Hinkle (a former organiser with the National Organisation for Women).[8] The new group collected rejections of the new term 'DSDs' from intersex advocates worldwide, arguing that the very framing of the handbooks revealed their true focus. There was no third handbook, only material 'for doctors and for parents but nothing intended for the actual child. There is a reason for this. The Consortium serves the interests of the two groups just mentioned at the expense of the child being managed.'[9] In Dreger's terms, she had disregarded the needs and perspectives of one group of stakeholders, addressing only two (doctors and parents).

Following from the earliest public arguments of the intersex movement, OII argued that the focus of intersex 'management' was the emotions of those challenged by intersex physiologies:

The propaganda in this handbook repeatedly brushes aside the serious issues of transphobia and homophobia which many of us have experienced from our earliest years and throughout life. The handbook is not about making intersexed children actually feel secure and comfortable with themselves but more about assuring the parents that their intersexed children will most likely NOT be transsexual or homosexual.

The whole reason for combining a lot of different conditions which have nothing in common medically under the umbrella term 'disorder of sex development' is not to treat real health conditions of intersexed children but to relieve the sufferings and anxieties that gender 'ambiguity' provokes within society.[10]

For these advocates, it was adding insult to injury to have their variations rebranded as 'disorders'. OII argued that parents were told that 'DSDs' were most likely not linked to any irregularities in gender identification, while doctors were issued with protocols for ensuring children's assigned sex and adult sex would align. The alternative, simply waiting to hear what children made of themselves, was spurned. Organisation Intersex International argued that the framing of 'disorders of sex development' was an interlocking one with so-called 'gender identity disorder' (today largely replaced with a diagnosis of gender dysphoria):

> It is always the child who is disordered in these handbooks. If the intersex child rejects the arbitrary sex assignment, they have another disorder. What started out as a disorder of the child's sex has become a disorder of the child's gender . . . At all points of the treatment protocols, the child is always wrong and suffering from a disorder.

In this way 'DSDs' rearticulated longstanding clinical fears that intersex people would grow up to be homosexual. Together, these two manuals attempted to reassure parents and direct doctors in 'managing' children away from transsexuality. Children would be subject to corrective procedures (surgical and hormonal) to minimise this new perceived risk. If they later opted to correct a wrongly assigned sex, they would be reclassified as suffering from another sinister acronym (from DSD to GID).

The debate between the newly founded Organisation Intersex International and the Intersex Society of North America became acrimonious, with Hinkle particularly taking objection to Dreger's repeated identifications of herself as a mother (seen as in bad taste as most of the intersex movement was childless for perhaps obvious reasons). But why did ISNA's managers ever believe that a movement focused on depathologising intersex people would accept 'disorders' as their new term of reference?

ISNA's role in the Chicago Consensus was decided not by the movement as a whole, but solely by the group's leadership – most vocally Alice Dreger and Bo Laurent. The pair shared a view that the intersex movement should frame their concerns in 'patient advocacy'. That meant adopting language that was palatable to medics (with a view to winning specific changes, argued for technically). Talk of 'hermaphroditic eros' and 'mutilation', once commonplace for the movement, had to be suppressed. The movement's concerns had to be detached from any overt affiliation with LGBT struggles (notwithstanding their earlier reliance on support from exactly these groups). Advocacy was to become presentable in polite company.

But this vision would neither extend beyond ISNA, nor hold the group itself together. By the end of 2005, Dreger had quit both the DSD Consortium and Intersex Society of North America, citing personal reasons. By all accounts, clashes with Laurent had apparently become unworkably common – perhaps the inevitable fate of a sibling-like bond. Divisions in strategy and style already visible in the 1990s became terminal. With its consciousness raising having soured into online acrimony, ISNA became inactive, then officially shuttered in 2008.

Defect, Disorder, Variation

ISNA's closure in 2008 followed years of dubious involvement in groups across the medical establishment. Open disputes about this redirection surfaced as a local activist group based in Portland, Oregon, the Intersex Initiative, called into question the Intersex Society of North America's collaboration with one birth defect research group.[11] Intersex Initiative's founder, Emi Koyama, had previously been an intern for ISNA, but saw this shift towards collaboration with eugenics-minded research groups as a dereliction of developing any *social model* of intersex. This social view was outlined by Koyama as contrasting with any conception of variations as defects:

> Intersex conditions are not what debilitate intersex people: it is the society's preoccupation with the concept of normalcy that does. While it is true that some intersex conditions are associated with physically debilitating medical conditions . . . studying the causes of intersex with an organization that studies 'birth defects' gives the wrong impression that intersex itself is limiting or undesirable.

Koyama didn't seem to receive a satisfying answer.

So how did a pathologising term that reduced intersex variation to 'disorders' become seriously entertained by the managers of the Intersex Society of North America? Writing on her personal website in 2005, Dreger acknowledged the criticisms 'disorders of sex development' had faced. Yet she justified the move since there was a need for a new 'logical system', agreed on by those she referred to as the 'stakeholders' in play:

> I understand completely why a lot of people feel like the term is a step backwards towards pathologizing and medicalizing sex anomalies. But here's the thing. The term seems to be helping. Really helping to accomplish those basic goals of the intersex rights movement. When I finished the handbooks and started distributing them, as I used 'DSD' instead of 'intersex', the medical professionals providing pediatric care immediately got past the usual defensiveness.

'DSDs' had not been the only available term for grouping those with atypical sex traits. Against the suggestion of Milton Diamond and others that talk of disorders or conditions could be replaced with the term 'variation of sex characteristics', Dreger cited a concern from clinical professionals that intersex people might be 'over-depathologised':

What about, for example, 'variations of sex development', as some have suggested? Honestly, I don't see that term flying in the medical system; I've asked about it, and it doesn't go anywhere. Part of the reasonable fear among medical professionals is over-de-pathologizing sex anomalies.

That there would be any serious risk of *excessive* depathologisation of a community whose members were still being subjected to routinised genital and gonadal cutting may seem peculiar. Additionally, this was a clear misrepresentation of the positions advanced by the intersex movement. No voices in the intersex movement had ever called for an abandonment of all therapeutic support for intersex people.

One specific variation cited by Dreger as rightly concerning clinicians was congenital adrenal hyperplasia (CAH), which often results in genitals described as 'virilised' for children born with XX chromosomes. In its salt-wasting form, CAH can require urgent medical intervention to prevent death. The specific use of CAH as an example would prove to be an ironic one for advancing 'disorders', as we'll return to. Yet its appearance in cases for a 'biomedical' understanding of intersex (rather than the social one developed by Emi Koyama and Morgan Holmes) should hardly surprise us. Lawson Wilkins's reputation, after all, was founded on his skilful and lifesaving use of stress hormones.

Others in ISNA presented similar arguments: Ellen Feder wrote that while there is an understandable argument against strictly biomedical conceptions of intersex, 'there is an equally compelling case that some of the conditions with which genital variation are associated bring genuine health challenges that require not less, but substantially more, medical attention than has been afforded them'.[12] Explaining why some form of treatment should be retained, Emi Koyama described what she took to be the shortcomings of talking about intersex physiologies as 'variations', or with other neutral terms:

87

I would personally like 'variation' or 'anomaly', but doctors don't treat 'variations'. And treatments are needed, not to perform unconsensual genital surgeries, but to correctly identify the condition, monitor potential metabolic issues, and provide psychological support and other medical help as the child grows older.[13]

In other words, some degree of pathological framing was required for clinicians to provide medical support at all.

So those within ISNA arguing for the term's selective use pointed to specific interventions required to resolve pressing emergencies (such as salt-wasting CAH) or monitor and mitigate commonplace risks such as brittle bones (osteoporosis) that demand categories for overarching clinical direction. Yet the argument made by the Organisation Intersex International against the new 'DSD' umbrella was exactly that it bracketed a range of variations with no unifying sense. Treatments delivered to intersex people by the medical profession include not only harsh interventions intended as 'correctives', but extended displays of medical neglect. The new system of carefully numbered 'rare diseases' did not change the fact that intersex people passing through clinical scrutiny were routinely being 'lost to follow-up'. The continuity in surgical harms was accompanied with an ongoing failure to collect usable health data for meaningful interpretation. That's because the focus was more on providing a new framework for clinical authority (with centralised teams of experts) than reshaping care around the existing criticisms voiced since the 1990s.

With Allies Like These

The turn to 'disorders' would split the intersex movement from some feminists who had previously been its most prominent allies. Specifically, the new framework was supported by several scholars who had previously taken a leading role within intersex advocacy. Alice Dreger, April Herndon, and Ellen Feder were all professional academics who had simultaneously held paid positions within the Intersex Society of North America. They'd overseen its transition from pioneering consciousness-raising group to basic NGO. The arguments presented by these erstwhile allies help show how successfully the 'consensus' came to be established among medical professionals by the end of the 2000s. These writings denigrated much of the existing intersex movement, dismissing the legitimacy of intersex advocates' self-representation: rather than debating intersex people openly, they cast doubt over whether any intersex community existed at all. To an audience often unfamiliar with intersex struggles, they made the case for segregating intersex struggles from the broader LGBT movement – abandoning the collaborative spirit of the 1990s movement. What's clear from the writings of these feminist academics is the weak grasp key movement 'allies' had not only of intersex, but also *gay* and *lesbian* life.

Incongruously, the place where this movement revisionism would be attempted was the scholarly magazine *Gay and Lesbian Quarterly* (*GLQ*). The special issue's title, 'Intersex and After', hinted at the determination of three authors to do away with the term 'intersex' altogether. While writing in one of the few peer-reviewed venues for gay scholarship, three 'allies' wrote with the full force and erudition allowed by their training as humanities scholars. Drawing from their experience as NGO managers working with intersex people, and bringing to bear the state-of-the-art in critical theory and the philosophy of science, they hoped to curb any sense of the intersex movement being meaningfully embedded with queer emancipatory struggles. Let's see what they came up with.

Alice Dreger and April Herndon's essay was titled 'Progress and Politics in the Intersex Rights Movement: Feminist Theory in Action'. Unfortunately, their political stance was strictly neoliberal feminism. This essay attempts to dismiss all autonomous intersex organising (startling given both authors had been paid members of ISNA) and seeks to justify the roll-out of 'disorders' as a means for dialogue between clinical professionals, intersex people, and their parents. Their arguments were twofold: first, that introducing the acronym 'DSDs' was vital to avoid confusing rows over who the term intersex included. Despite the fact that Dreger's historical training led her to write of the 'invention' of sex, they admit that a large number of clinicians may not deem Klinefelter's/XXY or Turner syndrome as intersex. This potential for confusion during invention is taken as so drastic that the 'disorders' framework serves as a necessary clarification. Second, Dreger and Herndon argue that it was misleading to consider intersex people a 'community' at all:

> Although people sometimes refer to 'the intersex community' as they do 'the lesbian community', this is somewhat misleading. There are online virtual communities of people with intersex, but large numbers of intersex people do not live together in brick-and-mortar communities, and only occasionally do they come together for meetings that are primarily about political conscious-ness-raising rather than about sharing information about particular medical diagnoses (like hypospadias or congenital adrenal hyperplasia) . . . such gatherings remain either irregular or infrequent.

Doubtless, many lesbian readers of *GLQ* were delighted to discover they had access to dedicated 'brick-and-mortar' hang-outs. (Lesbian bars are notoriously hard to find across the United States, with even enormous metropolitan cities such as Los Angeles going unserviced.)[14] Comparing the intersex and lesbian communities in this fashion was an especially curious choice, given how much of the 'management' of these variations had been about reducing the perceived risk of female-raised congenital adrenal hyperplasia patients from becoming lesbians. It also seems hard to believe that members of ISNA didn't meet with informal regularity, not least given the concentration of its advocates in the Bay Area (Northern California). Of course, this passage is not intended as a sincere comparison: Dreger and Herndon are trying to downplay and dismiss both the 2000s intersex movement and the work of consciousness-raising in general.

Strikingly, while Dreger and Herndon's essay references 1990s community-building materials, their interpretations of these documents and documentaries make little sense of these recordings (either in tone, or purpose). As an example of 'anxiety' over 'who should belong' as intersex, they reference the video *Hermaphrodites Speak!*, specifically one participant, born with hypospadias, jokingly introducing himself as 'a *real* hermaphrodite!' As the ISNA member filmed would have been fully aware, hypospadias was *not* treated by medics as an instance of true hermaphroditism. Indeed, hypospadias was used as a primary example of supposedly non-ambiguous intersex by the AAP in their declaration of intersex births as a 'social emergency': 'It should be recognized that most genital abnormalities in newborns do not result in an ambiguous appearance. These anomalies include hypospadias, in which the genitalia are clearly malformed, although the sex is unquestionably male.'[15]

A more obvious interpretation of the speaker's tone is self-conscious sarcasm: addressing his place in the insistent divide between male/female that the medical profession insisted upon, while rendering the entire exercise of setting intersex variations apart a farce. This was a darkly humorous send-up of *exactly the position* Dreger and Herndon's 2009 essay defended. Far from oblivious to scientific distinctions, the early intersex movement was prone to mocking the managerial work of medical professionals. (The same activist also refers to himself as a 'hypospadias monster'.) Exactly none of this spirit survived in these *GLQ* essays. With feminist allies like these, the intersex movement hardly had need for enemies.

In Ellen Feder's essay for the special issue 'Imperatives of Normality: From "Intersex" to "Disorders of Sex Development"', the philosopher and ethicist calls upon a wide range of thinkers familiar with critical approaches to science. She voices fears that usage of 'intersex' might establish 'looping effects'. In the work of philosopher of science Ian Hacking, looping effects create a category for observation which then generates populations around that observation. But the same is clearly the case for 'disorders': following the supposed 'consensus', many intersex advocates expressed fears about how these 'loops' would impact future generations of intersex people. As Hida Viloria reflected on their personal website:

> While some doctors and parents are, according to supporters of the term like Chase (co-author of the DSD Guidelines . . .), more comfortable referring to us as having 'disorders' than associating with a label supported by homosexuals and transsexuals, I do not believe adopting a pathologizing label to distance ourselves from these groups is a solution, to say the least . . . I know that it would have harmed my self-esteem to be raised under a term which named my difference a 'disorder'. Even complete ignorance about what to call myself was preferable as I was able to form positive beliefs about my unique qualities.

While Feder's essay argues for the conceptual elimination of 'intersex' in favour of 'disorders' to reduce the stigma around sex anomalies, there is an obvious problem. From a clinical point of view, disorders will always come with an implicit mandate for quick fixes. The flipside of reducing appropriate interventions to therapeutic moments, is a professional obligation to perform corrections where possible. Another kind of looping effect results: patients are generated through categorisation, while framing them as afflicted with 'rare diseases' establishes expectations for clinicians to provide treatments. As one Australian paediatric urologist remarked, one doesn't wait until a child has grown up before asking consent to fix a heart defect. Yet this same mindset applied to the fraught question of acceptable sex organs orients medics toward variations as problems to solve. As much as it attempts to *resolve* problems with sex, the clinical gaze surely *generates* them.

Feder's article does acknowledge the furious contention which the introduction of 'disorders' produced, citing the letters written to the *Archives* after the publication contested the supposed new consensus (ironically an echo of Laurent's 1993 letter to *Sciences*). Nevertheless, she moved on to oppose 'intersex' as a coherent category:

> While it is easy to make the case that differences in genital appearance should be understood as matters of variation, such terminology does not permit appreciation of the genuine health challenges faced by many individuals with intersex conditions.
>
> The objections made to the change in nomenclature seem to take for granted first that there are such things as 'intersexuals', which would render the characterization of the condition as a disorder offensive.

Feder aims to challenge what she calls 'an implicit understanding of intersex(uality) as analogous with homosexuality', which she says is 'misplaced' and risks 'trivializing' the physical injuries done to intersex people. But this argument supported a segregation of political struggles – one that had never been apparent in the history of intersex advocacy. The stakes for Feder are that the gay liberation movement *did succeed* in removing homosexuality from categorisation as a mental disorder. Yet Feder argued a contrary strategic path: the continued pathological categorisation of intersex people, facilitating support from the same profession whose transgressions had required a whole movement to oppose them in the first place!

Philosopher Robert Brandom has drawn a distinction between things that have histories and things that have natures.[16] Feder's argument demands an assumption that being gay is historical, while being intersex is natural. By this light, 'homosexuality' was responsive to the workings of historical and political struggles, but 'intersexuality' is an incoherent concept (better fragmented, then treated as a natural set of reducible maladies, by experts).

Joining Dreger and Herndon, Feder frames her essay as though it compares intersex with homosexuality – without such a comparison ever taking place. By the end of the 2000s (as most readers of *GLQ* would have known), gay life was unmistakably medicalised. While being gay had been depathologised in the United States since the 1970s (with the term 'homosexual' gradually falling into disuse), genitourinary medicine had dedicated GUM clinics which focused on preventing HIV seroconversion. Retrovirals had been available since the later 1990s, with testing resolving into automated emails and text messages informing patients of their HIV status. Retrovirals had already turned HIV into a manageable chronic health condition, with those receiving treatment typically reaching undetectable blood serum levels (the virus only surviving in their brain). The principle of 'undetectable = untransmittable' was so well-understood that it was a gay commonplace that the simplest way to avoid the virus was to select partners who disclosed they were positive (as those most infectious would usually be unaware, and thus declare themselves negative when asked). This breakthrough in curbing HIV/AIDS had not required a pathologisation of gay life (despite the best effort of right wing politicians).

A year after Feder's paper dismantling intersex was published, the first randomised controlled trial into pre-exposure prophylaxis (PrEP) would find that it had wholly prevented the gay men studied from testing HIV positive. This breakthrough was followed by a rollout of the drug in 2012. While Feder could not have guessed the imminence of PrEP, her *GLQ* piece seems badly dated. Western gay men were now to become medically treated irrespective of HIV status: retrovirals for those living with HIV, PrEP for those hoping to avoid it. Yet these changes were only partial: access to retrovirals and PrEP was heavily determined by access to healthcare, which varied wildly across national contexts and class position. That meant that these technological breakthroughs have only *exacerbated* existing community divisions along lines of class, nationality, and race.

Stigma persisted towards those living with HIV, just as it has done for the intersex. But no experts interacting with those living with HIV have reported that they could have been helped by a *more* pathological view of gay life in general.[17] Indeed, much of the stigma *within* gay communities has been a clear case of scapegoating: HIV was cast as the exemplary fate for those who'd contracted it through their marginalised lives (sex workers, gay or bisexual men, transgender women, and habitual IV drug users), thus leaving them doubly stigmatised.

The undeniably *political* shape of these healthcare breakthroughs is revealed quite easily through national comparison: in Britain this activism would continue doggedly into the mid-2010s because the state-run National Health Service (which provided most gay men coverage) still formally refused to offer PrEP until 2020.[18] Throughout the 2010s, a revived ACT UP worked alongside a community website (I Want PrEP) run by a single volunteer to both pressure government bodies and ensure ad hoc distribution continued in the meantime. In other words, gay life has been unmistakably medicalised, with struggles to relegate pathologisation (successful in the United States since the early 1970s) followed by campaigns against medical neglect concerning *specific* health needs.

So we can see that gay life was already extending the limits of clinical care (and noticeably stretching them beyond the directly therapeutic). The 'genuine health challenges' of twenty-first-century gay men were met through decades of community self-education and dedicated political struggle. This process was not an automatic extension of scientific breakthroughs: provision had to be won politically. Autonomous organising could never hope to fully overcome national divides. The mass availability of these drugs was not a given, but a direct consequence of health activism around HIV/AIDS that had started in the 1980s.

Do gay men have a nature, or a history? Both, of course. The same holds for those born intersex. With this in mind, Feder's argument seems to fall apart. During this process of political struggle for healthcare access, nobody directly involved suggested in earnest that being gay was really a 'sexuality disorder' (best recorded in a database). Such sentiments were the preserve of far-right shock jocks. Medical professionals did not require a purely pathological view of gay life in order to provide relevant healthcare for those living with HIV (or hoping to avoid seroconversion). Yet only the 1970s political campaigning to strike homosexuality from psychiatric categorisation as a mental health disorder allowed for any easy distinction between gay life as a whole, and HIV/AIDS as a specific risk within it. Only the *victory* of gay liberation against the psychiatric establishment ensured that HIV/AIDS could be treated as its own health condition, rather than an ailment that was synonymous with the psychiatric malady of homosexuality. (Early reporting prior to the HIV virus being isolated *still* referred to it as a 'gay plague' or 'gay cancer'.)

By the same token, at a community level, intersex people would never accept the imposition of the term 'disorders'. The overlap that had existed between ACT UP and '90s edgy intersex liberation rhetoric was no coincidence. Beyond their particular healthcare struggles, both intersex and gay people asserted themselves politically by refusing terms that didn't serve them. (The same year as the Chicago Consensus, the Gay and Lesbian Alliance against Defamation [GLAAD] convinced the *Associated Press Stylebook* to restrict use of the word 'homosexual'.[19]) Contra Feder, there was no clear reason the depathologisation campaigns successfully won by gay liberation would fail those pressing for more humane treatment of intersex physiologies.

Should we accept Feder's description of a 'visceral sympathy' that existed between gay men, lesbians, and intersex people? It's not clear that this perfectly *rational* display of solidarity existed solely at the level of the viscera.[20] There were obvious *reasons*, both strategic and historical, that the gay and lesbian, trans and intersex movements converged. Each of these movements' emergence had been one moment of the later twentieth-century counterculture, openly defying assumptions that the only viable life was lived through heterosexual households (with bodies reshaped to fit).

So if the intersex movement found itself extended platforms in transgender identity magazines, if they took to the streets chanting ACT UP slogans and were supported by gay and lesbian physicians and Transexual Menace, and if they were awarded an LGBT human rights prize, perhaps this was all simply a case of reasonably assessed shared cause. This integration was only to become more obvious across the 2010s (as the intersex movement reoriented towards human rights campaigning, routed through a network of LGBT global bodies). Feder, like so many allies, had wildly underestimated the historical savvy of intersex liberation.

By contrast, the managerial feminist game of setting up vying bands of 'stakeholders' to speak among can mislead: successful movements do not simply make the most of the positions their participants already exist in. They do not only articulate personal stances. They also intentionally *transform* the circumstances of our lives by providing us with points of contact that overturn the lives we'd previously lived. Typically enough for academic feminists of this era, Feder writes with the voice of management. Each stakeholder must speak in turn.

Finally, let's address the use and abuse of continental philosophy by the former ISNA leadership. In order to justify the use of 'disorders' instead of 'intersex', Feder, Dreger, and Herndon advance seemingly perverse readings of French philosopher Michel Foucault. Given Foucault is known for his resistance to natural scientists' and psychoanalysts' guiding notions of 'true sex', it was incongruous to see him marshalled in defence of male/female.

Yet Feder invokes Foucault's notion of 'normalization' to support the standardisation of the term 'disorders'. Feder argues that the introduction of the DSD acronym might render intersex variations 'disorders like any other', and therefore assist in ending the associated regime of shaming surrounding them. Scholars critical of the 'DSD' terminology have been at a loss as to how Foucault could be sincerely enlisted to support the introduction of 'DSDs', given that the French philosopher was among the history of thought's most vehement opponents of sex as a stable categorisation. Assessing Feder's essay, David Rubin writes: 'This is a perplexing move for a self-described Foucauldian.'[21] Philosopher Catherine Clune-Taylor wrote a paper in response the next year declaring DSDs a new disciplinary tool.[22] For those committed to fidelity to Foucault's method, seeing him invoked to justify a pathological vision of sexual difference seemed near inexplicable.

But the irony might have entertained the deceased philosopher himself. By this juncture, managerial liberalism was using Foucault to its own ends. By the 2000s, fidelity to the letter of Foucault was not required for most humanities researchers, but allusions could often seem expedient while rendering those discussed more docile. The touchstones thinkers of critical theory had become recontextualised in the idiom of new disciplines: 'medical humanities' and 'bioethics'. An erudite gloss for otherwise traditional thinking. Through these unlikely means, management of true sex could be defended.

From '90s Edgy to Intersex Ordinary

By the 2000s, the intersex movement appeared caught between two forms of fluency: using clinical terms sincerely or sarcastically. The intersex movement had always contained a wide range of rhetorical approaches. This was a matter of sensibility, as much as political stance. Thea Hillman's memoir, *Intersex (for Lack of a Better Word)*, offers a wry reflection on attending an anarchist event, Queeruption. Hillman observed a mismatch between ISNA activist styles following a disastrous panel:

I co-led a workshop with two other intersex activists, Hida and Xander, called 'Born Queer: Intersex: Fucking with the Sex and Gender Program'. I don't know who came up with the title. I understood it, but at the time I might have called it something more like, 'Intersex Awareness & Activism'. Today, I usually title my talks something like, 'Intersex Makes for Great Dinner Table Conversation'.

While those willing to take to the streets in the '90s were mostly of the harder edge, by the mid-2000s, group members with more conciliatory stances had come to the fore. References to 'Hermaphrodites with Attitude' were replaced with more anodyne people-first language: 'people born with intersex conditions'. Published materials and internal discussion emphasised the idea that intersex people wanted 'to live normal lives', tacitly downplaying queer connections.

This commonplace presentation of intersex people as wanting to be ordinary was a step change, considering the movement's countercultural origins just a decade before. This rhetorical move was twinned with a shifting relationship between intersex advocacy and feminism. Through the '90s, third-wave feminist theory had become increasingly focused on minorities, the abnormal, and the various processes of 'normalisation' that defined them. But frustrations had developed within the intersex movement over how much political support this really offered. Surveying feminist theoretical writing, Morgan Holmes's 2008 book *Intersex: A Perilous Difference* argued: 'Intersexuality was a departure point for a utopian appropriation . . . intersexuality as a mascot for sex radicals.' At once, the very *existence* of intersex variations was treated as a definitive marvel, while the positions advanced by the intersex movement were ignored. Singling out a particular collection, Holmes wryly remarked that 'in their introduction . . . [the editors] write that intersexuality is a liberatory state that will free us from the bonds of compulsory heterosexuality, but they fail to include any writings by intersexuals in the collection'.[23]

This was a bitter outcome for a movement that had pressed so hard to realise the principle of 'nothing about us, without us'.

Inevitably, the most lucid account of why feminism had come to treat intersex so instrumentally was offered by a women's and gender studies graduate, Emi Koyama. In 2000, Koyama wrote:

> I am very frustrated with how feminist, queer and postmodernist scholars exploit intersex existence merely for its sensational (and deconstructionist) value without considering the real-life implications for intersex people and the issues they are facing. Such actions do not educate the society about its oppression and erasure (both physical and social) of intersex people – it only further mythologizes them.[24]

This frustration would become *Teaching Intersex Issues: A Guide for Teachers in Women's, Gender and Queer Studies*, published by ISNA in June 2001, co-written by Emi Koyama and her former feminist professor Lisa Weasel. The pair wrote that for feminist theorists, 'intersex existence is viewed as a scholarly object to be studied in order to deconstruct the notion of binary sexes (and thus sexism and homophobia) rather than a subject which has real-world implications for real people'.

Treatment of intersex issues, Koyama and Weasel continued, was too often limited to using intersex people as a demonstration of complexity. Rather than outlining the relevant injustices that intersex people routinely faced, feminist theorists treated them as exemplary oddities. In this way, academic feminism performed its own kind of instrumentalisation of intersex, reducing intersex people to a deconstructive case in point, rather than being truly responsive to the intersex movement's challenges and concerns.

Regrettably, these charges ring true of even pioneering feminist scholarship published across the 2000s. In her introduction to her 2006 *Transgender Studies Reader*, Susan Stryker had little to say about the turmoil-stricken intersex movement, but called upon the example of their physiques to make a fairly typical deconstructive point:

> As the ambiguous bodies of the physically intersexed demonstrate in the most palpable sense imaginable, 'sex', any sex, is a category 'which is not one'. Rather, what we typically call the sex of the body, which we imagine to be a uniform quality that uniquely characterizes each and every individual whole body, is shown to consist of numerous parts – chromosomal sex, anatomical sex, reproductive sex, morphological sex – that can, and do, form a variety of viable bodily aggregations that number far more than two. The 'wholeness' of the body and 'sameness' of its sex are themselves revealed to be socially constructed.[25]

In this account, the 'palpable sense' of intersex people was to disrupt sex into its constituent elements beyond two-ness and wholeness. In the explicit, the intersex 'revealed' not the history of torture, mistreatment of children, castration, and medical concealment of treatment around stigmatised health conditions, but more simply the status of what was taken to be fixed and real as instead 'socially constructed'. That intersex people had 'viable bodily aggregations' that might astound those strictly wedded to sex as twofold was true enough. But this very obliviousness was bound up with both routinised harms and widespread incompetence. The 'social construction' doctors and parents agreed upon proved brutal in application. Altogether, this enlistment of intersex too often rested on a more conservative presupposition than we might pick out at first glance: these were still physiologies of note because they were *ambiguous* bodies.

On the other hand, intersex studies seems hard to reimagine without these grand conclusions for sex writ large: the titles that Dreger and Fausto-Sterling chose for their work invoke the 'invention of sex' or 'construction of sexuality' through 'sexing the body', while Kessler's book offered 'lessons from the intersexed'. Perhaps framing the oppressed as helping us grasp a process with much broader implications will always seem necessary, when bringing a minority struggle to light. But Koyama and Weasel had clearly identified a real problem within feminist pedagogy. Their guide advises teachers that many intersex students are reluctant to disclose their diagnosis, yet also that these classes may well be the *means* for them discovering their variation. Exactly this experience was related by intersex scholar Georgiann Davis, who describes reading academic feminism (specifically Kessler and Fausto-Sterling's most influential articles) in a humanities classroom:

> As evidence that I wasn't some sort of rare freak of nature, these pieces were personally (and later professionally) important to me. I remember thinking that if I was reading about intersex traits in a college classroom, they must be common enough. Still, as an undergraduate, I wasn't ready to disclose my personal experience with intersex.[26]

The increasing emphasis on the 'ordinary' ambitions of most intersex people was a sharp departure from the playful 'hermaphroditism' of the '90s. This was framed as a lack of motivation, as Koyama and Weasel put it: 'Don't be disappointed that many intersex people are not interested in becoming a third gender or overthrowing sex categories.' This position was to harden as the decade continued, and Emi Koyama's Portland-based local group, Intersex Initiative, attempted to strike a moderate stance on the question of 'disorders'. While reconstructing the case for 'disorders of sex development' proponents (Koyama herself concluded she preferred 'anomalies'), the initiative argued: 'Because the term "intersex" implied an identity rather than a condition, many "intersex" individuals – most of whom view themselves as ordinary men and women who happened to have been born with an unusual medical condition – never accepted the label.'[27]

While true on its face, this obviously begs the question of what it means to be 'ordinary'. Is this 'ordinary' the same sense of that word deployed by clinicians going about a genital exam? Is the 'ordinary' hoped for by parents from their newborn children the same as adult intersex people have in mind for their own lives? What the intersex movement's early years had revealed was not a broad population of former patients who now saw themselves as regular males or females with an unusual quirk. Instead, a sense of isolation and imposed ignorance was the prevailing norm. Contact with consciousness-raising movements allowed these plural self-understandings to be rethreaded.

In the pathological lens of clinical sciences, variations were understood mostly through a disjointed collection of symptoms. Intersex identification had surfaced only in context of life features such as fertility, menstruation, or muscle tone (always as relative diminishment, dysfunction against expected form, or perhaps excess/redundancy). But rarely were these breakdowns in expected bodily function grounded in the context that intersex people (and communities) would piece together for themselves. While many intersex people had *wanted* to be ordinary men or women, their movement had provided them with a means to come to terms with *why that had been so difficult to achieve* – and perhaps an opportunity to *stop* trying to belong to simplified sex norms.

What was revealed by the earlier intersex movement was how these variations are typically *hidden away* from those born with them. When parents and clinicians withhold information over the course of years, intersex people must form their own sense of themselves. The intersex movement had never relied on any one identity, but has instead guided participants through disintegration and recomposition. Consciousness-raising did not fashion any singular 'intersex self' to adopt, but collectively revealed what had been deliberately concealed. The intersex movement exposed anew an unexpected fragility of 'male' and 'female', and the horrors coldly enacted in prising them apart. Nevertheless, this argument of the default 'intersex ordinary' was to travel far. While mostly remembered for bringing the term 'transmisogyny' into popular feminist discourse, Julia Serano took up the cause of the normie hermaphrodite in her groundbreaking book *Whipping Girl: A Transsexual Woman on Sexism and the Scapegoating of Femininity*. Trained as a biologist, Serano was suspicious of the 'deconstructive' mode of feminism, echoing Koyama's complaints:

> I also find it disingenuous that academics in gender studies and sociology tend to concentrate rather exclusively on those gender-variant individuals who are most easily ungendered: transsexuals who have just embarked on the transitioning process, or inter-sex people who are in the process of being 'treated' by medical institutions . . . While these groups should be given a voice, what regularly goes unreported are the views of transsexuals who are ten or twenty years post-transition, intersex people who have lived fairly gender-normative, heterosexual lives . . . These populations of gender-variant people tend to have completely different experiences and opinions around gender. But their stories are never told, most likely because they are at odds with the positions and theories put forward by most academic gender researchers.[28]

That the majority of intersex people were either willing or able to live primarily straight lives appears here as a given. The intersex ordinary appeared even more bluntly in Serano's description of those with intersex variations as mostly leading 'fairly gender-normative, heterosexual lives'. By this account, intersex people could be expected to default towards the 'gender-normative'. Yet as we've seen, the whole edifice of clinical management aimed to reduce the odds of intersex people growing into gay, lesbian, or transgender youth. Medics had never treated the 'intersex ordinary' as a given: what the research of Kessler and Fausto-Sterling had revealed was that doctors were driven *exactly by the hope* that most patients could be rendered straight. While in the '90s Transexual Menace supported intersex advocates taking to the streets, by 2007 Serano's view seemed more supportive of them settling down in the suburbs.

Their Course

The patient advocacy approach recommended treating intersex as a sequence of 'disorders, like any other' (in the words of Ellen Feder). This approach was advanced by leading figures in the intersex movement, such as ISNA's founder, Bo Laurent. Why did this strategy fail? Patient advocacy attempted to win over medics who were often personally responsible for severe harms to intersex people. Through their dogged conceptual conservatism, these clinicians refused to either acknowledge those harms and make amends, or restrict themselves from repeating them. The medical profession's resistance to reform was stubborn, causing inevitable burnout among the intersex advocates who pressed them to change their practices. Intersex people and allies who were committed to this approach usually quit within a few years, often writing cynical and exasperated accounts as they left. Meetings with doctors were jarringly asymmetric in their ramifications for each party, as spoken to in the essay by Emi Koyama which began this chapter. For intersex people who'd faced medical harms personally, this mode of advocacy required retraumatisation: recalling and summarising injuries often during conversation with those who'd performed intersex surgeries or were being trained to do so.

In 2009, Alice Dreger began to write and agitate again on intersex, specifically congenital adrenal hyperplasia.[29] Through reporting and persistent blogging, she compiled academic bioethics writing against the use of fetal dex, along with her former ISNA colleague Ellen Feder.[30] At this point, Dreger was a professor of medical humanities and bioethics at Northwestern, and her targets were her own institutional size: Maria New (a professor of paediatrics, genomics, and genetics at Mount Sinai, where the intersex movement had staged a hijacking with the assistance of Suzanne Kessler back in 1996). And the preposterously named paediatric urologist, Dix Poppas.

After performing genital cutting on girls born with congenital adrenal hyperplasia, Poppas had been running 'clitoral sensitivity tests'. Poppas pressed a small vibrator on the girls' genitals, and asked them to rank their responsiveness between one and five. These studies also included papillary perfusion tests: Poppas pressed down on the clitoris until it turned white, then recorded how long it took for blood to visibly return. The youngest of these research subjects were six years old.[31] These practices were published without controversy by the *Journal of Urology*.[32] Dreger rebutted Poppas's defences extensively, resulting in public outrage, but not (as she'd expected) about the vibrators. Instead, the outraged readers of the popular press coverage had been previously unaware of CAH genital cutting altogether. Clearly the routine harms done to intersex children remained little known among the wider public and retained the power to shock. After a lengthy investigation, Weill Cornell Medical College found that Poppas had only performed a standard set of surgical procedures and aftercare.[33] (This is as scathing an indictment of the medical establishment as could be hoped for.) A subsequent study published in 2023 found that the 'nerve sparing' aspect of Poppas's technique for cutting clitoromegaly was greatly overstated.[34] After Dreger had spent several months focused on the affair but failed to stop Poppas in his tracks, she announced her final retirement from intersex advocacy in an essay bitterly titled 'Rejecting the Tranquilizing Drug of Gradualism in Intersex Care'. Gone were Dreger's hopes in diplomatic stakeholder brokering:

> I am fed up with being asked to be a sort of absolving priest of the medical establishment in intersex care . . . Being asked to be the speaker, the writer, the helper, or the whistleblower is increasingly making me feel – even while my *words* may be challenging the status quo – that my presence is shoring it up, by being part of a pretense that we have made real progress on the human rights issues before us.

Dreger's self-presentation here is dubious. While unambiguously on the side of the righteous in her work on congenital adrenal hyperplasia, we can see her once again depicting herself as a hapless intermediary. Rather than being a lowly go-between, she had headed the original DSD Consortium. Her words weren't challenging the status quo on intersex: by this point, they had become it. But what Dreger was finally, belatedly realising was that the harms done by clinical encounters were not only a conceptual matter, but a *struggle*.

Geertje Mak, Dreger's foremost critic in the scholarly history of sex, quotes a letter from one sexologist to another during the early twentieth century. The letter's author was affronted that his colleague had allowed a hermaphrodite to select her own sex. Instead, he wrote, the patient should have followed '*our* course'. Here, 'our' was a collective noun for the clinic. The same basic managerial mindset remained in play by the early twenty-first century: physicians came to delegate more of the decision-making to parents, as they processed these expectations through their new multidisciplinary teams. Yet the overarching *managerial* principle was retained: true sex could be sussed out by a skilled squad of professionals. For all her compassion with those being managed, Dreger had only honed that art. Dreger's work with the consortium was not moderating: it provided a *fresh language* to gloss a *familiar relationship* (medical abuse). One acronym segued from the last, and the cutting continued.

Despite Dreger's scepticism that an intersex community even existed, an international movement with ambitions that extended beyond the incremental reform of clinical care continued to challenge clinical practice. The new medical terminology would require the same approach used previously: consciousness-raising between intersex people, and agitation for depathologisation to bring in sympathetic apprehension of intersex from the wider world.

An Intersex International

The documentary *A qui appartiennent nos corps? Féminisme et luttes intersexes* (Who do our bodies belong to? Feminism and intersex struggles) follows a 2006 summer school organised by Organisation Intersex International France. The school was planned by Sarita Vincent Guillot, who was also the co-founder of the new Organisation Intersex International (OII) along with the US-based Curtis Hinkle. Bringing together a world-wide group of intersex attendees, the event set the template for the transnational gatherings of intersex people that OII and other groups would host more regularly over the next two dec-ades. Deploying sharp rhetoric, the intersex advocates gathered in France had developed art that addressed topics as varied as the history of John Money's clinic, to the appeal of coming to terms with dehumanising treatment through depicting oneself as monstrous.

This event followed a one-sided engagement of French inter-sex advocates with breakthroughs in the United States. As one account of their event published in French journal *Nouvelles Questions Féministes* (New Feminist Questions) shows, much of the Francophone intersex movement was familiar with the pro-gress made by Kessler and Fausto-Sterling in interplay with the Intersex Society of North America.[35] But this appreciation was by and large asymmetrical: while the introduction of 'disorders of sex development' was a topic of ferocious debate for the Anglophone intersex movement, in French parlance there was no question of accepting the term. Translated, the term 'sex develop-ment' appeared to address orientation, making it seem like an antiquated approach not to intersex, but *homosexuality*.

Beyond this philological quirk was a firmer political commit-ment. *A qui appartiennent nos corps?* shows the French intersex movement had retained the same focus on consciousness-raising and strategies of depathologisation found in the '90s-era Intersex Society of North America, including the sardonic spirit. For their part, the intersex movement had clearly achieved a more international integration by the 2000s, with the foundation of Organisation Intersex International triggering a proliferation of new and local groups and organisations refounded around participation in the new international.

The 'disorders' framework of the 2000s was not the first appearance of a certain Anglophone chauvinism on the part of US intersex activists. While the Intersex Society of North America was always explicitly transnational in scope, they had struggled to exhibit a genuine spirit of international collaboration. While the group had claimed victory after Laurent submitted an amicus brief to a Colombian high court ruling offering intersex children legal protections, scholars writing in both English and Spanish have questioned how much this ruling restricted the authority of surgeons.[36]

By contrast, from the outset OII took both political and institutional measures to cement operations across national divisions: imperialism was explicitly denounced and, showing their transnational language commitments, the group was officially registered in Montreal, Quebec (i.e., Francophone North America). This operation across languages meant that similarities and differences among national struggles could be fully responded to, honing an overarching understanding of intersex variations across the world. This approach allowed for local organising shaped around each community's specific needs. For instance, in Germany, legal struggles around intersex had long been shaped by jurists' enthusiasm for segregating transgender and intersex legal categories (typically interpreted as a distinction between psychological and physiological maladies, best scrutinised by the relevant specialist clinicians). In the German-language context, gender/sex split was never as strict as in Anglophone feminism, and relatively free use of the term *hermaphroditismus* (hermaphroditism) has continued in Germany up to today.[37]

The attempt to extend 'DSD' as a worldwide reordering coincided with the Anglophone world's War on Terror, which across the 2000s would transform existing forms of imperialism into a blunter, more brutal chauvinism. This backdrop matched the sheer optimism of American and British medics who rewrote protocols worldwide in an untranslatable form. One of the intersex movement's most powerful rejections of this is found in Argentinian intersex advocate Mauro Cabral's 2015 essay 'The Marks on Our Bodies'. Cabral wrote during the movement's failed attempt to have intersex variations depathologised by the WHO. Cabral linked medicalisation and colonialism in one breath (translated between two tongues):

> Three considerations about language:
>
> (1) for those who, like me, speak, write, breath, love and fight in a language other than English, decolonizing the way in which we are named multiplies to include not only medical speech but also the terms imposed by the Anglophone hegemony within international conversations on intersex;
>
> (2) the construction of an international intersex movement not only has depended – and still depends – on that hegemony, but has also considerably restricted the possibilities of other ways of communicating, including those of poetry, fiction, erotic, and other manifestations of 'inefficient' speech;
>
> (3) even against this double suture, the word 'intersex' still designates a persistent question, a scarred question that lies from tongue to language, a scar never fully healed, constantly reopened.

The earliest intersex advocates had adopted a presumptuous fluency in medical idiom to undercut fixed perceptions of medical competency. But the 2000s turn towards 'patient advocacy' resulted in a constriction both of political horizons and acceptable terms for self-understanding. 'Hermaphroditism' had to go, so that advocates could better focus on the fool's errand of clinical reform. Yet the persisting scar named by Cabral remained, to be addressed by new tongues and struggles over the next decade.

A Twist of Self-Consciousness

An impasse was opened by the new regime of 'disorders', which we are still living through today. As clinicians continued to refer to their patients with terms explicitly rejected by autonomous intersex organisations, they disrupted any hope of free dialogue on equal terms. Having invited Laurent to address them in 2000, clinicians would revert to form for the rest of the decade: dismissal and truculence towards critics, with feigned obliviousness towards their critiques.

This was a bitter moment in the intersex movement's history. As we've seen, the movement's earliest advocacy had begun with letters to feminist scholars, who were easily hooked into supporting the nascent movement. At its inception, the intersex movement heralded its community building with titles like 'Intersex Awakening' in special issues of transgender magazines and proud appearances on the streets of Boston alongside members of Transexual Menace. But now, to better facilitate the 'disorders' shift, intersex people would be presented quite differently – as a docile group of permanent patients. This liberal view would ultimately prove corrosive. With ISNA dissolved, the work of contesting pathologisation began anew. One movement memoir written by intersex advocate Kimberly Zieselman recalls:

> Looking back at the times I've used the term DSD, I can't help but wince. When I first made my discovery, I preferred the medical-sounding terminology. I thought *intersex* was more of an identity term that seemed popular outside of the United States. The people who were identifying as intersex were also predominantly identifying as queer. I hadn't liked the term because it sounded like 'inbetween sex' – or maybe it was more my straitlaced upbringing that made me afraid of a term that seemed to put so much focus on the word 'sex'. I had to break down my own squeamishness – really, my own pathologizing.

That rejection of the term 'disorders' was more widespread out-side of America is affirmed by Zieselman's account:

> For up to a full decade after the publication of the consensus statement and launch of the term *DSD*, there remained rampant controversy in the intersex community over its use. Intersex activists throughout (much of) the rest of the world were extremely concerned about the medicalized nature of the term, which had been coined by doctors who clearly benefited from pathologizing our intersex bodies. The term DSD helped to justify medical interventions such as surgery to 'fix our disorders'.

Zieselman tells us her changing stance was based on the group's youth activists, who took clear offence at the term being used even in self-description.

The word 'disorders' provided a hazy conceptual framework that attempted to replace what had been both 'pseudo' and 'true' hermaphroditism with a single umbrella term. But even if we restricted our understanding of reproductive anomalies to those possible to identify as 'disorders', shouldn't conditions such as endometriosis (the growth of uterine tissue and often cysts beyond the limits of the uterus) be included? Or if endometriosis *was* recategorised as a 'DSD', what use would a direct relative of someone with that 'disorder' have for a guide that instructs them on how to break the news to their extended family?

In truth, DSDs were never intended to name *any* anatomical dysfunction concerning the reproductive system. More specifically, they named physical variations perceived to have chaotic outcomes *for sex as a simple split*. These particular quirks of the body were disturbing for doctors and parents to encounter. The term 'disorders' simply rebranded a familiar set of challenges not to *health* but to *male/female*.

At ISNA's 1996 protest in Boston, Max Beck had argued that the palliative impact of these surgeries was not oriented to the children experimented upon, but instead soothed the anxieties that played out among their parents, physicians, and broader culture. The introduction of 'disorders' would seem to be another case of this pathological projection. Once again, the main focus was therapeutic: referring to their patients as 'disordered' helped physicians to lay their minds at ease, to soothe their consciences, and convince patients to authorise the interventions clinicians saw fit. Previously physicians had referred to 'pseudo-hermaphrodites' to tame knowledge forms beyond the limits of their training. Now their appeal to classical myth was replaced with a comprehensive database. Like so many ambitious projects of the twenty-first century, the key to 'DSDs' was in declaration, not completion.

Terms used to describe intersex variations revealed a long-standing interplay of clinical category and clinician's phobias. There had been many terms used over the decades to voice the ongoing sense of unease physicians felt when surveying sex's full diversity. In the early 1920s in Kentucky, Dr. Leon Solomon wrote up a medical report after an encounter with what he referred to as a 'strange creature', 'queer individual, 'strange fellow', and in his title a 'woman' (inverted commas in original). While she had come to him requesting an abortion, upon an examination Solomon was shaken to discover what he called her 'hermaphroditism':

> Upon entering the room, to my amazement there stood, nude, a veritable wolf in sheep's clothing, with all of the outward habiliments of a man. I felt that a hoax was being played on me and am free to admit, I did not know whether I was angry, frightened or embarrassed. Gazing first into a women's face, then at a large male organ of procreation was sufficient to produce a queer sensation.[38]

The woman refused to let Solomon investigate whether she had testes, as he'd wished to. Still mystified and titillated, he concluded the paper in pious terms: 'An All-wise Creator sometimes deals with His handiwork in a manner beyond mortal understanding.'

These disturbances to physicians' psyches only intensified once intersex people began to organise. That intersex people had achieved political militancy through their shared exchanges left medics with a 'queer sensation' of frustration and amazement. Let's repeat Dreger's assessment of the situation by 2004 once again: 'Paediatricians did not want to ascribe the heavily politicized (essentially queer) identity of "intersex" to babies, so among themselves they continued to use terms "true hermaphrodite" and "pseudo-hermaphrodite".'

With the introduction of 'disorders', these queer-fearful medics attempted a simple psychological fix: projection. It was intuitive for the medical profession to rebrand intersex as a set of reproductive 'disorders' in the 2000s. Labelling them 'disorders' was their way of setting their chaotic minds at ease. As best they could, they buried the speaking pseudo-hermaphrodite. But they would not find their target laid to rest so easily.

A Language Game with Loaded Dice

Some within the intersex movement had argued for 'disorder of sex development' for limited practical ends. Adopting this lingo from medics is usually appealed to as 'pragmatic'.[39] Intersex Initiative's director, Emi Koyama, suggested using 'intersex' for political organising purposes, while deploying 'DSDs' when in conversation with medics. Anick Soni, the founder of British peer support group iCON UK, defended the use of language 'mirroring' (following the lead from your conversation partner), particularly in the context of peer support.[40] But *pragmatism* has another meaning – one which can help us understand much more easily the clash of the *expressive* that the 'disorders' controversy unleashed.

In trying to frame a natural order for sex around its atypical forms, medics and their collaborators inadvertently formed a *community* which used its own logical idiom to oppose them by providing quite another way to speak of sex. They attempted to overwrite 'intersex', and failed.

For philosopher Robert Brandom, a community plays a decisive role in the use of words – with exchange and refinement of vocabularies continually drawing communities into life. There's good cause to prefer this sense of 'community' over the sense used earlier by Dreger and Herndon (whose emphasis on purpose-owned buildings seems slanted towards the resources available to a particular tier of urban gay men). A community in the semantic pragmatist sense is not defined by how much real estate they own, nor even by how often they meet in person, but by their shared tongue. It is this commonality that allows for the social institution of new terms, and a spirit of trust.

We've seen that ISNA's former managers Dreger and Herndon argued that speaking of an intersex 'community' was misleading. Whatever truth there is in this assessment is surely best decided by lesbians and intersex people in dialogue (perhaps led by those who overlap!). Let's complete the comparison: does a lesbian community stop being a community should their one 'bricks and mortar' bar in town close down? Even if a series of messy, interlocking break-ups leaves none of them living together, has lesbian community been extinguished? No. Not as long as they retain their own reasoning and logical idiom, as long as they share tongues together. The shuttering of any dyke bar is a tragedy, as are some lesbian break-ups. But these moments are not the death of a community. For as long as one woman in conversation can tell another that their rebound is more of a futch, some kind of community survives.

To work as a *community* in this way, all one needs to do is offer and receive reasons. Communities offer themselves accounts of their lives, using distinctive terms. These vocabularies are fit for the particular purposes of those developing them, while those beyond these conversations learn their breakthroughs long after the event – mastery of these shared words is displayed casually long before these vocabularies can be pinned down and recorded. Communities serve as a location for intimacy and informal contact, and are a wellspring of *rational deliberation*. That's because communities of this kind are a unique means for mutually developed idiom, and the source of reasons fit for confronting the circumstances we face down together. (We speak most beautifully when surrounded by those who we believe will be able to hear us and grasp our meanings with the lightest guidance.)

There is an *expressive* content to these reciprocal exchanges: you notice the terms used by those conversing with you, and infer conclusions from what they tell you. But community members also keep each other in check: within communities, meanings can be quickly clarified and confirmed. (Brandom calls this moment 'deontic scorekeeping'.) We keep track of words as those we're speaking to use them, and press them to clarify as their reasoning is in motion. Often it suffices to simply notice that they're using a word as they usually wouldn't. Commitments to shared positions are continuously questioned and reaffirmed: we use terms in ways which stretch the understandings of those we're speaking with. That process of mutual exchange reworks our grasp of topics through heated discussion – or without us fully realising it. The interplay of the reasons we provide, and what sense those we're speaking to make from our words, continues as a back-and-forth. Whatever the limits of reason are, we can only work them out together. That's why conversations are so often remembered as turning points in our thinking, and single meetings can transform our sense of the world (and our place in it). Communities reason together and form around these reciprocal exchanges, offering terms reshaped around the points made. It can't be denied that intersex people, who have challenged clinical reason since the 1990s, constituted a community in this sense. A new *fluency* was emerging, shaped around this new movement.

When I first attended an intersex international conference in Austria, my casual use of the word 'conditions' in conversation drew evident winces. When it was patiently explained that 'variations' was the preferred term, I found myself stopped in my tracks. Was having a 'condition' truly a thing to regret? Before I knew it, my own idiom had been reshaped: 'intersex variations' rolled off my tongue by the next morning of the event. This tiny yet decisive conversion in my conceptual apprehension of atypical physiques had unfolded so totally that even looking over old emails or chatlogs made me wince. A minor moment of correction provided an entry point to a new immersion in a developing idiom, and the community formed around developing this back-and-forth.

Often apparently 'semantic' splits may play a *pragmatic* role as full arguments are elaborated upon, and divides made clear. For instance, the interACT youth who couldn't bear to hear the word 'disorders' pass the lips of one of their peers were simply operating as a community. Refusing any reference to 'DSDs' established a new community, in contrast with earlier communities' playful pastiche of medical terminology. In different ways, these cultivations of language were how the intersex movement came to *reason together*: by extending an understanding of their social conditions to the wider world.

While the move towards 'disorders of sex development' by the medical professions was intended to soothe and stabilise their own condition of political chaos, for the movement, the 2000s were a clarifying decade. As one of the 'disorders' framework's most spirited opponents put it: 'OII is not of the opinion that this is a controversy simply about terminology . . . OII has objections to the DSD Guidelines and the underlying abuse of power used in imposing this term on us without consultation.'[41] Through their thoroughgoing rejection of 'disorders' terminology, advocates positioned themselves against a whole managerial framework of thinking.

Beyond Sex Coding

The 2000s challenged the self-consciousness breakthroughs won by intersex advocates in the '90s. As soon as the intersex movement faltered from this basic orientation, infighting ensued and key organisations fragmented. What was needed now was not feigned unity of purpose, but actual works of *translation* and *comparison*.

Following the challenge of the intersex movement, in the twenty-first century clinicians waived their former command over 'socialization', attempting a much simpler appeal to parental expectations of their children's bodily forms. While previously 'intersex' named human hermaphroditism as existing in its own right (albeit only *pseudo-*), now those who'd been intersexuals were solely identified via their developmental 'abnormalities'. They were transformed from outspoken 'intersexuals' to muted victims of 'rare diseases'. Thankfully, this rebranding failed to take hold: 'DSDs' would remain in the realm of clinical jargon. The movement responded with an upswell of international organisation, which would continue through the 2010s. By that point many of those involved in 'patient advocacy' had burned out of the movement. They were replaced with advocates who had met through dedicated websites such as Bodies Like Ours (founded by intersex advocate Betsy Driver), and local groups of the Organisation Intersex International.

In his article 'The Marks on Our Bodies', Mauro Cabral recalls his childhood encounter with medics, who took him to be a defective girl:

> The gynaecologist, the endocrinologist, the surgeon and his team, they were all nice people, polite and well-meaning, but absolutely incapable of accepting what I had to say; they could not accept that my body was fine as it was, and could not accept that I identified myself as a boy who liked boys. From their perspective, my flesh, my identity, my sexuality, my whole life was coded in terms of a diagnosis – and, according to that diagnosis, I was defined as malformed.[42]

For as long as these acts of presumption continue, advocates of intersex liberation will need to forge communities *against* those moments of clinical encounter. From the 2010s, the global dimensions of this struggle would become clearer, as break-throughs in consciousness would proliferate and come to popular attention worldwide.

The global intersex movement sought to respond through their own escalation, demanding that the enshrined right of medics and parents be replaced with protection of intersex as a human category. Human rights campaigning replaced the more docile drift of 2000s-style intersex advocacy, as advocates became exhausted by pretending to believe doctors.

4

Herms as Humans

I was born like this. I don't want any changes.

I am a woman and I am fast.

– Caster Semenya

Since her womanhood was first called into question around 2009, mid-distance track runner Caster Semenya has been prone to laconic statements expressing her total lack of interest in the controversy. The South African athlete typically contrasts jargon-rich interrogations of identity to her resolute dedication to running itself.

Since Semenya was a teenager, reporting officials and amateur sexologists have delighted in treating her womanhood as a technical question. Their speculations have taken a technical tone, with fussing references to chromosomes, blood plasma comparisons, gonads, and 'disorders' masking their obvious discomfort at seeing a powerful black physique. Resisting efforts to reduce her outstanding sporting achievements to so much isolated flesh, Semenya has remained entirely straightforward. As the title of Semenya's memoir *The Race to Be Myself* suggests, she treats controversy as a sideshow to her life's true purpose. That contrast fuelled public sympathies: her refusal to respond in biomedical terms is an achievement in its own right, given the intense (and often cruel) speculation that began when she was only eighteen years old. Through her refusal to bow to pressure from the press and international sporting bodies, Caster Semenya has served as an icon for both South Africans and intersex people worldwide. Her refusal to comply with authorities' demands for hormonal suppression coincided with an insurgent growth of intersex advocacy across Africa.

Semenya became the focus of a dispute around intersex athleticism in 2009, after winning gold at the International Association of Athletics Federations (IAAF) World Championships. Semenya's running time of 1:55.45 shaved her previous personal best by 8 seconds, a shocking improvement. Between this outstanding achievement and the runner's lean and muscular appearance, the body responsible for the race (since renamed World Athletics) insisted she enter a process of 'gender verification'. The results, reported while the championship was still underway, found that she had atypical levels of testosterone. In 2011, World Athletics introduced a rule setting a ceiling on acceptable levels of serum testosterone (a maximum of 10 nmol/L).

As this dispute continued, it generated an increasing amount of outrage because it seemed that Semenya was being personally targeted. Documents published in 2019 revealed that throughout this process, track officials had argued in court that Semenya was one of several 'biologically male athletes with female gender identities'. Then in an intriguing twist of circumstance, in 2011 Semenya was retroactively awarded the Olympic and World Championship 800m gold medals. The original winner, Mariya Savinova, was exposed for doping and received a lifelong ban. Savinova had bragged on film about using both testosterone and another androgen, oxandrolone (which Savinova explained would flush from her system within twenty days). This irony was compounded in 2015: while they were pressuring Semenya to diminish her endogenous hormonal levels, World Athletics stood accused of ignoring thousands of similar doping cases across a decade.[1] At the start of the 2010s, Semenya conceded to these demands for her to take anti-androgens, imposing an artificial handicap. But the side effects were too powerful, so she quit the medications and adopted a stance of open defiance towards the sporting authorities (which she's held to ever since). For their part, World Athletics continued to cast this as a question of unverified 'gender', tacitly aiming to mislead the world into assuming Semenya was a trans woman.

Through the rest of the 2010s, Semenya's career became bogged down in the process of appeals routed through bodies such as the Swiss-based Court of Arbitration in Sport, her outstanding athletic achievement surveilled by arcane bureaucratic bodies. But despite this major distraction, her running only improved across the decade. By 2016, South African sports writers had come to write of her in melodramatic terms, with one calling her a 'ticking timebomb' for the inevitable controversy that would follow her continued career (and certain success). Another who'd followed her career closely since the 2000s remarked, 'She has become the poster girl for hyperandrogenism.'[2]

Semenya's enthusiasm for keeping her career on track seems indefatigable. Recently she's focused on overturning national records in different races: the 400m at the 2018 African Athletic Championships (49.96 seconds), and the 300m at the University of Johannesburg in 2020 (36.78 seconds), after which she remarked: 'Track and field, you will see my face. I'm here to stay.' After this last triumph, Semenya explained she was aware her versatility was unprecedented: 'I try to do crazy stuff. You run and win titles from 200m to 5000m, no one has ever done that in the sport . . . But I am up for it.'[3]

Much about the case of Caster Semenya is obvious through her detractors and supporters: those supporting Semenya's exclusion from running cite snippets of her leaked medical reports, often reducing the situation to a pair of letters, or anatomical references. In this way the contempt for black *flesh* surfaces in these accounts. The root cause was clarified in 2023, when a spike of contempt followed her appearance in black tie with her wife, Violet Raseboya (who dressed glamorously). Various online personalities declared this as definitive evidence that she is a male interloper – apparently never having seen a butch/fem couple previously. So the reason for investigation was a crude and racism-saturated assessment of her appearance, as much as shock at her sporting prowess.

Contrastingly, Semenya's supporters have treated her as emblematic of South Africa's status as the 'rainbow nation'. From the outset of the controversy, Semenya was supported by South Africa's ruling African National Congress party (ANC), which has governed the country by enormous majorities since its decisive role ending the apartheid regime. Responding to the original round of controversy, the ANC and the Young Communist League of South Africa denounced the racism of evaluations of Semenya's appearance: 'It feeds into the commercial stereotypes of how a woman should look, their facial and physical appearance, as perpetuated by backward Eurocentric definition of beauty.'[4] Many remarked on the clear racist presumption that was exhibited by everyone from a minority of Semenya's white competitors, to right-wing commentators. Popular social media hashtags such as #HandsOffCaster and #JustDoItForCaster demonstrated widespread adoration for both Semenya's sporting success and her defiance.

Semenya further received the support of both local and worldwide intersex advocates. In a piece which acknowledges Semenya has refused to address the controversy in detail, US advocate Hans Lindahl writes:

> People have long tried to identify a 'true' sign of sex on the human body; in earlier centuries, intersex people were defined by, and forced into social positions based on, their gonads. When that proved cumbersome, medical authorities shifted toward looking at their genitals. When genitals proved to have loopholes and gray areas, chromosomes became more appealing, an answer written in the genes. Except that elements of complex categories like sex, which are made into social differences, can't be neatly and universally pinpointed. That's the kind of thinking that brought us scientific racism.[5]

One feature of the controversy which would appear repeatedly in these disputes around female athletes was the leaking of medical reports. This kind of 'leaking' is a practice that defies the basic norms of medical data and patient confidentiality, yet with intersex athletes it has become par for the course. When medical reports are furtively distributed this way, what is revealed by the physiques of the intersex appears only through the clinical lens at its most hostile. Rather than positioning healthcare as an ongoing exchange of expertise, leaking makes clinical science the 'last word' in a running conflict. The speculations and faux-objective assessments become a private law, or definitive judgement. 'Leaking' has to be understood as its own violation, both discrediting and revealing the entire process at work. The medical authority as it is appealed to by Semenya's critics is manifestly *not* one operating under conditions of sincere trust and ongoing discretion.

Semenya's responses to being the object of such controversy have been consistent: she has never been anything besides a girl or a woman. One unlikely celebration of Semenya's steadfastness occurred towards the start of the controversy in September 2009, when the popular South African magazine *YOU* ran a front cover featuring Semenya in a makeover photoshoot (appearing alongside such enticing titles as 'Gay Mormon Guy in a Million!') The runner's hair had been released into a perm, and she wore a black dress, gold loop chain, and matching bracelet. The headline ran: 'WE TURN SA'S POWER GIRL INTO A GLAMOUR GIRL – AND SHE LOVES IT!' The makeover was clearly a one-off, intended to evoke reaction by obvious contrast to her typical persona (impeccable butchness). When Semenya was later shot for *ELLE*, her usual butch comportment was back in force: she was clad in a Nike T-shirt and two-piece denim, a familiar icon rather than an oddity.

To appreciate Semenya's resistance against the coercive frameworks and medicalisation that threatened her career, we first need to locate her as one of many athletes from the Global South being punished for what Western medics now diagnose as 'disorders of sex development'. Second, we need to grasp the particular national context of South Africa, which had long fostered an intersex movement and was the first country to formally protect intersex people.[6]

Throughout this book, we've found two key framings of intersex people resurface across contexts: that they exceed the expected norms, or that they are born incomplete (requiring professional help to 'finish off' their physiques). Intersex people are usually cast as either excessive or under-developed as a prelude to their attempted elimination, or at least being rendered invisible through surgical or conceptual means. Physicians proffering explanations and pressing for operations more often present intersex as 'unfinished'. However, in both cases, much the same cutting can be justified: intersex forms are depicted as either impelling completion or sacrificial excision.

The controversy around intersex sporting achievements targeted athletes from Africa, India, and Central Asia. The obvious economic disadvantages faced by women from these countries makes it all the easier to cast their sporting achievements as undeserved. But equally, this framing reveals the absurdity of calling these variations 'disorders'. The supposed 'disorder' triggering hyperandrogenism is a disability operating without an impairment: the implication is that there is an upper limit of achievement conceivable for a woman, beyond which some natural order is breached. Within this imagined orderly form of sex, sporting achievement demonstrates a woman's commitment, effort, and talent – while for the intersex, any athletic performance should be seen as instead indicative of a male physiology.

For their part, athletics governance organisations referred to the testing of suspected intersex athletes as 'gender verification' – leaving it unclear whether they were simply using the term 'gender' as a euphemism for sex, or pulling on transmisogynistic fears that virilised women were actually men in disguise. This spectre was raised by an IAAF spokesman during the original Caster Semenya controversy in 2009: 'However, if it's a natural thing, and the athlete has always thought she's a woman or been a woman, it's not exactly cheating.' This equivocation between trans or intersex women was not accidental: the association intends to delegitimise their target either way (a female-assigned woman not 'exactly' cheating, but the next worst thing).

The racism latent in these discussions has to be addressed frankly. Repeatedly, the managers of these grandiose athletic associations insinuated (and sometimes outright stated) that the entire problem was caused by the failure of hospitals and midwives in Global South to detect and eliminate the visibly intersex before they became adult virilised females. This was a task which these institutions took as their duty to complete. Global sporting authorities talked in terms of 'gender' as they sought to cast doubts around the *sex* of these women to justify biochemical handicaps, and otherwise plainly unnecessary cutting.

Those who were more compliant with the edicts of sporting bodies have reported they suffered greatly from it. Ugandan mid-distance runner Annet Negesa turned whistle-blower after having suffered years following a World Athletics–sanctioned gonadectomy. Negesa had been told that she would be able to return to her career within a few weeks of the surgery, but the reality was that Negesa's treatment was negligent. (Doctors provided her with no replacement hormones, which led to joint pain and fatigue.) As Negesa put it, the surgery shattered her hopes of a career, and thus her identity (as a runner as much as a woman):

> I was no longer a person who has importance to anyone . . . I was useless to people because I was no longer racing. I lost my career, I lost my scholarship, I lost income, and I was no longer able to help my family financially. I lost everything.[7]

As well as having fewer resources to support their athletes (in everything from training to legal battles), poorer nations also would offer dim prospects for athletes who'd dedicated their adult lives to their sports, only to be suddenly discredited and medically mistreated.

Caster Semenya experienced much the same crisis during an interlude of several years on anti-androgens, which also left her deeply ill. Given the weak understanding of intersex physiology we've encountered throughout this book so far, it should hardly be surprising that experimental treatments intended to deliberately weaken and curb sporting prowess might have such an impact. In Semenya's case, after her experience on anti-androgens, she resumed a determined and open resistance to the sporting establishment's attempts to delegitimise her career's achievements.

The role played by androgens specifically in this controversy bears careful examination.[8] Clearly testosterone levels *for those with sensitive receptors* play a role in muscle growth (as do estrogens). But equally, testosterone holds a mythologised position in these discussions. In Rebecca Jordan-Young and Katrina Karkazis's 2019 book *Testosterone: An Unauthorized Biography*, they highlight the *cumulative* nature of the unfounded attributions of prowess to androgens. Without a rigorous examination of the effects of differentiated levels among women, testosterone is appealed to vaguely but with such monotony that the associations between virility and this lone steroid become further entrenched.

In the case of intersex athletes, assumptions are often made about how androgens are processed. In reality, hormonal processing matter varies as wildly from body to body as hormone levels themselves. As receptors came to be fully understood by the end of the twentieth century, a spate of overdiagnoses of androgen insensitivity seems to have followed, with many advocates reporting their diagnoses were revised in their lifetimes. (This makes it doubly cruel that public discussions rely on the leaked documents of official medics, who are assessing a single snapshot.) Hormonal receptors affect how each body processes the sex hormones circulating through blood and tissues, but they are rarely tested. Full-body karyotype (which pulls chromosomal data from various body parts, rather than just blood plasma) and receptor testing are often not available in either Western nations, or those targeted by intersex scandals. While sporting bodies attributed the non-detection of intersex athletes to 'less developed' nations' weaker healthcare systems, in reality, mosaic genetic testing and receptor sensitivity scans have not been reliably available in the West either. As such, our understanding of the links between androgen levels and performance was much more tenuous than was widely acknowledged. A much wider variation in both receptor sensitivity and chromosomal mosaics likely exists than we currently appreciate, with unclear ramifications for sporting performance. Seemingly freakish achievements will always be the mainstay of international contests such as the Olympics, and the limits of achievement are not being approached scientifically.

Virilised women were not just feared because their excess of manliness fuel might give them an undue advantage. This controversy was also used as justification to coerce athletes into genital cutting that would target no discernible sporting advantage. Once again, horrors performed against intersex people by clinicians were not hidden, but published for peers to consult. As a *New York Times* reporter summarised:

> Sports officials referred four female athletes from 'rural or mountainous regions of developing countries' to a French hospital to reduce their high testosterone, according to a 2013 article in *The Journal of Clinical Endocrinology & Metabolism*. The authors, many of whom were physicians who treated the women, describe telling them that leaving in their internal testes 'carries no health risk', but that removing them would allow the athletes to resume competition, though possibly hurt their performance. The women, who were between 18 and 21, agreed to the procedure. The physicians treating them also recommended surgically reducing their large clitorises to make them look more typical. The article doesn't mention whether they told their patients that altering their clitorises might impair sexual sensation, but it does say the women agreed to that surgery too.[9]

The racism at work in these sex investigations is exhibited unmistakably when these women are described as being 'from rural or mountainous regions' of the Global South.

In this account of sex and civilisation, a tidy and unmistakable split between male and female is the prerequisite for entry to civilised life. If childbirth and rearing outside of the imperialist core features less intersex genital cutting, this is surely a sign of the region's relative backwardness (confusingly for these accounts, traditional female genital cutting practices are *also* taken as an indication of primitive inferiority).

If we distinguish between a choice and the circumstances surrounding that choice, we can see clearly how difficult it becomes for these women to defy these Western-based sporting bodies. These athletes had already suffered career-long institutional disadvantages compared to their European counterparts: from weaker support with coaching, to more intense sexism when committing their lives from adolescence onwards to sports, to more costly travel from their remote countries, with less easily secured visas.

Semenya's rejection of anti-androgens foreclosed a potentially intensifying regime of body normalisation: the managerial figures of World Athletics clearly were not directing their attention purely towards some hormonal injustice. Whatever the relationship between androgens and human stature, strength, and muscle endurance, the fact that World Athletics ordered and oversaw the cutting of clitoral tissue reveals the real game. No case can be made for a 'virilised' clitoris providing a sporting advantage. The sporting bodies' 'gender testing' enforced conformity to narrow expectations around the acceptable limits of sex. In the same way that Semenya would have been directly disadvantaged in her institutional struggle if she had declared herself proudly 'intersex', these women were aware that compliance was tacitly required for their sporting careers to continue. The true concern wasn't that they were unfair competitors, but that they possessed an *excess of female tissue*. The condition of womanhood for these athletes was, accordingly, the removal of this supposed excess.

While they frame their behaviour towards intersex athletes as a confirmation of the athletes' 'gender' and an attempt to avoid deception by those of another (true) sex, these sporting committees are actually expressing their contempt for the physiques of these athletes, through an imposition of sex differentiation to an arbitrary standard – at whatever sacrificial cost.

These sporting officials have used their leverage over women from rural backgrounds in the Global South to push unnecessary surgeries onto athletes, failing to support them in recovery, and obliging them to undergo hormonal recomposition treatments with unclear side effects. They've done so mostly quite calmly and officiously, supported by lawyers and hired medics. Like the clinicians who evolved their concept across the 2000s, their principle of 'management' of intersex led through to elimination. To say at this point that World Athletics should be disbanded would be too mild a suggestion.

The virilised woman who appears in phobic fantasies isn't defined by any measurable blood level, but by her achievements – her way of passing through the world. When Semenya reached the end of her mid-length bouts still seeming like her placid, almost tranquil self as other world champions looked on in awe, she drew adoration and disdain in equal force. When Semenya brushed off the speculations of right-wing pundits and boosted her performance by taking up sprinting as well, we can see exactly the figure that makes more hidebound believers in sex as twofold tremble. Semenya received support from across South Africa: a nation with a long history where 'intersex' was treated as a scholarly focus for racism, and as an emancipatory movement.

In Amanda Lock Swarr's book *Envisioning African Intersex: Challenging Colonial and Racist Legacies in South African Medicine*, Swarr shows that apartheid-era sexologists vigorously explored claims that black South Africans were disproportionately prone to 'true hermaphroditism'. G. P. Charlewood's 1956 book *Bantu Gynaecology* was only the most famous of the many papers. Swarr shows that this fertile vein of race science was founded on a statistical misinterpretation, with a chain of hazy citations of citations eventually leading back to a shoddy master's thesis – resulting in something like an academic's game of telephone. By baselessly casting black Africans as disproportionately prone to being 'true hermaphrodites', these scientists stitched the governing ideology that civilisation had to be safeguarded by the National Party seamlessly into studies of defective sex.

Just as South Africa's fabricated sex research was bound up with its racist political order, its intersex movement appeared through apartheid's downfall. Sally Gross was a Jewish South African living in exile until 1999, at which point she returned to found Intersex South Africa. The group focused on both community work and legal advocacy. Remarkably, South Africa was the first nation to officially enshrine constitutional protections of intersex people, with the 2003 Sex Description Act offering formal rights to correct documents and secure name changes. (This was a bittersweet victory for Gross, who had already been delayed from returning to the country for three years while changing her legal documents).

Despite these official breakthroughs, the social conditions for intersex people across South Africa remained harsh. Local intersex advocate Babalwa Mtshawu reported in 2019 that traditional midwives and healers were still killing children born visibly intersex, while surgical cutting was also becoming increasingly common in clinical hospitals.[10] A year before her tragic and premature death in 2014, Sally Gross had turned to thinking through intersex oppression in terms of 'social death' (a term she drew from Jamaican American historian Orlando Patterson's work on slavery). Gross wrote of the life-long indeterminacy intersex people could experience, as imposed by a society that refused to anticipate them as a 'shadow existence'.

In a 2009 column, Gross wrote expressing both solidarity and sympathy for Semenya. Following a self-deprecating remark about the pair's relative fitness, Gross shared a story of emergency room medics referring to her as 'he' in front of her, and refusing to stop when she presented her (hard-won) legal documents:

> The way in which Caster Semenya's sex is being questioned reminds me of my emergency room experience. A patriarchal sex-police claims the right to determine her very identity, regardless of the consequences for her. As I have pointed out elsewhere, the 'gender verification' process is anything but objective and scientific. It is moot whether any intersex condition actually gives athletic advantage in the first place.

In South Africa, unwavering support for Semenya came not simply out of a sense of craving for local sporting achievement, but also legacies of shared struggle. While this was a powerful national context, it was also a continental one: African intersex groups would become highly active across the early twenty-first century. While facing diverging circumstances from nation to nation, these advocacy groups would achieve an increasing spirit of collaboration across the Global South.

Intercontinental Breakthroughs

Both the Intersex Asia Network and Intersex Africa Movement were founded in the late 2010s. The rapid proliferation of interlocking local groups worldwide that followed has received support from three huge LGBT 'consortium' organisations: Astraea Lesbian Foundation for Justice, the International Lesbian, Gay, Bisexual, Trans and Intersex Association (ILGA), and Global Action on Trans Equality (GATE). The Astraea Foundation hosts and funds continental community meetings, bringing together advocates from across national contexts. Since 2011, ILGA has supported projects in Africa and Asia and worldwide meetings attracting intersex people from across the globe. During the pandemic these moved online, with sessions addressing themes such as 'Intersex Joy' addressed by advocates from Africa, Asia, Europe, and the Americas.

In a cute flourish, GATE's intersex subgroup describes its aim as 'seeding intersex politics to reforest sex monoculture and root diverse resistance'. Their mission statement is echoed by one of Intersex Asia's founders, Hiker Chiu, who describes their role as not directing but rather 'incubating' the formation of groups in new national contexts.

Rather than demonstrating any radical differentiation in movement aims from continent to continent, advocates throughout the world generally talk about the same conditions of shaming and silencing. While the circumstances can prove harsher in rural areas especially, many accounts of intersex advocates accord with those found in the rest of the world. When interviewed by other intersex people as part of the Interfaces project, Nthabiseng Mokoena related a story of overcoming her lifelong submersion in stigmatisation, closing off her submission, 'No Body Is Shameful'. But this had taken a long journey. Like many intersex people, Mokoena introduces her story by relating a childhood filled with deception from her parents. Finally in 2011 she was diagnosed with partial androgen insensitivity, and confronted her mother about what her birth had been like. After refusing to answer, her parent finally gave way:

What she told me was that: *'The only thing that I wanted was for you not to feel as hurt and ashamed as I felt after I gave birth to you.'* Because she gave birth to me at home, and not at a hospital, and there were midwives there, and in African culture, unfortunately, the birth of a child is the mother's responsibility and if there is something 'wrong' with the child the blame goes to the mother, and so she felt extremely isolated after giving birth to me. And she said to me: *'All that I ever ask is that you not feel the same pain that I went through after giving birth to you, and it's not that I was ashamed that I gave birth to a child like you it's because people put me in that position.'*[11]

We can see here how even a parent that *refused* to sanction the worst available harm still found herself locked into the logic of 'management'. While Mokoena attributes this shame to African culture and the midwives, there is a similar sense of responsibility otherwise played off by doctors following visibly intersex births. In this instance, being born outside of a clinical context may have helped Mokoena escape harm physically, yet she was still harmed by the prevailing interphobia of her society. Just as is typical in the West, Mokoena struggled with medical expenses and accumulated mistrust after repeated mistreatment by public hospital staff:

> So, it took a long time for me to actually accept myself, and because I've never been operated on . . . the shame, the shame . . . all that I wanted to do was to get an operation for a long time in my life, and I hated going to the public hospital because over and over again I became this guinea pig for the doctors. I became so abused by the doctors to a point whereby even when I got sick, and I was seriously sick, I could not go to the doctor.

Finally through meeting other intersex people (presumably most of whom had received surgeries), she found that her overriding desire to be corrected abated, and instead became thankful that she had avoided this harm as an infant.

Working to overcome these widespread experiences of harm inflicted by families and medics both clinical and traditional, African intersex groups have become adept at networking through internal and world-facing web sessions, from Zoom seminars to Twitter spaces (each bringing together advocates and perspectives from several nations).

The Ugandan Support Initiative for People with Congenital Disorders (SIPD) was founded in the late 1990s, making it one of the oldest African intersex groups. SIPD campaigns both on a community level and through pressuring Africa-wide governance bodies to pass measures such as the African Commission's recent

'Resolution 552 on the Promotion and Protection of the Rights of Intersex Persons in Africa'. The resolution formally protected infants across Africa from unnecessary genital cutting.[12]

Intersex Nigeria has hosted various online discussions open to participation across the world with titles such as 'Intersex: Unpacking the Dynamics Within our Community'. Locally, they ran events including a joint Lagos Pride symposium and gala night in the country's capital. The group's legal advocacy includes trying to get intersex surgeries outlawed under anti-torture legislation. In a touching video addressing younger intersex people still coming to terms with their variation, the group's executive director, Obioma Chukwuike, reassures them: 'It's the right time to be born. If I was given birth to now in this present year, I'd see information about my experience or share. I can actually find my tribe easily.'

The 2022 documentary *InterAfrika* interviewed intersex people from across the continent about their upbringings and political work. Within a few minutes, the film shows us how normative violence runs both through clinical practice across Africa, and beyond it. One interviewee reports that a sense of inadequacy inspired them to visit traditional healers, while another recounts stories of parents going into debt to afford professionalised hospital corrections. Intersexuality is often conflated with homosexuality, in contexts where homophobic laws are either newly proliferating, or a living legacy of British colonialism. While *adult* intersex people are often treated as objects of pity rather than targeted for violence (if passably heterosexual), many infants and children are treated more harshly. Especially in rural contexts, many infants are still simply murdered by parents or traditional midwives.[13]

Whereas the sporting bodies we've mentioned presented intersex genital cutting as a marker of civilisation, from the perspective of these African advocates these harms are variations on a theme. Whether they are killed after birth or surgically hidden from view (in the genteel Western style), violence against intersex people remains widespread. Different means are directed towards the same end: societies with visible hermaphroditism eliminated, at whatever price. African intersex advocacy began in the late 1990s, and through the twenty-first century a proliferation of groups have reshaped intersex liberation as a global movement. Both local struggles and international collaborations have required the intersex movement to collectively resist colonial inheritances. As decolonial philosopher Alex Adamson has it: 'Intersex activism is not reducible to arguments about sex or gender or sexuality, but rather reveals how these concepts arise with geopolitical arrangements of knowledge and power.'[14] In other words, to reveal the shape of sex can only mean shaking up the history of imperialism.

Variations on the Human

Through the 2010s, intersex advocacy came to refocus around human rights campaigning. This reorientation allowed for a strategic uniformity even as groups proliferated internationally. Whereas in the post-war twentieth century the pressing concern for clinical sexology was to manage 'hermaphroditism in humans', in the early twenty-first century clinicians were making efforts to remove the concept of intersex variations from the natural category of human. In response, the intersex movement asserted that they were *people* who warranted uniform protections afforded against dehumanising treatment. Though the intersex movement increasingly came to bypass national bodies, these appeals were heard in detail by experts not directly implicated in existing harms done to intersex people.

The turn to human rights was an intuitive shift for intersex advocacy. Several advocacy groups reflected this change in their names, including Intersex Human Rights Australia and Intersex Human Rights India. This revitalising trend contrasted with the widespread burnout caused by 'patient advocacy'. Advocating through global governance meant interacting through hearings around topics such as torture and childhood development. These experts were less likely to be directly involved in the offences under discussion, and had a broader grasp of the relevant topic of concern. This proved a more promising avenue for advocacy. Whether in healthcare, children's rights, or sports, these campaigns have established intersex people as deserving of comprehensive protections. Often this work is couched in terms of securing 'fundamental rights'. Via well-publicised appeals to expert bodies, this work has often bypassed less promising professional and national networks, and resulted in a proliferating volume of knowledge that now needs to be pressed home locally in order to finally end these routine harms forever.

What emerged from this interplay of advocacy and expert opinion was a new consensus: in an echo of the old juridical principle of establishing hermaphroditism in court to allow some degree of traversal between male and female entitlements and identities (or vice versa), now 'the intersex' were affirmed as requiring thoroughgoing protection by a constellation of official governance bodies. Innumerable reports on abuses against intersex people in various localities were released, along with formal censure of nations lacking safeguarding of intersex 'fundamental rights' (i.e., basically any nation-state). While medics had cast the term 'intersex' as outdated and misleading, it came to serve the movement set on undermining their authority perfectly well. Less consistently, formal protections have appeared on the national level – first in South Africa, most recently in Greece.

In other words, one expert's 'management of differences in sex development' is another's 'ongoing human rights abuses against intersex people'.

There are obvious risks and limitations attendant to participating in global governance bodies and working through transnational consortium NGOs. How these will be navigated remains to be seen. This new approach reshaped intersex advocacy on an organisational level, with both a proliferation of more and more groups across new national contexts, and the establishment of continental-level community organising by the end of the 2010s.

A reorientation towards global governance bodies was greatly enabled by the existing international shape of intersex advocacy's organising: the 'early adapter' emphasis on online communications seen in the 1990s bloomed with the rise of social media and mass availability of video editing software. Direct production and distribution of personal accounts led to viral distribution of discussions among intersex advocates.

As the intersex movement reoriented towards local struggles distributed worldwide, researchers delved into the neocolonial scope of sexology. Lena Eckert's *Intersexualization: The Clinic and the Colony* shows that Gilbert Herdt and Robert Stoller collaborated across the 1980s to introduce what they called clinical ethnography.[15] The clinical establishment had long behaved as if they could simply impose their biomedical understanding worldwide. Their use of colonised peoples was extractive, drawing the basis for both professional training and pet theories about 'psychosexual differentiation' across ethnicities. In the Dominican Republic, Stoller and Herdt collaborated with Julianne Imperato-McGinley to research what she called 'male pseudo-hermaphrodites' with 5-alpha reductase deficiency. Typically raised as girls, these children would then have what was taken to be a male puberty. In their bid to understand the cultural integration of intersex people, the researchers began testing them in ways that exposed them to new scrutiny by their peers. The introduction of medical examination by all accounts intensified prejudice against these youths in subsequent years, and may even have introduced new slurs for them. The story is still repeated today by the popular press as a quirky tale of human diversity.

In this way, neocolonialism came to extend its science of sex (by this point centuries old), drawing in new 'case studies' and pushing a clinical framework of true sex across new horizons. The intersex movement today exists in the shadow of this moment, striving to overturn both harmful imposed understandings and resist local prejudices and damaging customs. At this point, global governance bodies have come to serve both as a forum for representation, and in the case of sports, opponents in a contemporary battleground.

5

A Struggle without a Centre

This account so far has unfolded like a lens panning out, beginning in Boston and drawing out to watch the interplay of intersex liberation as it emerged across the Global South, now leading a dialogue with the West. This view lets us understand what was attempted by European and US medics and geneticists in the 2000s, and why they failed. Their aim had been intersex knowledge's *centralisation*.

This strategy was quite explicit, and it operated on two levels: first, 'centres of excellence' would be home to multidisciplinary teams; second, knowledge of intersex was restricted to clinical professionals (from surgeons to psychologists). While billed as a 'modernisation' fit for the twenty-first century, this strategy actually remodelled intersex healthcare around the centralisation that had already been able to dominate healthcare practices worldwide (with university clinics run by sexologists who wielded a combination of clinical authority, influence through research publications, and popular influence through talk show interviews). Hatched out of this was a vision of prestigious central bodies for clinical care – which, due to wildly uneven resources across national contexts, would never be realised. While use of genetic testing had expanded since the 2006 consensus, both data-sharing and the framing of treatment around multidisciplinary teams had yet to take place:

A team consisting of paediatric specialists in endocrinology, surgery/urology, clinical psychology, and nursing was only possible in 31 (41 %) centres. Of the 75 centres, 26 (35 %) kept only a local DSD registry and 40 (53 %) shared their data in a multi-centre DSD registry.[1]

But conceptually too, this framing of centralised clinical jurisdiction rode roughshod over local understandings of sexual difference. The 2000s saw an attempt to marginalise local understandings of sexual variations, just as they sought to bury any explicit reference to the Western/Mediterranean mythological figures of hermaphrodites.

Against this attempt to concentrate and restrict knowledge, the affiliated groups of the Organisation Intersex International provided a counterweight. Community meetings produced statements approved by participants. But there was no attempt to bind members to follow directives between nations: the intersex movement came to rely on internationalism without a central committee.

The Travails of Twenty-First Century Solidarity

The intersex movement has increasingly come to rely on support from large transnational LGBT organisations. A strategic unity that was already obvious in the early advocacy of the 1990s has now been cemented by organisations, with institutional bodies with far greater funding and access than any one intersex group could hope for running projects focused on intersex advocacy, and hiring full-timers from the movement.

Yet this move linked intersex struggles unmistakably with queer and trans people at the exact moment that homophobia and transphobia have become a guiding preoccupation for the global right. Take one *Dateline* report on Kenya, which featured footage of a protest by local advocates attempting to win legal recognition. One Kenyan MP joined the protest, and explained that his own albinism left him intuitively sympathetic with the intersex people and their cause. However, when the American interviewer asked him about gay rights, his face fell and he curtly replied that the intersex movement shouldn't have anything to do with that.

An advocate from a southern African nation remarked upon these difficulties at a panel discussion hosted by ILGA-World. They explained that while protests outside hospitals as they'd seen in the United States were inspiring, the audience had to understand such tactics weren't viable in their nation. As hospitals were government buildings, such a tactic would amount to defying the state. Advocacy which didn't run the risk of being 'disappeared' had to happen through the official channels overseen by the ruling party (which the group actually had been using with some hopeful breakthroughs). The nation's former leader had outlawed gay relationships as part of his chauvinist bid to stay president for life, meaning connections to queer groups also had to remain underground.

What this shows us is that intersex advocacy will look divergent in the alliances it can forge openly. The clinical determination on discerning 'true sex' becomes particularly salient if that conclusion is tethered to the legality of one's relationships (whether marital, sexual, or inheritance). As Georgiann Davis wryly recalled:

> I vividly remember queering my own marriage in 2001. On a rainy October Saturday in a suburb of Chicago, I walked down the aisle in a traditional white wedding dress and married a cisgender man who, like me, has XY chromosomes.[2]

(Davis tells us her complete androgen insensitivity syndrome was originally described in her records as 'testicular feminization'.) After her next check-up, the specialist who'd removed her testes responded approvingly to the marriage: 'She has recovered well from surgery and is married and doing well.'

In other words: sex is a legal principle of division in ways which are never external to 'sex' as it appears on the level of apprehension. The expressive face of sex appears in lawyers' debates or sceptical police stops, as much as the clinics of endocrinologists or cosmetic surgeons. Legal dimensions of sex can be either more binding or permissive than anatomy, since they are undeniably responsive to political struggles. As Geertje Mak has shown us, we can only grasp the terms and ramifications of clinical application of sex *concepts* if we account for the *prevailing legal norms* which these evaluations cast shadows across.

Transphobic legislation has studded the rising tide of the global right, with legal norms affirming the lawfulness of intersex surgeries spelt out more explicitly than ever before. The laws were pushed by the governing parties of places including Hungary, where a law prohibiting identity documents from bearing any sex save that on a birth certificate was introduced by the ruling party, Fidesz, in 2020. While directed at formally outlawing transitions, this further made the assessments medics offered at birth binding, without recourse for correction. As LGBT rights continues to serve both as a shibboleth for 'humanitarian' interventions, and the definition of anti-West politics by regimes such as Russia, Uganda, and Hungary, this dissonance seems sure to heighten. In 2023 the Russian Federation introduced a new law to bolster their faltering war effort, banning medical transition entirely. Yet specific exemptions were carved out for intersex infants and children – demonstrating that the focus of the state was not to prevent cutting but to stabilise 'sex' as two legal forms, each supposed to be binding. The rise of the global right is spelling out how sex is stabilised legally: transition is outlawed, while clinical domination of intersex physiques is enshrined as legal.

In Europe, bans on non-consensual intersex surgeries have succeeded at the continent's margins: Malta, Portugal, and most recently Greece have banned intersex surgeries. In Greece local struggles broke through with support from ILGA-Europe, who released a video on hate speech against intersex people both in a clinical context and broader society with an accompanying animated video summarising their findings.[3] Intersex Greece also submitted a report to the government while it was formulating its National Strategic Plan on LGBTQI+ Equality, getting a dedicated section on the plight of Greek intersex people included, with an emphatic opposition to non-consensual surgeries.[4] A week prior to the final vote, the secretary of Intersex Greece spoke in front of Greece's parliament, recounting how two obstetricians had pressured her 'very insistently' to terminate her child for being XXY.[5] The vote passed easily.

Censure and Data

While many LGBT activists have warned against the rise of 'homonationalism' supporting Western imperialism, intersex advocacy is regrettably unique in that relevant offences against human dignity are to be found in basically any nation-state. This has resulted in a sizable quantity of reports condemning these practices by expert bodies including the UN Special Rapporteur on Torture, the Committee for the Rights of the Child, the Council of Europe, the EU Basic Rights Committee, the EU Agency for Fundamental Rights, and the African Commission on Human and Peoples' Rights.

How much practical use these statements will serve remains to be seen: the movement has recently won surgery bans (in Greece for instance) or other formal legal protections (such as in Austria) by pressing connections with local ruling parties and winning supreme court rulings (the Philippines). Further pressure is required to ensure that these official protections are being realised consistently. There's reason to be concerned that national bans won through pressure exerted by global governance bodies on imperialist peripheral countries will simply result in 'paper bans', with the de facto continuation of familiar harms. Following heavy pressure through global governance bodies, Indonesia moved to officially ban female genital cutting in 2006, only for the Ministry of Health to reverse course. The only demonstrable change was traditional cutters becoming marginally less popular, with female cutting taking place more often in a medical setting, often by nurses on newborns.[6] Clearly a shift directed by local groups is required to uproot these practices from convention, rather than paper bans to appease global governance structures. The contemporary intersex movement has benefited from its fragmentation into advocacy that works through the local contexts that these advocates are embedded in. Familiarity with local legal traditions and languages will be required to achieve progress through juridical means. While transnational solidarity expressed through conversations, collaborative projects, and fundraising has been a blessing, this movement will only succeed if it avoids the temptation of management.

The rising tide of worldwide recognition for the intersex movement's insights has begun to be verified in more comprehensive ways. Often, papers have expressed longstanding claims of the intersex movement in terms more appropriate for fields such as legal studies and public health.[7] Featuring lines such as: 'Our qualitative study revealed that prevention of non-therapeutic medical interventions on the bodies of children was understood to be the key method to achieving equality for intersex embodied people' and titles such as 'Intersex Studies: A Systematic Review of International Health Literature', this literature can feel like a more anodyne version of insights offered for decades by the intersex liberation movement. Yet this accumulation of rigorously compiled data provided a breakthrough in the objective understanding of mistreatment faced by those with intersex variations worldwide.

The new century has also seen free development of autonomous resources, providing an extensive set of introductory material from beyond the clinic. In a collaboration with an LGBT student organisation and a European equality body, OII Europe produced their own guide for parents, introducing them to the prospect of raising an intersex child without pathologisation.[8] Their 'toolkit' was released in six European languages. Former OII head Hida Viloria co-wrote a book with Biology Professor

Emerita Maria Nieto, *The Spectrum of Sex: The Science of Male, Female, and Intersex*, in 2020. The same year, Jay Kyle Petersen published *A Comprehensive Guide to Intersex*, based both on his research and his own experiences as an intersex man. This new set of introductions suitable for the 2020s supports a new hermaphroditic humanism: marshalling knowledge to help those who've passed through unbearable and dehumanising treatment recover. When Kenyan preacher Apostle Darlan Rukih visits a young intersex woman, Maureen, filmed by US news show *Dateline NBC*, she closes a period of isolation and despair. Maureen remarks of her youth: 'I would have been better as a fruit to be consumed, or as a dog to be killed.' These sentiments are not unusual for intersex people emerging from their solitude. How can we make them a thing of the past?

Solidarity When Most Required

In 2012, Hida Viloria wrote a letter to the UN: 'A Call for the Inclusion of Human Rights for Intersex People'. Viloria then headed the Organisation Intersex International. While the UN fields any number of letters, this one was apparently well received: Viloria was invited the next year to speak at the UN's Human Rights Day event on a panel entitled 'Sports Comes Out Against Homophobia', with tennis player Martina Navratilova and basketballer Jason Collins.

Presented at the second International Intersex Forum, hosted by ILGA, Viloria's text was co-signed by the leaders of the groups that made up OII Europe, in addition to Morgan Holmes, Mauro Cabral, Pidgeon Pagonis, Sally Gross, and Julius K. Kaggwa (founder of Uganda's SIPD). This missive represented the intersex movement as it had now reforged itself: global in scope, and politically distant from any patience for re-pathologisation.

Viloria's letter is remarkable in several ways: it foregrounds the use of fetal dex treatments (used by doctors attempting to eliminate congenital adrenal hyperplasia features in the womb), even before mentioning surgeries. Opposing any division between homo/transphobia (pushed in erudite form by the likes of Feder and Dreger) and intersex rights, Viloria argues intersex variations leave children more exposed to harms from their family on exactly that basis: 'We recognize that because intersex traits are detectable at or before birth, intersex people are more at-risk for homophobia and discrimination against gender-variance than other members of the population.'

The language of DSDs was swiftly rejected: 'We point to the fact that it adds to discriminatory attitudes by portraying intersex traits as illnesses in need of correction.'

But most remarkable about Viloria's letter is its opening hook. While the letter mentions Caster Semenya among other intersex athletes being mistreated, it begins with another track runner: Pinki Pramanik, from India. Pramanik was accused of rape by a woman who claimed she was her partner. (Pramanik describes her as a neighbour and stalker). By her accuser's account, Pramanik was secretly male, while Pramanik claimed a voyeuristic photograph of her had been taken. By the time Viloria wrote, Pramanik had been arrested and put through a successive barrage of testing. As with Semenya, not only Pramanik's medical reports (which declared her a male pseudo-hermaphrodite) were leaked, but also an examiner's photo of her naked body.

Indian criminal law followed its former colonial power, Britain, in defining 'rape' as something that had to be done with a penis. This left Pramanik's legitimacy as a legal female a matter of considerable importance, unclearly entangled with her supposed variation. (What would Andrea Prader say?) Viloria's letter was resolutely in solidarity: 'We, and many others, are asking: why are the rape allegations against Pramanik only valid upon her being shown to be an intersex woman?'

It was hard to deny that intersex people required specific protections: diagnosis could unleash harsh treatment against them, both clinically and informally. The focus, rather than being directed at the offence she had (or as it emerged, had *not*)

committed, had shifted to Pramanik's supposed hermaphroditism. Hida Viloria's advocacy for Pramanik would be fully
vindicated by history: the accusations were revealed to be a
stitch-up by Pramanik's local enemy, Avtar Singh (who'd been in
dispute with her over a large parcel of land which Pramanik had
been awarded by the government of West Bengal). By Pramanik's
account she had been 'virilised' not by any intersex variation, but
by testosterone shots she was ordered onto by her trainers for
boosted performance. At the time, however, this was less clear, so
Viloria continued with the proviso concerning the ongoing case:

> We make no statement regarding the question of whether violence
> has occurred, but merely argue that Pinki's 'sex' should be irrele-
> vant to the investigation. It is not that we call for the investigation
> of the complaint to cease, but that we call for the body of the
> defendant not to be made a public spectacle, or otherwise mis-
> treated because of her supposed embodied state.

This vignette was a high-stakes narrative with which to open an
appeal to a global governance body, but with Viloria's delivery
seemed a perfectly obvious adherence to point of principle. Viloria's reorientation of intersex advocacy through a human rights
framework took the form of unflinching and unconditional solidarity between intersex people.

Human Rights Are for Hermaphrodites Too!

This slogan heads the page of the International Covenant on
Civil and Political Rights 7th Report on Intersex Genital Mutil-
ation Human Rights Violations of Children with Variations of
Reproductive Anatomy.

This report followed up on the way legislation supposedly
offering protection to intersex children was truly instituted after
2021. Despite this juridical breakthrough, the report estimated
1,900 unnecessary surgeries continued in Germany annually. In

response to the new law, parents had simply stopped having their children officially declared intersex (and as such part of a protected category).[9]

Together, the slogan and study show the unexpected potential that human rights advocacy has to retrieve and sustain the spirit of early "90s edgy' protests and community building. With the turn to global governance bodies, intersex liberation struggles were at risk of being co-opted into professionalised activism and trained to speak with the voice of management (in other words, at risk of becoming boring). Yet human rights campaigning provided the intersex movement with alternative venues for developing their positions. From the earliest days of the Intersex Society of North America through to truly global groups such as Organisation Intersex International and ILGA World, this struggle has blended the participation of sympathetic endosex experts and direct advocacy by intersex people ourselves.

Human rights rhetoric has been criticised for its tacit dereliction of non-human animals. Yet during the fierce debates around the introduction of 'disorders', one board member of the Organisation Intersex International who had trained as a biologist argued the loss of 'intersex' as a human state would upset almost a century of research that had examined the ways in which humans extend from the natural world. The geneticists overseeing the 'DSD' term were not so bold as to extend their new category across all other species. As Bhakti Ananda Goswami writes:

> The effect of this change will be to cut-off human intersex from the context and continuum of all other life on Earth. So no longer would a web search for 'intersex' yield references to plant, animal and human forms of intersex, including natural XY-female or XX-male sex-reversal, spontaneous sex-changing or transsexual or homosexual relevant animal research. Instead, only certain very limited atypical human conditions would be web or library searchable under the new very narrowly defined

and professionally controlled and pathologizing term 'Disorders of Sex Development'.[10]

In truth, our grasp of human sex has always been closely bound with comparative animal studies, with natural history segueing into clinical care through methods that range from the speculative to the cruel.

The term 'hormonally intersex' first appeared in the essay by Richard Goldschmidt, which, as we've seen, had a far-reaching influence on conceptualisations of intersex people. However, very little of the paper directly addressed humans: Goldschmidt had conducted careful studies on the moth *Lymantria dispar* and announced he had found several that were neither male nor female. This 'intersex butterflies' discussion became animating for German interwar sexology, including the circle around renowned sexologist Magnus Hirschfeld.[11] The butterfly enthusiast Goldschmidt seemed to have only a fleeting interest in the implications of hormonally intersex variations in humans, paying closer attention to proving that 'inner secretions' solving the longstanding puzzle of the freemartin. These cattle appeared morphologically (and often behaved) like bulls. Two papers the year before had shown that these cows began as twins, merging surviving female and absorbed male through a process called a chorion fuse.[12] In 1917 Goldschmidt compared the case of freemartins to several other animal species, making passing remarks concerning humans which were then wildly extrapolated from.[13]

Pioneering paediatric endocrinologist Lawson Wilkins had collaborated with a French embryologist named Alfred Jost, who had refined the art of vivisection on animals *in utero*. Eventually, as historian of science Nathan Q. Ha describes, Jost set about experimenting with prenatal rabbit castrations:

He removed the gonads from both male and female rabbit fetuses while they were still developing inside their mother's wombs. The castrated, female fetuses developed reproductive structures nearly commensurate with normal females, but strangely, the castrated male fetuses did not. Internally, their masculine ducts stopped developing and disintegrated, but their feminine structures continued to grow as if they were females. Their external genitals also developed into a clitoris and vagina instead of a penis and scrotum. Jost extrapolated from this experimental evidence to construct a theory of sex differentiation that made the presence of testicles the primary determinant of male sexual development. Testicles produced hormones that both encouraged the development of male structures and inhibited the development of female structures. Without potent testicles, all individuals would develop along female lines.[14]

If anything, the 'sex reversal' view Jost developed was still more gonad-centric than that agreed upon by many earlier twentieth-century sexologists. Wilkins swiftly extrapolated from this finding, speculating that his human patients with Turner syndrome (XO chromosomes) were 'male pseudo-hermaphrodites' who had passed through another version of the 'sex reversal' process.

More cheerfully, the intersex movement has exhibited a fondness for hermaphroditic animals: the Intersex Initiative set a snail to appear as its avatar in web browser tabs. Basque territory–based intersex advocate Mer Gómez alludes to the indistinguishable genital structure of hyaenas in their book *La rebelión de las hienas: relatos corporales de personas intersex* ('The rebellion of the hyaenas: Body-stories of intersex people', published 2022). Other contenders from the animal kingdom speak to specific variations: as black-and-ginger fur is encoded in a different chromosome than white, 1 of every 3,000 calico cats is male (XXY).

For the time being, the preservation of 'intersex' as a term of art for understanding animal life (and chemical processes) but not humans presents rich opportunities for both opportunist right-wingers and the least reflective scientific researchers. The eccentric visionaries of the global right have become increasingly alarmed about the impact the mass production of petrochemicals and widespread pollution caused by microplastics will have on sex differentiation. Poetry scholar K. J. Dykstra observes the same anxiety in natural science research, citing one example of this apocalyptic view of intersex with the remarkable title 'The Increasing Prevalence in Intersex Variation from Toxicological Dysregulation in Fetal Reproductive Tissue Differentiation and Development by Endocrine-Disrupting Chemicals'. While providing no evidence for intersex variation increases from *human* studies, these researchers compile a sizable body of research concerning amphibians. The numerous authors have not even finished *defining* intersex variations before they make their true concerns plain: 'With early surgical intervention of children presenting with [intersex variations] no longer the preferred medical management practice, and with parents electing to delay surgery until development of secondary sex characteristics, the number of children with IV will increase.'[15]

This paper (published the same year as the discussion of CAH as 'risking' lesbianism) presents an increase in intersex variations as a twofold threat: the first from a sprawling ecological disaster, and the second a collapse in 'management'. Lively bioethical discussions about fetal dex and selective abortions have been replaced with a vision of society swamped by intersex births. Waves of ecological crisis produced by decades of cheap petroleum and its plastic by-products seem set to continue for the rest of our lifetimes (and without systemic changes in production, end many of them). Yet the right is vague concerning how this might be corrected, derailing even liberal ecologist measures – while as clear-eyed as ever at the human menace they fear will emerge as a degenerative consequence.

In response, the intersex movement should be clear: even those of us declared freakish, unnatural, or the offspring of toxic waste share the same natural order as those who condemn us. Frogs, newts, humans, and alligators all deserve a habitable planet, whatever their sex(es).

Impatient Advocacy

The move towards declaring intersex people victims of isolable 'disorders' came accompanied by significant organisational changes within multidisciplinary teams. The global intersex movement responded by eschewing 2000s-style patient advocacy, instead embracing human rights campaigning.

Why did patient advocacy come to be replaced by human rights organising worldwide? Patient advocacy had always required the foreclosure of broader alliances between intersex people, and those with overlapping struggles. While the medical establishment is likely to be recalcitrant in any case, across time earnest engagement with even seemingly sympathetic surgical teams had burned out advocates. A persistent cultural conservatism sustains the clinical justifications for radically nontherapeutic surgeries. In particular, medics are prone to a knee-jerk scepticism towards any kind of counterculturalism or self-advocacy. In an interview, geneticist Eric Vilain made explicit the division which many physicians had long relied on: 'I call the ones who work with us advocates; those against us activists . . . We're trying to listen to the community, but by the same token we're committed to producing data and evidence.'[16]

Throughout this book, I've carefully avoided using the worst slur known to the history of science: activist. While blunt, Vilain was far from a marginal figure: he was hired as an expert by the International Olympics Committee, one of several grand sporting bodies overseeing controversies around intersex athletes. Yet he was also a longstanding supporter of the intersex movement: recalling that they were shut out of the process of scientific and clinical discussion despite high proficiency, Vilain says they were dismissed as 'zealots'. Working alongside intersex advocates, he did not perceive indeterminate genitals as a disaster: the worst outcomes were parental rejection. Yet by the time of this interview, Vilain's stance seemed to have hardened in favour of clinical sovereignty: 'You're basically calling doctors torturers when they're doing something considered standard medical practice . . . I'm not opposed to guidelines, I'm opposed to things that completely alter medical practice in an irreversible way.'

Inadvertently, this spells out *exactly the appeal* of framing non-consensual intersex treatments as human rights violations. It's perfectly possible that 'standard medical practice' be dehumanising, cruel, and unjustifiable (as the briefest review of his medical field's own history would demonstrate). And the *complete alteration* of medical norms is always what the intersex movement has aimed for.

One of Vilain's colleagues, the psychologist David Sandberg, performs the typical *displacement* of clinical responsibility from clinic to private household: 'Parents are scared. You just don't dictate to them and say "get over it".' (This is the same 'stakeholder shuffle' we've seen so much of already: doctors blaming parents for decisions made within the distorted framework they've been provided.). Reading between the lines, the turmoil caused to the medical profession by the intersex liberation movement seems clear.

But just like a romantic breakup, the way harsh news is delivered doesn't stop it being true. The era of clinical command is slowly coming to an end. If anything, doctors should be relieved that advocates' boiling rage is usually expressed on their personal websites and in consciousness-raising videos, rather than face to face. The consistent commitment of intersex advocates to non-violence has been an obvious contrast to the devastating injuries many participants were administered clinically. ('Militant' intersex advocacy has remained militant only in the French sense.)

One report from Britain's *Guardian* newspaper sees a clinical professional attempt to undermine decades of intersex advocates' criticism of non-consensual childhood surgeries: 'A small group of people who have had surgery and are understandably unhappy will detract from a genuine picture of a whole load of people not being unhappy. It's tricky to write off surgery on the basis of that.'

The shocking modesty of expectations set with the majority 'not being unhappy' suggests that this medic is aiming to avoid further investigation of available data, or perhaps hoping that there is none. The reporter continues:

> Surgery in infancy is more straightforward than later in life, Woodward argues: tissues are easier to operate on and heal better, and the distances to bridge are smaller. Performing an operation before a baby can remember the trauma spares them the distress of going through it as a teenager. Plus, no one has expertise in operating on young people old enough to give informed consent. 'If everyone is too worried about doing the wrong thing by these children now, and we say, "Let's leave it until they're 15", who's going to do the surgery? It isn't going to be a paediatric urologist. It's not like there is a generation of surgeons out there who will have had any experience of this very niche surgery. I just worry that people will become too scared to do anything for fear of doing the wrong thing, and then be putting off a problem that will be a real surgical challenge. Surgeons are getting less experienced, if anything.'[17]

Tacitly, Woodward admits how widespread infancy and early childhood surgeries still remain. We can also see a total refusal to imagine that a happy and full life could be lived without them: the 'decision' is a question of *when*, rather than *if*. Intersex advocates have given cause to doubt this since 1996, with those who escaped surgeries sharing their testimonies quite openly. That babies won't remember procedures is belied by an overview in *Surgical Neurology International* which reports: 'Research suggests that strong painful procedures or repeated mild procedures may permanently modify individual pain processing.'[18] Besides which, the idea that doctors might perform human rights abuses because retraining is a nuisance seems like a problem for physicians to address, rather than infants to endure. Finally, those able to consent (if indeed they choose to) will be able to have some say in the *expressive* dimension of sex, through being consulted on basic options.

While unusually blunt and self-interested, the testimony quoted here is typical. Two interviews conducted with intersex surgical specialists by Human Rights Watch in 2017 echo this sense of inertia, given that these procedures have become standardised *professional* norms:

'If this is your career as . . . part of your professional identity, if this is a specialty you've become known for, it is very hard to back away from it,' she said. 'I think that there are going to be a few doctors . . . who really built a career on providing normalizing surgeries. It's going to be very hard to back away and say, 'yeah there's maybe another way maybe a better way to care and support these families.'[19]

More recent justifications have included conflating statistics around the suicide rates found among transgender youth who had experienced clitoral cutting during infancy or childhood:

The girl with the big clitoris – do we make it look good before puberty or do we wait? In a perfect world, no of course we'd wait. But it's not a perfect world and parents know that – parents say: look I'd love to live in a place with that kind body and not get any grief . . .[20]

Such justifications assume that physicians can accurately guess the later identifications adopted by those they are cutting. Dismissing blanket bans on non-consensual surgeries as mere 'perfect world' idealism, they set to one side the ongoing trauma caused by permanently removing erogenous tissue from young children. As Human Rights Watch's own report has it:

A dearth of data on outcomes for intact children does not support defaulting to conducting irreversible and medically unnecessary surgeries that carry the potential for harm. Indeed, the available medical evidence points overwhelmingly in the opposite direction: that the well-documented harms of these operations should be a primary factor in doctors' recommendation to defer them until the patient can understand and consent to (or refuse) the procedure.

This immediate riposte offered by the report's author demonstrates how flimsy clinical reasoning can appear to external experts. These accumulated studies and reports may not serve as a direct constraint on medical authority, but they further challenge the objectivity of medics' deliberations.

These interviews have given a glimpse of the intractable resistance that advocates of clinical reform have been met with. Medical practitioners' conservative attitude towards social change seems to have moored their compulsion towards radical interventions, outlasting decades of criticisms and mounting evidence for harms done. Surgeons have adapted their case by making references to prevailing racism, or the plight of transgender youth rejected by their families, to vaguely construe not the *prospect* of social change normalising visibly intersex children, but its *impossibility*.

Tiger Devore's intersex advocacy predates the movement: he appeared on talk shows across the 1980s (including the uniquely popular *Oprah*).[21] These talk shows were notorious for their freakshow sensationalisation of delicate topics, but for Devore they provided a platform to speak openly about the harms done to him. Born with hypospadias, he spoke frankly about both being a gay man, and the extensive surgeries which had left him devastated. By the 2010s, Devore had been committed to reconciliatory dialogue for years, continuing through the Accord Alliance that had replaced the Intersex Society of North America. Devore's open letter announcing that he was quitting this approach explained that he had followed the route taken by his moderate wing of the movement, only to find it fruitless:

It is now abundantly clear that medicine and the research community continue to co-opt patient advocates in order to silence them by giving us the impression that we had access to influencing medical practice and research ... The surgeries will stop, by legal action, and by recognition of the rights of the child to bodily integrity and self-determination over the psychological comfort of the parents who don't want to have given birth to a 'deformed' child. The experiment of surgery on genitalia to 'normalize' naturally occurring variants that pose no medical risk has failed. The faster the medical community recognizes this and stops this arrogant practice, the smaller the settlement funds for non consenting experimental subjects like me will have to be. The standards must move from a pediatric, to a fully informed adult model of consent to elective surgery. Anything less is a continuing abuse and assault on innocent infants and children.

By floating 'legal action' and 'settlement funds' as the means to end medical mistreatment, Devore was suggesting a strategic path that still merits full exploration. In many localities, pursuing *civil claims* against medics might be more successful than attempting to institute criminal charges against them. The drawback is that these would most likely be lodged by parents who had a change of heart (as by the time those injured directly come of age themselves, statute of limitations restrictions could exempt medics from prosecution).

'Patient advocacy' consistently generated burnout in advocates, but the moment they gave up on winning surgeons around, they often became newly enthused and imaginative in their work to prevent clinical harms. A similar case is found in the writings of Mish O'Brien for OII, who explained how she came around to the anti-pathologisation politics espoused by the group. When O'Brien was living in Britain, she had engaged in extensive informal conversations with paediatric physicians at the University College London Hospital. These 'backchannel' dialogues led the OII advocate to believe that professional conduct was being modernised as demanded by her movement – with cosmetic practices being abandoned. But upon being pressed by a friend to find support for these claims from the clinicians in writing, O'Brien discovered a co-authored statement from 2010 which affirmed the continued need for operations. This text asserted trainee medics that 'ultimately, it is the surgeon's responsibility to undertake surgery for genital ambiguity if considered necessary, to restore function and achieve an acceptable cosmetic outcome'. Far from being reserved for functional ('plumbing') necessities, the same injuries Mish's organisation had always agitated against were continuing well into the twenty-first century. This apparent duplicity left O'Brien shaken:

> So, I have to admit some dismay at this, as this completely contradicts my understanding of the situation . . . I can only conclude that when I was told that things were changing, either I misunderstood what was meant, or was being misled.[22]

Concluding after a lengthy quotation from an ethicist also sanctioning surgeries, Mish tells us her stance has hardened: she once believed that surgeries were primarily to correct psychological anxieties on the part of parents. But really, doctors were fabricating emergencies:

> What is the emergency? I used to think 'socio-medical emergency' referred to the trauma of parents, and helping deal with that. But actually, the only urgency here is in carrying out procedures before the child gets to a point where they can have agency.

In 2020, Morgan Carpenter, an intersex advocate who directed the Australian intersex movement towards a focus on human rights, faced off against two practicing paediatric specialists based at the Royal Children's Hospital Melbourne (both also full professors at the local university) in a filmed dialogue, hosted by the Annual Melbourne Medical Student Conference.[23] John

Hutson is introduced in glowing terms as the author of textbooks used by the medical student who arranged the event, making what follows still more alarming. Sonia Grover presents the more reformed face of contemporary clinical practice, diplomatically framing treatments as both much improved technically, and more humane in approach. Grover uses the example of a family of migrants to Australia, who were anxious about introducing their child to their extended family and having them realise she was 'not a normal girl'. She tells us extensive conversations with these parents convinced them not to perform surgeries, saving this migrant family from itself. Carpenter could barely restrain scoffs in reply:

> I find quite concerning any assumption that people from a particular ethnic background might have more difficulty than people of a majority ethnic background, when there's not much evidence to say a widespread understanding of intersex variations exists *anywhere* in the world let alone in Australia . . . or in our white bread suburbs.

Here Carpenter was puncturing a move of *displacement to parents* that more 'modernised' medics had come to perfect since the 2000s. Numerous instances could be found of hospital 'multidisciplinary teams' instructing family courts to allow surgeries. Carpenter references the case of *Re: Carla (Medical Procedure)* where after a dispute, a child already clitorally cut was sanctioned a further gonadectomy. To believe Grover, clinicians were navigating the often backward sentiments of parents, gently directing families away from unneeded harms. But this was a moderate managerial *fantasy*. By contrast, her colleague John Hutson offers a blunter account of interactions 'managing' intersex children:

> From my point of view, I'm not worried about the rights of the child or moral issues when I see a baby. I'm worried about how

the parents are reacting to the fact that they have found that the baby isn't what they were expecting. And my job is to try and help them come to terms with that, with whatever, you know, tools are available in the medical toolkit to fix them. To help them, if they think that's what required. And most of the time, I'm looking after children with CAH, where they have got genitalia that are not either normally female or normally male, but are looking different. And the parents are very stressed by this because it is not what they were expecting because your average parent has never heard about intersex or DSD and they are expecting it to look obviously like a boy or a girl and my problem is trying to help them come to terms with the fact that it isn't looking the way they were expecting and what are we going to do about it.

Hutson's reply attempts to reassert the irrelevance of moral inquiry, or indeed consultation of any documents beyond those covering clinically relevant technical questions. This rant shows that the legacy of framing intersex people as 'unfinished' is still a living one. Indeed, this clinical ideology has been reaffirmed by the overall shift to discussions of these variations solely as a cluster of 'disorders'. While not oblivious to the challenges posed by intersex advocates, Hutson demonstrates succinctly how the narrative of continual 'surgical evolution' allows doctors to discount the lifelong dysfunctions caused by surgical interventions. By the very nature of these surgeries, the extent of damage done to sexual intimacy will become clear only in subsequent decades, by which point methods currently being applied to children and infants will supposedly have progressed:

So one of the difficulties here is that the intersex community of the world are often, are often responding to the fact that they might have had treatment on themselves in infancy or childhood that turned out to be wrong, because we didn't know at the time how to make it better.

But every day we are learning how to do it better and better, and we are never doing it for what we think is inappropriate or unethical reasons, we are always trying to do it for the most ethical and the most efficient way, but that does not mean that we are perfect. We are clearly not perfect. But we are trying to, doing it better and better.

As Carpenter replies: 'There is a narrative of scientific progress and there is a claim that improved surgical techniques are a meaningful response to a very different question about the necessity and appropriateness of surgery in the first place.' What these doctors could not grasp is that their careers were not just directed toward the *nature* of sex development. They are also shaped by a great *historical weight*, playing their own role in sex's ongoing history. The linear narrative of surgical progress is self-serving: it's soothing to imagine one's career is at least justifiable in context of the gradual, cumulative art of honing medical science (answering precise, technical questions). It would be a much rougher landing to accept continuities between intersex surgeries and lobotomies, or clitoral cutting performed by clinical nurses across Indonesia.

O'Brien and Carpenter's experiences show the seemingly Sisyphean task of building dialogue with those directly responsible for clinical harm. This asymmetric burden threatens to drain out all who commit to reform of the medical profession. Both accounts require justifications for the unjustifiable: that some babies are born unfinished, that tremendous progress has been made in recent years to improve that being corrected, that the topic could never possibly be understood by those not drilled in clinical jargon, and that those who attempt to are probably best dismissed as 'activists' (with no scientific standing, and dubious sanity). This is a gruesome mischaracterisation of the intersex movement. From the outset, intersex advocates have presented arguments that are carefully framed and tonally restrained rather than fanatical or strident. Their arguments were closely informed by feminist researchers of clinical science, who worked in active collaborative dialogue with them. The movement originally pressured clinicians themselves, hoping that abusive practices could be quickly abandoned if exposed carefully and dryly. But it was exhausting to witness clinicians' displays of blatant incompetence and their tendency to justify their cruelty as necessary. When the medical profession stubbornly resisted advocates' efforts, they were compelled to work through expert bodies and global affiliated groups instead. The twenty-first-century intersex movement, which retains the subversive core of '90s edgy activism, is now charging the medical profession with *human rights abuses*, and operating in contexts where this accusation can be pressed home decisively.

Today's intersex advocacy has both expanded to continental-level autonomous organising, but also entrenched its focus on particular healthcare institutions. Focusing on particular institutions responsible has become a means to ending the non-consensual 'civilising' cutting practices that they established across generations.

A New Consensus

To understand how Global South intersex advocacy came to directly inform that taking place in the imperial core, let's return to the same city that had hosted the supposed 'consensus' replacing intersex as a term of art – Chicago.

Moving into the 2010s, the advocates of the Intersex Justice Project would achieve a set of breakthroughs carried through the legacy of 1996's Boston revelation (from autumnal New England to the windy Midwest). These achievements would be further inspired by the connections the group had established with the international intersex movement. Far from providing command from the imperial centre, Intersex Justice Project members were surprised to discover how quickly legal breakthroughs were possible for chapters of the nascent Intersex Africa Movement.

By the later 2010s, efforts on both a state and national level to move towards outlawing intersex surgeries had stalled. In 2017, long-time intersex movement target the American Academy of Pediatrics released a newly softened statement to mark Intersex Awareness Day (that occurs every year on 26 October, marking the Boston protest). Conspicuously avoiding the word 'disorders', the AAP half-heartedly declared: '66,000 member pediatricians, pediatric medical subspecialists, and pediatric surgical specialists are committed to the health and dignity of all children, including children who do not easily fit into binary gender categories.'[24]

US intersex advocacy came to focus on Lurie Children's Hospital. In a moving video, Pidgeon Pagonis stood outside the building, recounting the harms they'd received within. As the campaign continued, employees of the hospital broke rank, openly supporting the demands of intersex advocates. As Pagonis remarked afterwards, the precise focus of their campaign had a practical necessity: 'Four years of pinpointed pressure on one specific clinic at Lurie, that was the first step – not just fighting for ending intersex surgery in the whole country, but saying, "We have limited resources. What can we do?"'[25]

InterACT staffer Hans Lindahl argued that the breakthrough should be followed by reparations and free support for the generations of injured intersex people: 'There's a population of decades' worth of damaged intersex adults who have nowhere to go. There's no adult intersex care specialty.'[26] Pressing home their success, from 2021 the Intersex Justice Project repeated this tactic of direct and named targeting of Weill Cornell (part of New York-Presbyterian Hospital). As a child, Sean Saifa Wall had received a gonadectomy at Weill Cornell, which was the workplace of aforementioned CAH paediatric 'researcher' Dix Poppas.[27] Where the conceptual historian Alice Dreger failed, the movement has proven doggedly determined to make harms against intersex children a thing of the past.

True to the movement's origins, the Intersex Justice Project's protesters began interacting with feminist academic Elizabeth Reis, who explored their successes in her second edition of *Bodies in Doubt: An American History of Intersex*.[28] In 2015, Wall's essay 'Standing at the Intersections: Navigating Life as a Black Intersex Man' appeared in a collection of intersex life narratives. The essay demonstrated Wall's redirection of the intersex movement towards advocacy that worked to upset the US 'colour line', along with medical authority. Like many of these accounts, much of Wall's story concerns his family. While his siblings had also been born androgen insensitive, Wall was the first spared surgery by his mother. Wall's family life was overcast by his parents' anxiety that he appear passably feminine, and eventually he was given an adolescent gonadectomy followed by hormonal treatments. Wall found these interventions transformed him in ways he couldn't easily live with. As he recounts things, Wall's development was one that played out *over* him, offering him limited opportunities for autonomy or directive involvement. As he puts it: '*At no point did anyone ask me what I wanted to do with my body.*' For Wall, transition was as much an act of reversal as replacement, as much about rewriting his physique in his own terms (at last) as correcting how he was identified.[29] While accounts such as this are sadly common, the birth of another political movement clearly infuses his essay – Black Lives Matter. Multiple relatives from Wall's extended family were imprisoned, harm done by managerial medics matching that meted out by police and prisons:

> As a Black intersex man, I have witnessed the impact of state-sanctioned violence on my family and my community, both from the police state and medical community. I charge the police state and the medical community with state-sanctioned violence: Each targets non-normative bodies – the former through incarceration and execution, and the latter by means of surgical and hormonal intervention. As a Black intersex man, I stand at the intersection

bearing witness to how this violence has incarcerated my friends and loved ones as well as being subjected to medically unnecessary surgical intervention.

In the United States, Wall's reading of non-consensual intersex surgeries as 'state-sanctioned violence' was timely. By the 2020s, a restless phobia became an animating focus for the state-level Republican Party. Bills were introduced outlawing doctors from providing medical support to dysphoric children, with trans healthcare framed as acts of 'mutilation'.[30] These laws included provisions exempting intersex interventions (and in some cases also male circumcisions) – the law was to facilitate only the genital cuttings which stabilised sex.

The *selective* nature of these bills, outlawing and legalising in the same moment, demonstrate that Wall is perfectly correct to identify intersex harms as unfolding with the state's sanction.[31] While Devore's letter about quitting 'patient advocacy' might lead us to believe civil claims are a means forward, this reflection directs us towards an immersion in broader struggles. Those incarcerated or hassled by law enforcement have suffered alongside those 'managed' by medics (and many have endured abuses from both). This theoretical linkage is timely: laws permitting specific harms against intersex people have become more explicit than ever.

Even forcing hospitals to abandon harmful practices to intersex people would not be a final victory for liberation. As a report from one expert in Greece immediately following the local government's ban on surgeries put it, there remained a need for more thoroughgoing protections: 'The prohibition of discrimination must be horizontal and must pertain to every life circumstance where the intersex person "encounters" the state.'[32]

The Intersex Justice Project's confrontational approach to the medical profession and explicit integration of global connections to intersex advocacy groups worldwide marked a profound break with American intersex advocacy's earlier drift into NGO liberalism. Both theoretically and practically, the Intersex Justice Project addressed the 'colour line' organising challenges faced by all political groups in the United States. Recent intersex advocacy out of Chicago suggests the future of the larger movement: rejecting any segregation of intersex liberation from other struggles as unnecessary and unhelpful. Instead, they purposefully elaborated on latent connections to other social struggles (especially anti-racism). The interplay of international dialogue led directly to escalation. Rather than issuing instructions to their Global South counterparts, Pagonis and Wall found themselves stepping up operations to match their successes. Their newfound ambition was inspired by breakthroughs more easily possible outside the imperial core. In a total contrast to the view of mediation between 'stakeholders' (cutters and cut), the strategy of the Intersex Justice Project was to operate in *solidarity* with those 'known over' and subjected to routine harms. Intersex liberation will require further *reciprocal* exchanges between those so injured, wherever those offences have happened. Liberation of this kind plays out not through the wisdom of the centre spilling outwards, but as a back-and-forth between contexts and positions.

Veils and Embraces

Jeff Cagandahan was one of the founders of Intersex Philippines. During a meeting of Intersex Asia, he recounted a childhood filled with a sense of displacement and freakishness – sadly typical for intersex upbringings. During puberty, Cagandahan and those around him found no language to 'articulate what I was going through'. Instead, he became the object of vicious gossip. Raised as a girl, he was expected to veil himself to attend Catholic liturgies. For Cagandahan, this provided little clarity: he described the practice as being draped in a 'symbol of feminine purity in the eyes of God, and society', one which he could never have fully filled.

After being tested while still a schoolchild, he was told the classic mantra 'It's easier to dig a hole than dig a pole' by physicians, who refused him phalloplasty. Regardless, Cagandahan decided to live as a man, staging an extended legal struggle for recognition. The court demanded Cagandahan's chromosomal analysis and blood work, which was duly submitted. Initial victory was followed by a three-year wrangle of appeals, with the case passed through to the Supreme Court. The adjudicators stated they could neither decide such an 'intimately private' matter for any intersex individual, 'much less' did they have standing to insist on surgeries to reduce CAH virilisation. The judges affirmed that each decision ultimately belonged to the intersex citizen themselves:

> Respondent is the one who has to live with his intersex anatomy. To him belongs the human rights to pursuit of happiness and of health. Thus to him should belong primary choice of what courses of action to take along the path towards sexual development and maturation.

The wording of the ruling reverses the priorities in the sexological exchange cited in our last chapter by historian Geertje Mak. In this ruling, the *course* of life for intersex people in the Philippines was formally declared to be *their own concern*.

While the press still reported on Cagandahan as a 'woman with two genitals', the ruling was a breakthrough for his organisation: with this legal precedent set, Intersex Philippines refocused to press for similar access for other intersex people across the country. Many local intersex people still can't afford the legal advocacy and medical testing required for legal sex reassignment. So along with the usual peer support and political advocacy, Intersex Philippines runs an economic support fund to help people navigate the costly process of juridical-clinical scrutiny.

What does this case show us? When Cagandahan juxtaposes his veiling with his assertion of legal authority over his own 'life's course', he shows a rejection of being *hidden away*. While he was draped through religious veiling, clearly Cagandahan had no prospect of a fruitful life through continued concealment. When Cagandahan openly claimed his manhood through the local court of law, when he shed symbolic purity forever, he exposed himself to the typical fears of hermaphroditism. Even the court's comment on setting aside his 'male tendency' through congenital adrenal hyperplasia from their rightful obligations fuelled the local media into a typical display of sensationalism and stubborn ignorance. But this indignity didn't discourage his advocacy: having broken with this childhood shrouding, drawn into public view and cast in freakish terms by a cruel press, he could not close his eyes to the divisions which prevented others from living openly.

For W. E. B. Du Bois, references to 'the veil' accompany his better-known theoretical lens of 'double consciousness', the state of split apprehension of oneself and one's circumstances. Du Bois saw this ambivalence as defining black American life: one moment the same observer could see herself as a privileged imperial subject (an American), and the next be reminded of the dehumanising circumstances that could not be escaped (blackness). Neither America's pre-eminence in a brutal global pecking order nor the horrifying treatment faced by its racialised minorities could be denied, yet sustaining both clearly in view could be maddening in its own right. Hence the 'veil' held these two truths apart, ready to be twitched aside at any moment. While 'double consciousness' implied either being split, or else superimposed, 'the veil' alluded to the delicate sense of being shrouded between views, caught between perspectives that continuously shifted between registers of apprehension. To survive, black Americans could neither consistently forget they were human, nor fully believe it.

Du Bois sometimes suggested the veil could be cast aside, revealing the truth he drew readers towards. When addressing society, the veil addresses the *obliviousness* that his white readers had otherwise sustained about black life in America. But equally, the veil could divide any black person's perception of *themselves*: in one moment they regard themselves unmistakably American, human, and a participant in society . . . But only a twitch to set the veil aside would reveal themselves as nothing of the kind.[33] The veil could serve each of these roles, which was why the state of double consciousness proved maddening for black Americans. While the structures of racism could appear to be an intergenerational curse, they were also a font of wisdom. As Du Bois put it, being black in US America meant one had been 'born with a veil, and gifted with second sight'.

With each side of the racial divide held apart by this veiling, encounters with those living simpler lives could leave black people shaken. Unveiling could leave them aware of their relatively convoluted identifications, while also allowing them to witness first hand that they were unnecessary. In Du Bois's deeply moving 1903 reflection on the loss of his child (*Of the Passing of the First Born*), he wrote that even his apprehension of his own child seemed inflected by the United States' race science: 'And thus in the Land of the Color-line I saw, as it fell across my baby, the shadow of the veil.'

Anti-colonial revolutionary Frantz Fanon developed a twin concept that he called 'twoness'.[34] In Fanon's writings on French domination of metropoles in the Caribbean and Africa, we read of the tormented state ensnaring black colonial subjects. Aware of themselves as humans, they were simultaneously aware that their every gesture and word would be evaluated through a dehumanising lens by ever-present colonial voyeurs. To overcome these conditions of colonialism, Fanon called for a 'new humanism'. This book concerns a hermaphroditic humanism: a future where medical harms are prevented from repeating, and an embrace of forms previously scrubbed from the record.

The moment of casting aside the veil is one that we must approach in our own time and way – but whenever we can achieve it, the hidden is revealed. As the intersex movement came to assert themselves as human, they also came to make renewed reference to *joy*. Sean Saifa Wall has returned repeatedly to a particular moment in his advocacy that shows us what the future might hold after the unveiling of intersex liberation. In an interview with British scholar and model Dani Coyle, Wall explained that he drew inspiration from Underground Railroad organiser Harriet Tubman's maxim that one had to simply save as many as possible. Wall continued:

When you asked me what 'intersex joy' means to me, I thought about holding an intersex child who has not been harmed. When I was living in Atlanta this mom (of colour) reached out to me, saying she gave birth. Let me tell you when they say 'Oh we don't do that anymore, we believe in choice': some hospitals do, and some of them don't: this was in 2019 and literally doctors tried to force her to do surgery on her kid. So don't believe the hype, folks! But she reached out to me because she'd seen my story . . . she was like: 'I don't want to do surgery on my kid.' And I remember when I went to visit her, I saw this child. And I held this child, and I went: 'This is why this is important.' I may not be able to reach the ears of parents and doctors, but if I can save one child, if I can save two, the work is being done. For me, holding that child was joy. It was a blow to the system: I can die right now, because I'm holding a child which has not been harmed.

By sharing his story with the world, Wall had changed one mother's mind, sparing lifelong suffering. Through unflinching advocacy, political struggle can lead through to these moments of simple joy. Breakthroughs that were once scarcely imaginable become intuitive as they enter the present (then reset the future).

Returning to the Dateline clip: when Apostle Darlan Rukih meets Maureen, we witness a moment of intersex mentorship in the twenty-first century (mediated through the dubious production standards of *Dateline*). Apostle's claim to be a religious leader was clearly not without controversy. Dismissing Apostle's claim to be intersex, a rival preacher *Dateline* interviews shifts from depicting her as a con man through outlining his suspicions about her anatomy, to appealing to the sanctity of marriage: 'I couldn't leave [her] alone with my wife.' This specific fantasy: Apostle being untrustworthy left unaccompanied with a woman, contrasts with Apostle's maternal meeting of a younger intersex woman, which *Dateline* captured. When arriving, Apostle is met with a welcoming song from what seems like Maureen's entire township. Performers harmonise, singing 'Welcome, welcome, welcome: our guest!' while dancing between trees. Apostle immediately grasps Maureen close to her. (In an off-key reading, the journalist voiceover describes Apostle as a 'celebrity holy man', seeming to affirm hateful local voices which reduce Apostle to a male.) The next scene sees the two seated together. Addressing Maureen's life achievements, Apostle speaks slowly and deliberatively: 'Those who *were* ashamed of you now regret it.' The preacher modestly sets aside any role in the community's newfound regret, as the next scene brackets their one-on-one conversation, with Apostle delivering a rousing gospel a capella before departing. After the meeting, Maureen seems calmly overjoyed: 'I now see there are others like myself. I feel more human now.'

Whether in the Philippines' high court or Austria's, rural Kenya or Atlanta, the intersex movement has pressed to overturn old harms for coming generations. Drawing back the veil means learning not to flinch at horrors, but also never forgetting the freakish joy of mutual recognition. The movement's victories are a living blessing, a legacy that can be held close. These breakthroughs may concern the laws of a whole nation, or two sharing an unforgettable embrace. But a new sense of human variety is surfacing, bound together with a new science.

6

Sex in the Wreckage

Surgical interventions diminish intersex traits while normalizing the male and female body.

> – Georgiann Davis and Erin Murphy,
> 'Intersex Bodies as States of Exception'

Writings on intersex surgeries since the liberation movement began have merged critical reflections on overarching processes to stabilise sex with deeply personal reflections from those who've been subjected to them. Iain Morland is one intersex theorist whose writings focus on what (failed) attempts to justify intersex surgeries reveal to us about the shaping of sex, picking apart the appeals to 'clear visual sex' offered by parents authorising these procedures:

> The proponents of surgery evoke various looks or glances that are supposedly enabled by surgery – the look in the locker room or when the diaper is changed; or the glance at the urinal, at the swimming pool, at bath time, or in the bedroom. These scenes of looking at sexual difference are evoked to justify the alteration of both cosmetic and functional aspects of genitalia . . .

> Those in favour of surgery portray the sight of genitals prior to surgical alteration as a scene of disaster. In the words of a major medical textbook, 'Genital ambiguity in a baby is almost as devastating in the delivery room as a perinatal death.'

Being born without clearly differentiated sex is treated as a visual crisis that surgery is framed as a remedy for. Yet Morland argues this sense of sex is misguided: sexual difference does not appear in any *one* body but is created by the distinctions drawn between them. It's for this reason that procedures performed on intersex children can often serve not to diminish or mask their variations, but place them under a spotlight.

Intersex procedures as still widely practiced have the potential to ruin the lives of those subjected to them. These procedures can be profoundly damaging irrespective of the 'severity' of the variation they aim to resolve: those with variations doctors rank as 'mild' or 'minor' often face extensive barrages of procedures, as both Iain Morland and philosopher Christopher Breu's accounts attest to. Morland's intersex treatment included at least fourteen procedures (mostly before he could meaningfully consent). His theoretical writings pinpoint the cosmetic idealism that these operations lapse into:

> Intersex surgery instates male and female as monolithic and incontestable categories while simultaneously exceeding their naturalness and inevitability by its technology of sexual construction . . . Surgery is exorbitant, hyperbolic in its logic. Intersexed genitals are modified not with reference to any existing gold standard of genitalia – for instance, a plaster cast of the surgeon's own on a plinth beside the operating table. They are altered in accordance with certain fantasies: the endlessly mammoth penis . . . the immeasurably spacious vagina . . . the infinitely delicate clitoris.[1]

As Morland has it: 'Such body parts do not exist; they are fantasies about how genitals ought to be.'

Rather than salvaging an underlying form, these surgeries impose an ideal onto intersex children, both through the procedures themselves and through their suggestive work in framing how the children should interact with their own bodies. As much as the lasting anatomical injury done to intersex children, harm resides in the framing of these procedures: internalisation of a necessity for 'correction'. It's only through political struggle that intersex people come to find new, adequate terms for themselves. Writing of his own experiences, Breu sketches this unspeakable moment:

> I knew it as an experience long before I knew it had a name. Even now that I know it has a name – my condition is called hypospadias – it's not always clear to me how adequate the different names are . . . what the relationship is between those names and my embodied experience.[2]

Without meaningful contact with adults who've lived full lives with these procedures, intersex youths typically regard their atypical sex as a source of freakishness, to be struggled with:

> I felt internally different but appeared, when clothed, the same as any other, alternatively cute (if I may say so myself) and awkward, growing boy. Yet I felt secretly monstrous, that I was different in precisely the areas with which our culture is most obsessed. My experience finally was one of profound confusion.

Since these variations are hidden from most of their peers, young intersex people typically adopt a strictly 'medicalist' understanding of their variations (one treatment following the next). Yet as surgeries continued, Breu describes the disintegration of trust in his medical professionals:

> It was one of wanting to and finally not believing my doctors when they suggested that the next operation would be my last. I learned to see my doctors as antagonists, people who thought they had my best interests at heart, but who I began to suspect didn't.

In reality Breu (years after intersex liberation had begun) was running into a problem already familiar to advocates: the damage done by surgeries was cumulative, as scar tissue proved increasingly difficult to manipulate or 'correct' in the operating theatre, leading to further procedures.

Morland describes how, in adulthood, the surgeries' therapeutic value seemed less apparent to him: they increasingly aimed to correct damage done by previous procedures, and only improved his quality of life at intervals now measured in months, instead of years.

These surgeons were grappling with what Breu later came to call the *non-binary* face of sex, but which we might otherwise call its plasticity. Breu argues that even critical appeals to 'gender' are too easily shaped around an assumption that sex takes a simpler, twofold form than identification.[3] Moves to replace all reference to 'sex' with 'gender', Breu argues, fail to capture how these surgical harms appear irrespective of personal investment in any specific identity. And the notion of a stable, two-part sex (to serve as a solid counterpart to gender) is belied by the chaos that ensues when surgical fixes to 'normalise' genitals are attempted. Clearly sex is both more varied and resistant to 'correcting' into a twofold shape than is usually imagined. Gender theorists have emphasised *assignment* as a social process that those subjected to it may not be able to live with later. But as writings from those subjected to childhood intersex surgeries show us, one childhood sex assignment does not look like the next.

Being Known Over

Being intersex is not any one experience. Intersex variations are usually taken to be based on an 'incongruence' between genetics, measurable physiological processes, and resultant anatomy. The intersex movement has shown that suffering follows directly from the 'smoothed over' understandings of sex that intersex physiques disrupt. The sense of 'freakish' isolation intersex people often report from childhood follows from their direct embodied experiences being categorically denied. Intersex people are asked to disbelieve what they see in the mirror. Existing between conventional views of possible sex produces a continuous sense of being known over, smoothed down, brushed over – and denied wherever possible. Intersex emerges from those whose lives are jostled between understandings of exactly which two forms are to be expected. These oppositional understandings (male vs. female) have proven durable and persistently popular, whatever the level of complexity demonstrated by scientific investigations. For as long as sex appears as two strictly exclusive sets, intersex people will exist between wherever these lines are drawn, occupying zones declared 'fuzzy' and better passed over. The dominant idea that human sexual difference is simple and twofold directly produces a category of people excluded from such definitions.[4]

Living an incongruent life brings the cost of profound personal turmoil. As well as the *physical* forms of anatomical and physiological variations as we now understand them, there will be a need to introduce a wider audience to the *existing harms* done when physicians ride roughshod over human physiological diversity. Intersex people live at odds with sex taken as a simple reality, a split that 'everyone knows'. Vehement defenders of sex as twofold split appear wherever it is challenged. Even those intersex people who avoid direct exposure to medical harms will find themselves in social contexts that deny their experiences outright. During an interview with the Interface Project, Austrian intersex advocate Alex Jürgen recounted:

> At the age of 12 we learned in school about male and female anatomy and one day I sat down in front of a mirror with my anatomy book and started discovering myself and it didn't take long for me to see that it wasn't the same – the book back to me. The book. Back to me. No. The floor under my feet disappeared in just one second, and I didn't know what I was. '*Freak*' was one of the words that came to mind, and I wanted to talk with the doctor immediately because I felt that I couldn't trust my parents anymore.

As the doctor told me about my testes everything got worse, and I lost myself completely.[5]

After contrasting their own form to the expected shape of things (male or female), the interviewee consulted a medical professional and experienced belated clarity, and identity collapse. This is what it means to be *known over*: the basic contours of one's form defying the limits of popular education and conventional expectation.

For Alex Jürgen, this sense of isolation was not to last: a lengthy legal battle was followed by a 2020 Austrian Supreme Court ruling. The court ruled against the local state's refusal to grant Jürgen identification matching their intersex status. This decision enshrined the rights of intersex people to legal documentation marked neither male nor female, a victory following years of agitation and outreach by Austrian intersex advocates.[6] Jürgen had been a founding member of the local advocacy group, VIMÖ (Verein Intergeschlechtlicher Menschen Österreich). The group used this legal struggle both to build their profile, and win a legal precedent for intersex people across Austria. These adolescent experiences of displacement impelled Jürgen towards determined advocacy as an adult.

Consciousness-raising groups can change the way intersex variations appear to those born with them. Through moments of political and pioneering legal struggle, shared experiences of isolation can become points of unity. Limiting understandings imposed on intersex people can be compared and collectively overturned. Intersex personal crises, the sense of being *experientially overwritten* by prevailing understandings, can give scope to successful campaigning.

Intersex people are directly at odds not only with the underinformed, but also those who have sustained a *commitment* to sex as a dyadic (twofold) form. That means stigma and hostility towards those with intersex variations is not simply the working of 'ignorance' or a lack of education, but rather the dominating face of clinical expertise and those willing to rely on these terms to delegitimise understandings with other origins. As we've seen throughout this book, clinicians would rather change reality (perform irreversible surgeries on infants) to fit their ideas about sexual difference than adjust their ideas to fit with the complex reality.

Far from being oblivious, medics clearly felt the need to demonstrate their mastery of the irregularities of intersex physiques. Their professional training also made demands on patients: when human variance was incorporated into medical training, intersex physiologies became objects to examine in detail. In many cases, there was a blithe disregard for consent of those under this observation, part of the broader culture of routine dehumanisation of intersex patients. As Jean Butler (one intersex person interviewed by feminist science researcher Katrina Karkazis) recounted:

> I had genital inspections every single time I went to the doctor. And not only that, I was used for training. It'd be me, my mother, the doctor, and then there'd be about a dozen others – nurses, residents, interns, medical students – and they would all be standing around looking at my genitals, and the doctor would be making comments, and I'd be lying there passively while this was going on. I finally rebelled. I just refused to go to the hospital.[7]

This recollection shows clearly the distinction between professional training as an act of elevation, and any sense of cultivating a meaningful relationship while providing therapeutic support. As much as any anatomical familiarity, the trainee nurses and doctors were being introduced to a lopsided relationship, where they observed those reluctantly placed on full display. To be *known* in this sense by the medical profession demands the passivity Butler describes: the rebellion she ultimately settled upon meant facing down the routine medical neglect intersex people are accustomed to.

Medical treatments aimed primarily to double up on the existing *knowing over*: efforts to scientifically sketch intersex variations move seamlessly into attempts to make them disappear. This sense of being overwritten, and *hidden away*, could operate at the level of personal encounter. But it otherwise appears through the development of limited and pejorative medical concepts: bodies are cast as 'over-virilised' to justify cutting, as 'under-developed' to urge testosterone injections or implants. Let's return to Alex Jürgen, who tells us consulting a doctor caused them to 'lose [themselves] completely'. The risk of triggering such a breakdown appears throughout Natalie Delimata's book *Articulating Intersex: A Crisis at the Intersection of Scientific Facts and Social Ideals*. Based on her interviews with medics, Delimata introduces the term 'disinterpellation' to name this moment of rending through existing self-understandings. While in social theory 'interpellation' identifies the moments where key interactions with institutional authorities call us 'into being', disinterpellation names the reverse: the moment authoritative oversight causes our previously stable points of recognition to give way. But is easing moments of disinterpellation the best we can hope for? Clearly, the most humane place to begin is not to revise intersex anatomy, but the textbooks.

Improving our knowledge of sex is not primarily a matter of cataloguing dysfunctional forms (as 'rare diseases', 'disorders', or whatever else) but rather expanding popular horizons of differences to be typically expected. This shift would require a broad range of media, from the biology textbooks already mentioned, to educational videos and popularising accounts relating the harms already done by forceful overwriting of human variation. Much of this work will sketch out atypical difference, but also further serve as a corrective to prior oversimplifications. What stands in the way of these measures' success is the sedimented weight of convention and tradition, but also the more *active* foreclosure which today's professionals remain wedded to. (The medical profession is set against intersex liberation not only as a status, but a commitment.)

While sexology as informed by John Money and his successors had stressed the need for shrewd predictive work early in the lives of intersex children, those making these decisive interventions had limited training in the cultural ramifications of their decisions. Medical school could hardly have prepared clinicians to predict the rapid clip of social change from the later twentieth century into the twenty-first – nor the paths and prospects of those living lives beyond the 'ordinary'.

Intersex variations show the need for integration of history of medical sciences with current treatments. Some living intersex people across one lifetime have been diagnosed first as either male or pseudo-hermaphrodite, then again as the other, and are now considered to have 'disorders of sex development'. This was most notable in the cases of XXY/Klinefelter and Turner syndrome, which in the mid-twentieth century were swapped back and forth as forms of 'male' and 'female' pseudo-hermaphroditism, as researchers tested patients with crude chromatin swabs.[8] Today medics will typically assert with equal confidence that all Klinefelter patients are male, and Turner syndrome patients female (without any apparent regard for the self-understandings offered by patients themselves). Some argue that neither even constitute a 'DSD'.

These oscillations demonstrate that our emergent comprehension of these variations will leave any understanding of sex provisional across the longer term. Intersex liberation requires an overhaul not of physiques, but what is commonly known.

As we've seen, the early intersex movement responded to this treatment with playful and sardonic deflation of clinical authority. Now, the new modes of knowing which have already been developed out of this resistant movement need to be deepened. The early movement showed the world that medics and parents were hiding the truth of intersex from the children and youth with these variations. But much was also being hidden from medics and parents *themselves*. The true ramifications of these procedures were only made clear at this point, through the forceful efforts of intersex advocates and those they recruited to their cause.

Parents played varied roles in 'knowing over' intersex people: families are often selective and calculating about the information of medical procedures and diagnoses they give to intersex people. Too often, the significance of procedures and treatments is downplayed first by doctors, and then again by parents now invested in the process of normalisation. Beyond these personal stories, groups advocating for parents have been operative for years, seeking to both justify and legally protect interventions that intersex people themselves often take to be both harmful and permanently delimiting to life options. Increasingly, these groups have counterposed the need for autonomy on the part of intersex people with the 'privacy' they consider families (parents) entitled to. In Ellen Feder's research, extensive interviews provided as comprehensive an overview for the parents of intersex children as Suzanne Kessler had achieved in her mid-1980s interviews with intersex-specialist doctors. In her 2014 book, *Making Sense of Intersex: Changing Ethical Perspectives in Biomedicine*, Feder presented the arresting argument that parents related to their intersex children not with disgust or discomfort, but *envy*.

As the book continues through the arguments of a parental advocates' 'Bioethics and Intersex Group', Feder thoroughly rebuts their justifications for intersex surgeries under the principle of 'family privacy'. After the 1990s 'Hermaphrodites with Attitude' phase of intersex advocacy shook clinical authority, clinicians ceded authority to parents in order to stabilise the practice of genital cutting. Feder brings to bear ideas ranging from German philosopher Immanuel Kant's conception of duty, to Maurice Merleau-Ponty's notion of bodies being animated by 'I can' motions, to dissemble parent-advocates' expedient justifications for genital cutting. (It's hard to imagine how they might respond to this book-length close reading of their reports.)

As the intersex movement mastered new means of sharing the experiences their consciousness-raising sessions had brought to light, innumerable family histories became overturned. The 'privacy' of the family was rocked by widespread public discussion. The ethical impact of the intersex movement was intense: the '90s were a moment of awakening. The movement developed a defiant idiom, appropriating clinical terminology to undermine medical authority. Yet the twenty-first century may see the household as much as the clinic become a focus for intersex struggles. Intersex struggles are presented in a very different way in movement rhetoric, to how they are in memoir. Movement accounts are most often told through the history of sexology, with parents appearing passively and at the margins of the archive. In memoir, the harms done by our families often appear as early as the opening of the first chapter. Such is the evident weight of parental expectations, introductions of parents usually precede intersex memoirists telling us who *they themselves* are. The anxieties intersex children vicariously absorbed from their caregivers typically appear as these narratives' dramatic foreground. As one advocate for the Intersex Justice Project began their account: 'My story is one of the threads woven into the tangled skein that is my family.'[8] As much as they're enmeshed in clinical claims to authoritative knowledge, intersex lives are bound up with the expectations, dreams, and fears of private households. The twenty-first century would see the ambitions of the medical profession curbed, and bring families' involvement in the harms done to intersex people into clearer view.

Clandestine Communities, Liberatory Knowledge

hypertrophy: Literally, too much meat. How much is too much? More, madam, than your sister has; less, sir, than you will have when we are through.

– 'The Murk Manual'

This book has tracked the development of clinical concepts as they were applied to intersex people. From 'spurious hermaphrodites' to 'disorders of sex development', these terms of art have pinned pejoratives to the topics they purport to define neutrally. But since the later twentieth century, this history has equally been one of resistance: clinicians are now not the only authority who compile glossaries, and never will be again.

'The Murk Manual' was a piece originally published in the 1997 ISNA Intersex Awakening takeover of trans identity mag *Chrysalis*. The title is a typically sardonic reference to the Merck & Co. medical manuals that cover everything from clinical diagnoses, drugs, and tests to, yes, disorders. This A to Z is written with the caustic wit that defined the '90s movement: a cynicism which was unforgiving and provided no clear exit to the horrors it presented and pastiched.

Since then, the movement has shifted towards the register of global governance and social media: new audiences have been found, and new coalitions formed. The twenty-first century will be defined by the increasing dissemination of this knowledge *beyond* the confines of the clinic. A more human future would orient us away from medical hoarding and the extraction of knowledge at the expense of those living through perfectly ordinary irregularities. We can already see a glimpse of the future in the existing tendency of intersex advocates to familiarise themselves with clinical terms of art and reapply them for their own ends. The extension of this may look like a return of 'Hermaphrodites with Attitude': new strategies of subversive appropriation and fresh forms of countercultural struggle.

Advocates made the dehumanised status of intersex clear through actions that contrasted with the objective pretensions of clinical science: protests, satirical comics, amateur documentary interviews, dedicated websites, and now social media. These forced sex to be discussed in new ways and continue to pose fresh challenges, gathering testimonies left scattered and lost by clinicians.

The future demanded by intersex liberation is one where this expressiveness is the primary concern for those who live out the consequences. That means that questions of physiology and anatomy should proceed from the basic principle of 'nothing about us, without us'. Those who do not display this personal autonomy need to be doubly mindful and respectful not only of sex's lability, but the *limits* to which any imposition can be reversed. Not everything written can be overwritten, with numbness and scarring imposing permanent limits.

The expressiveness of sex appears in how it demands explication. Rather than settling, sex becomes known through *differing* idioms, fashioned for practical ends. None who look upon sex will do so with clear eyes, nor reshape it with sterile hands. Rather than serving faithfully as the bedrock of any objective view, sex demands participation, and prompts those handling it to spell out their commitments (even more than they realise: accounts intended to simplify will drip all the more with metaphors, unwitting assumptions, and subtext). Sex is not inevitable or predictable, but carved into the observer's own form – or all too often across those of others around them.

As well as suggesting a certain modesty clearly *not* exhibited by clinicians to date, the challenge of the intersex movement is bound up with the crisis posed by endocrinology. Although farmers have known about gonads for thousands of years, it wasn't until the early twentieth century that they were understood in context of the full range of hormonal glands. While sex has existed since before recorded history, our full physiological understanding remains embryonic.

Previous studies have understated the depth and tenacity of the intersex movement in marshalling medical knowledge and learning for their own ends. Having examined themselves and several images of various vaginal configurations found online, seventeen-year-old Sydney informed their mother that they most likely had a microperforate hymen, and would require medical examination.[9] Predictably, their doctors initially dismissed their self-diagnosis, remarking that 'lots of women don't know their vaginas' (Sydney is non-binary). The doctors inspecting Sydney were at a loss, eventually calling in a trainee medic who offered that the opening resembled a diagram from her medical textbook. This resulted in the medics (finally) returning to the term they'd initially been offered by their patient. As Sydney lacked medical insurance, and therefore could not afford less invasive scans, the doctors scheduled an exploratory surgery to determine the next course of action.

Let's linger on the knowledge exchange at work in this brief vignette. Far from illuminating their patient, the medical professionals were *unfamiliar* with the relevant diagnosis (a microperforate hymen). As Sydney puts it, the professionals were not who 'brought that word into the room'. Correcting paid and trained professionals becomes a matter of course for intersex advocates. As well as disregarding Sydney's self-understanding (referring to them as an oblivious woman), the medics demonstrated deficiencies in their own terms (having to be educated by their untrained patient and a trainee).

Another account by an advocate of encountering a doctor at age ten reflects that by 1999, information on complete androgen insensitivity was widely available both online and via support groups. Yet the clinical encounter proceeded as if web searches were still not possible:

> Despite all of this, I was standing in the office of a doctor who knew nothing about my body. He did not direct me to any actual support, and for the next twelve years I went from doctor to doctor, none of them really knowing what to do with me.

Resorting to Google searches, she mostly found celebrity gossip concerning models that used the term 'hermaphrodite' freely. Yet with hindsight, medical obliviousness was still better than the 'best practice' of the late '90s:

> As hard as all of this was, in a way my doctor's lack of knowledge turned out to be both a blessing and a curse. I felt cursed and ashamed of this different, 'broken' body that couldn't be 'fixed'. I felt like a problem that nobody had the solution to . . . It wasn't until I was older that I discovered the blessing amongst all of this pain. As it turns out, my doctors were so entirely ignorant about my condition that they didn't know how to remove or even *find* my internal testes.[10]

While this account describes a more passive victory than Sydney's (who brought the correct terminology 'into the room' despite their lack of training), it shows us the familiarity required of advocates. After a life of being expected to embody femininity by his anxious mother, another intersex advocate describes physicians swinging between open resistance and blithe admissions of their own professional inadequacies:

> When I decided to transition from female to male, I was met with resistance from physicians because they incorrectly assumed all people with AIS identify as women. In the beginning of my transition, doctors would often tell me, 'I read a chapter on intersex conditions back in medical school', or 'we don't know how to work with people like you' or flat out, 'your body is too weird'.[11]

Witness the constraint of action that intersex people encounter quite quickly: an intersex physique *or* a transitioning one is a challenge enough in isolation, but *both at the same time* makes physicians think back hopelessly to med school. The flipside of all of this is that advocates have come to master multiple medical tongues. This asymmetry arose through mass availability of online glossaries, searchable images, and dedicated niche communities. Each of these developments allowed a determined amateur to gradually amass relevant terminology, testimony, and points of comparison. While advocates were already beginning to master knowledge along narrow themes in the 1990s, it has only become easier since.

Formally or casually, it's clearly easier to sustain state-of-the-art familiarity with any one topic when 'plunging in' alongside like-minded nerds. It's exactly this mutual immersion with the available experts which the so-called Chicago Consensus of the mid-2000s ensured medics would not have access to. From the 2000s, medical practitioners moved to consolidate their pathologising grasp on intersex variations, attempting to make intersex *people* disappear altogether. But these efforts only drew them farther from understanding the challenge posed to them. Medics, by establishing an idiom directed towards soothing their unease at clinical authority being undermined rather than sincerely reconciling with the intersex movement, cut themselves off from contemporary knowledge. They could not participate in the fluent discussion that became typical for advocates. Meanwhile, intersex community self-education has flourished, meaning we can't satisfy ourselves with grasping the history of intersex solely through histories of sexology. The struggle for intersex liberation begins precisely at the limits of medical concern.

For intersex advocates, terms of art reflect the ends that they've pursued. Out of all the ways we could explicitly address sex, intersex communities have largely chosen a more humane appreciation of human physiological diversity. Intersex advocates have sought to undermine the clinical justifications of their routine mistreatment, while meeting the needs of their specific variations autonomously. Their vocabularies were developed towards a shared political purpose. Selective use of terminology (vehemently opposing the use of 'disorders', say, or opting for 'variations' over 'conditions') is *how* these communities take shape. Through sharing not only their experiences but interpretations of them, advocates quickly made everything from satirical countercultural readers to local political campaigns possible. Through their tenacious effort to foreground experiences previously sidelined and silenced, the intersex movement obliges us to *infer* sex anew, requiring a revised attempt to explicate the tangled state of sex. This was made possible through direct interplay between advocates themselves and sympathetic feminist researchers. Those subjected to medical abuse could refashion themselves as full respondents. Following that legacy, advocates have had a deep involvement in channels of knowledge both critical of clinical science and operating beyond its limitations.

Knowledge is not simply a bind that intersex advocates have contrived to wriggle free from. Equally, knowledge has served as a *means* for liberation: new understandings of intersexuality that advocates cultivated purposefully to disrupt the prejudices of medics and parents working through their physiologies. The research of intersex communities contrasts with the professionalising ends of medical expertise. Rather than illuminating all who encounter it, the professionalisation of clinical knowledge establishes tiers between the elevated and gently deceived. Consider the doctors who refer to 'differences' to parents, but 'disorders' among themselves. That approach followed directly from their previous readiness to use 'hermaphroditism' during internal discussions while deploying euphemisms (including intersex) when addressing families and patients. It's exactly that *tiering* that became challenged by the intersex movement: jargon that had previously bounded the limits of elites was reappropriated and redistributed to new ends.

What's required now is a further intensification of the existing deprofessionalisation and dissemination of knowledge. Here intersex people are likely to find obvious allies: as an increasing number of right-wing states move to outlaw both medical transitions and abortions, reproductive healthcare needs will be resolved by networks of self-provisioning and clandestine care. There will be more points of convergence than ever between the communities that provided intersex people refuge and relevant information where medics have failed. But this moment requires the unique insights that intersex liberation has gathered to be understood on their own terms. What the intersex movement has expressed since the '90s more than anything was a productive numbness. Navigating scar tissue, ongoing surgeries, and other treatments that were unclear (palliative or causative?), and overcoming years or decades of secrecy, these communities seized upon knowledge to satisfy unmet needs.

This political breakthrough left us with questions that clinical science could never hope to answer. How much meat is too much, really?

Baby X as Intersex

What happens if you tell a group of people that an unknown baby is a hermaphrodite?

'Baby X' studies blind test social assumptions around sex. Researchers screen footage of an infant child or toddler to a group of research subjects, typically dressing the females in blue and the males in pink without revealing their actual assigned sex. Inevitably, behaviours are interpreted quite differently depending on whether the infant is understood to be a boy or girl. Most often, behaviours which register as distress in girls are interpreted as anger in boys. Boys are described as curious or ingenious manipulators of their surroundings, and girls more often as cautious and shy.

A variation on these studies was conducted by John Delk, who registered reactions to a twenty-two-month-old infant.[12] The medical students tested duly labelled 32 percent of the activities from a supposed 'hermaphrodite' baby as masculine, but only 19 percent of activities were labelled masculine in the case of the 'female'. It quickly becomes apparent that many medics' and parents' fears and anxieties are grounded in this same conflation of indeterminacy and maleness, while 'between' male and female, hermaphroditism is slanted against the still-widespread denigration of girlhood and the lifelong feminine. Even a baby 'hermaphrodite' is intuitively understood as an active agent.

In these bigoted yet predictable apprehensions of the indeterminate as male (active) we can hear echoes of Ovid's original narrative of Salmacis pulling Hermaphroditus into her embrace, a scene described as a wrapping of serpent folds around an eagle: an unlikely overpowering followed by the two being merged together by divine will. Hermaphroditism is compelling because of the prospect of twinning beauty and force.

Most 'Baby X' studies have rather more predictable answers than Delk's variation. While feminism achieved breakthroughs across the later twentieth century, perceptions of children clearly too young to account for themselves remain stubbornly shaped around the male and female. Indications are even present that this differentiation is culturally entrenched. For example, 'gender reveal' parties are defended as an intuitive and obvious 'tradition' despite the fact that they clearly originated in the twenty-first century, not to mention the wildfires, plane crashes, and explosive accidents associated with the most overblown of such parties. These starkly differentiated reactions to male and female infants shape their upbringing and self-development profoundly. Anne Fausto-Sterling has described the split in how boys and girls are treated from the youngest age as triggering 'cascade-and-feedback effects'.[13] Since her tongue-in-cheek fivefold sex divide back in the 1990s, Fausto-Sterling has elaborated an increasingly thoroughgoing account of how the interplay of upbringing and identity develops during early childhood, through what she now calls a 'dynamic systems framework'.[14]

Katrina Karkazis and Rebecca Jordan-Young are two researchers with a shared method and shared commitments, an affinity obvious well before their co-written masterpiece, *Testosterone:*

An Unauthorized Biography (2019). *Testosterone* is a book-length critical account of contemporary endocrinology and the enormous body of writing around androgens by non-experts. The book demonstrates comprehensively that the mythology around androgens is both baseless (given decades-old research) and persistent into the present. As this book has shown, Karkazis and Jordan-Young both have, more than anything else, a sharp eye for the *ideological* workings of natural science research. That is, ways in which seemingly neutral evaluations and measurements are set around terms and thresholds that are quietly adjusted as presuppositions shift for broader social reasons. And then how stray studies and minor papers become extracted from their original conclusions to fuel those existing presuppositions across broader society.

Karkazis's 2008 book *Fixing Sex: Intersex, Medical Authority, and Lived Experience* is a tour de force marking the maturation of feminist studies of intersex into full incorporation of perspectives of those harmed by medical practices. Accounts from intersex people and their families appear alongside (and against) the working concepts of clinicians, along with their own testimonies. She shows how medical professionals had been insulated by their steadfast focus on ensuring that intersex people were heterosexual and never transitioned (what Catherine Clune-Taylor called a priority of 'securing cisgender futures'). The overriding focus on conventionally heterosexual patient outcomes had allowed them to conceal every possible harm that accumulated towards that end:

> An individual who accepts his or her gender identity and is married (i.e., heterosexual) would, by the criteria of most studies, be said to have had a successful outcome; but these criteria tell us very little about how individuals adapt to their condition and its treatment, shame or stigma they or their parents feel about their condition, the strain or challenges the condition poses for family and personal relationships, and the experience of being different.

Karkazis's account of the continued pathologisation of intersex children develops the argument that pathological framings *fuel* existing mistreatments through clinic and family. *Fixing Sex* resolves in an unflinching critique of pathological conceptions of intersex. As Karkazis puts it:

> The disease-model approach to intersexuality, which broadly includes conceptualizations of, treatment practices for, and anxieties about gender atypical bodies and creates a profound insecurity about the body and being, and one's right to ownership of both, affects lives in meaningful ways.

Rebecca Jordan-Young's essay 'Taking Context Seriously' is the cornerstone of her 2011 book *Brain Storm: The Flaws in the Science of Sex Differences*, which takes apart the entire field of 'brain organisation' studies. These studies purport to isolate the key differences in sex. These researchers studied personality traits and behaviours of children with classic congenital adrenal hyperplasia who were raised as girls. Following an ingrained belief that 'virilised women' were prone to violence, lesbianism, and other 'masculine' qualities, these studies focused on topics where medical treatment would leave children most impaired, and least 'representative' as a comparative sample.

While few papers would spend a moment reflecting on their history, 'brain organisation' views came to the fore after John Money was discredited by Milton Diamond, sparking a renewed interest in detailed studies of hormonal conditions in the womb. Just as Richard Goldschmidt had studied the bovine freemartin to develop his notion of 'hormonally intersex', the brain organisation faction of sexology would focus on classic CAH patients with XX chromosomes in order to entrench their view of in utero flows of inner secretion. Sadly, human societies are both more complex and brutal than a cows'.

Lesbianism was taken to be a definitive act of gender nonconformity, and an avoidable negative outcome for homophobic parents (via use of the steroid hormone dexamethasone). But the sexuality of those with CAH was irrevocably shaped around clitoral cutting. Varieties of these procedures claiming to be 'nerve-sparing' proved to be greatly overhyped. Even after these surgeries, penetration was not always possible. Jordan-Young suggests that this inspired bisexual women to explore a range of sexual avenues – although clearly the association of CAH with lesbianism was wildly overblown, even with this considered. The legacy of numbing surgeries followed by retraumatising examinations meant that as adults, women with classic congenital adrenal hyperplasia had unusually few romantic partners (an outcome of little interest to 'brain organisation' researchers).

'Gender conformity' was not a neutral concern in households raising classic CAH girls: doctors often explicitly warned parents to expect 'tomboy' children. Many from the intersex movement report that their parents would scrutinise their bodies obsessively for signs that they were developing according to cultural convention. (Indeed, this was often the case even with non-classic CAH variations which didn't cause larger genitals.) Psychological development of those born with this variation was heavily impacted by repeated medical visits, as often as every three or four months. Far from simply resolving and monitoring metabolic issues, these would often involve repeated genital examinations towards no clear end. Interviews with CAH parents and patients by Karkazis make it abundantly clear many parents were navigating how doctors were using these routine and seemingly non-therapeutic genital examinations as training opportunities, at the expense of their children.[15]

Disregarding harms done to CAH children *after* being born, brain organisation researchers believed that their 'womb virilisation' was a most decisive moment. Karkazis notes that even when researchers mention the extensive treatments and examinations classic CAH girls receive, they typically treat them as a blessing:

They routinely assume that *treatment can only limit or counteract the effects of the illness or . . . the early hormone exposures.* That is . . . treatment can only *help* patients be more like normal, health comparison groups . . . Yet given that 94% of the 35 women in this sample had clitoral surgery and vulvoplasty, and 66 also had vaginoplasty, it would seem more reasonable to frame the poor outcomes as *because* of the medical care, rather than *despite* it.

Jordan-Young reached something of a professional breaking point as she came to the same conclusion, using a range of frames to try to grasp the stubborn obliviousness of the field she is disassembling: 'agnotology' (the study of ignorance, doubt or misinformation), the 'epistemology of ignorance', or simply the *not-known.* Jordan-Young's essay on CAH context moves as if she was trying to reassure the reader that she is *not* asserting what page after page of evidence would otherwise suggest:

Let me be clear: I am not implying that clinicians involved in the medical treatment of intersex individuals are malevolent. Karkazis painstakingly documents clinicians' dedication and even passion to improve treatment for their intersex patients – but she also reveals that they are so deeply invested in the idea that genitals can and should be 'fixed' that they fail to consider how their treatment does, in spite of their very good intentions, harm their patients.

However, Jordan-Young and Karkazis avoid a more obvious conclusion: this is not an epistemic problem, but a political one. Spinoza once asked, 'Why do people fight for their servitude as if it were their salvation?' Grasping why they fight for their continued mastery *over others* is more easily answered. The intersex movement did not simply expose harms done to those who took part. It also shook forever the purported objectivity that clinical authorities had claimed for themselves.

These researchers are happy to assume that medical professionals have largely benign intentions, and that 'tunnel vision' makes them oblivious to the catastrophe they generate. Rather than cruelty, medical harm can best be understood as akin to cosmic horror. But at what point do examinations, often described by those receiving them as 'violations' or akin to rape, become more callous than oblivious? An asymmetry has opened between a movement writing its own satirical glossaries and cartoons, and their punchline: a profession that refuses to listen, that always believes another twist of clinical Greek or acronym will be the last word. A moment follows where the 'veil falls', and intersex people are left scrabbling to account for the reasoning behind damages done. On the one hand, knowledge of oneself as human. On the other: dehumanisation made routine, all decked out in professional flourishes.

The focus for coming years will surely not be passing moral judgements on clinicians' inner monologues, but making it harder for the harms they've done to continue (irrespective of the exact reasons they might have felt moved to do them). What's still unresolved from the earliest days of intersex advocacy is an ongoing *challenge to the command of clinical reason:*

- Intersex people are *known over*, and came to realise that in a way that reshaped the reshaping of sex forever.
- *Communities develop their reason together*, honing terms for their own ends, both through clandestine channels and open involvement in the broader world of reasoning.
- *Sex is expressive*, in that sex will be spoken about. Each of us devises, adapts, and revises terms suitable for that task.

So, Can We Be Reasonable?

Voices of continuity in the medical profession were quick to dismiss the intersex movement as a group of 'zealots' who wish to ban even life-saving medical interventions, or 'activists' who disregard the norms of scientific knowledge. Yet as we've seen, scientific reasoning was never absent from intersex advocacy. This movement was birthed through a dialogue with feminist researchers of clinical psychology and developmental biology. Appearing at the end of the twentieth century, intersex advocacy closed an era which had seen understandings of sex chaotically rewritten. Following these origins, intersex advocates have been shrewd in their networking with scientific researchers, playfully subversive, prone to comedic understatement. Far from snarling militancy, the intersex movement has been characterised by a delicacy and precision. Advocates' dispassionate affect contrasted with the routine brutality they'd received.

Intersex advocates did not disregard clinical jargon, but reappropriated it. They exchanged unique personal testimony at inward-facing gatherings and reported their insights publicly to expose the widespread nature of medical incompetence they had endured. Consciousness-raising formed a base of knowledge that counterposed the continual shedding of relevant data and follow-ups by clinicians and medical researchers, who left intersex people 'lost to follow-up'. From the 1990s, the intersex movement presented a case against clinical mistreatment beyond the understanding of those they confronted (their dethroned former experts).

Intersex advocacy produced new forms of knowledge from the ruins of clinical sex. This confluence of reference points and styles allowed for medics' devastating and deceptive treatments to be recast in terms many outsiders simply could not bear to read. The political challenges posed by the intersex movement are best understood outside the context of the professional work, surgical refinements, and conceptual developments performed by medics. 'Clinical management' is only half the picture. We have to bring into view the creative and defiant work of intersex *people* to redefine their circumstances and reclaim their physiques' character. This is the ethical work of the intersex movement: to turn ordeals of routine mistreatment and longstanding neglect into lives worth living. The writings of the intersex movement are a polymorphous medley of the best understandings to hand: history, physiology, literature, histology, feminism, phylogenetics, deconstruction, endocrinology, Merck, mythology, fifty shades of Foucault.

Conclusion

Entanglement
(*Intersex* Poems, Hermaphrodite Statues)

> For our ancient nature was not what it is now, but of another
> kind. In the first place, there were three sexes among men – not
> two as now – male and female – but a third sex in addition, which
> was both of them in common, whose name still remains, though
> the thing itself has vanished . . .
>
> – Plato, *Symposium*

Intersex liberation ended a great silence. Lost medical records
and personal recollections that had previously been hoarded in
privacy were retrieved and shared more openly. Prior to the intersex movement, depictions of intersex physiologies came twinned
with mythology. These depictions usually showed us how twinning of the sexes was widely *longed for*. In ancient Greek
mythology, the character Hermaphroditus appeared as one of the
Erotes (winged gods, closely linked to sex and romance), a merger
of beautiful male and female flesh. Hermaphroditus did not pose
a threat to conventions of desire and matrimony, but actually
affirmed them instead. One philosopher from Lesbos, Theo-
phrastus, suggested that the fourth day of the month was
associated by the superstitious with Hermaphroditus, falling as
an auspicious day for a wedding.

The first template for hermaphrodite depictions attested by the
historical record is attributed to the ancient sculptor Polycles, with
copies of his work in bronze and stone becoming commonplace
across antiquity. In the 1600s, sculptor Gian Lorenzo Bernini created a detailed carving of a stone mattress for one of these ancient

statues, a sleeping hermaphrodite, which was set up for display. Bernini's work was so skilful that visitors to the displayed statue are said to have reached out to caress the fabric. In this depiction that was widely copied by the 1700s, we find a portrayal of hermaphrodite as indeterminacy made resting flesh. This comes from a trick of approach: the statue's shoulders are bent such that its face and ass align. From this view, the piece's physique was modelled to resemble Aphrodite (or Venus). By contrast, frontal view would reveal both the statue's full breasts and genitals.

The assumed intention of the sculptor was to purposefully mislead those first encountering their work. Each view is only partial, and a viewer passing the 'rear-facing' approach might not recognise the statue as a depiction of Hermaphroditus (perhaps taking the maiden for her mother, Aphrodite). But it seems facile to question which view provides insight to the figure's 'true sex': rather, the statue tests viewers' existing familiarity with the art-form, and that of human bodies (what shape of groin is a round pair of buttocks and soft face expected to accompany?) The serene countenance of the sleeping hermaphrodite serves as a counterpoint to the imagined voyeur: whatever shock is caused by her indeterminacy glances off the mute indifference found in her repose.

Alongside the development of hermaphrodite figures in ancient Greece, versions of these statues were spread across the Kushan Empire (which extended across today's North India and Pakistan, through central and west Asia). In the Kushan era, deities from an array of contexts were brought into a mottled pantheon. Greek deities were borrowed, along with the use of the Greek language for administration. A new type of hermaphrodite appeared: a standing figure split between two sexes, down the middle. Surviving Kushan-era carvings feature a figure with half a scalp of matted hair, the other half combed and threaded with flowers.

By the rise of the Gupta Empire across South Asia, these statues became known as *Ardhanarishvara* ('half-female Lord' or

'Lord who is half woman'). By this point, these figures were taken to depict the deity Shiva joined physically with the goddess Parvati, merging the divine male and female energies into a single generative form. The *Ardhanarishvara's* female half wears a lotus around the neck and carries a bloom or sometimes a parrot. Her skin is often green, or dark. Their male half usually has a broader shoulder, flat chest, and fuller waist, and is clad in pearls, with a sacred thread across his chest and docile serpents surrounding him. In some depictions, the bifurcation is played up across the face: the male half has half a moustache, or a sacred eye. These depictions became ubiquitously popular, and still appear in almost every temple devoted to Shiva.

While these figures merge male and female sex aspects, they are not exactly egalitarian. Most present the statue's right (dominant) half as male. By contrast, the Hindu school Shaktism usually presents the statue's right side as female, reversing consort and liege.

Regardless, depictions of this hermaphrodite from the Gupta period on emphasise a popped hip stance, known as the 'triple bend position' (*Tribhaṅga*). This position sets the body in three directions: one through the slightly bent knees, another around the hips, and then once more through the shoulders or neck. As well as serving to exaggerate the curving form and poise of the statue's female side, *Tribhaṅga* also serves to angle the statue's arms (sometimes three or four, occasionally as many as eight) around this emphatic orientation. This pose seems to undercut the male dominance of majority depictions: the predominance of the right side visually against the three-part motion led by the hip. Hermaphroditism here appears as slanted towards the feminine: not just an assembly of incongruent body parts, but a physique setting a unity of opposites into motion.

Some ancient Greek and Roman depictions shared the *Ardhanarishvara* statues' visual emphasis on hermaphroditism as displayed through the positioning of limbs. A collection of statues and bronzes now known as the Dresden pattern hermaphrodites portray a hermaphrodite bound in struggle with a satyr (the half-goat icon of unchecked lust). These two excessive figures wrestle together, both the hermaphrodite and satyr appearing naked. While in the *Ardhanarishvara*'s presentation of female and male divine energies the suggestion is harmony and unity, here they directly clash for physical mastery (with the female dominant). Whereas the sleeping hermaphrodite carved by Polycles exposes onlookers to their own desire by their orientation towards this slumbering form, in the Dresden group statues this longing is externalised. The satyr's writhing limbs wove into his lust's object, his throat gripped, and his longing held down. While not

Figure 3. Cast of a satyr and a hermaphrodite. © Ashmolean Museum, University of Oxford

tamed, the hermaphrodite's wanton suitor is held at bay, or in submission. Contrasting with the impassiveness of the better-known *Sleeping Hermaphroditus*, this hermaphrodite is fully immersed in motion, and struggle.

The conflict between the two forms (and their eight limbs) was known in Greek as *symplegma* – entanglement. Just as the popped hip of Gupta-era sacred hermaphrodites provided a visual centrepiece, the dynamic entwinement of the Dresden pattern statues' limbs allowed sculptors to showcase their skills. This state of *entanglement* is key to understanding the often fraught yet overlapping development of the intersex movement among accompanying counter-cultural moments: feminism, gay liberation, and transsexuality.[1]

Transition and intersexuality have too often been treated in counterpoint: the first a matter of resolving identity, the second a clinical crisis (that generated 'gender', as we know it, along the way). Struggles for the liberation of women, gays, and trans people had become bound up with intersex liberation by the end of the twentieth century, through shared *political struggle*. These movements had thought together, shared publications, and took to the streets together.

By the twenty-first century, attempts to segregate these struggles began in earnest, yet denials of the entangled form of social struggle could only go so far. Let's turn from ancient carvings to the contemporary *working through* of people confronting their childhood mistreatment.

'Intersex' is the name of two pieces, both published in 2015. 'Intersex', by Juliana Huxtable, is a fragment of poetry which addresses the angelic. *Intersex*, by Aaron Apps, is a memoir that addresses the animal.

Huxtable begins with the divine, and debris: an angel opening an embankment gate, pushing through a decaying threshold. Huxtable's angel opens the gate to channel a flood of history: we pass between flesh and divinity, in direct challenge to the worldly powers. Our attention is pushed from flesh to the professions, from those who live in the wake of sex's bifurcation, to those who'd engineered that flimsy divide: 'CORPOREAL FIGURES WHOSE POWER INSPIRES A SLIPPAGE OF FEAR TO PANIC IN THE VIBRATING SOULS OF DOCTORS, LAWYERS, PRIESTS AND BIOLOGISTS.'

In a few words, the poem slides through the history of hermaphrodites: from divine forms in merger, to the disintegration of expert reason (clerical, juridical, clinical). Advocacy by self-declared intersex collectives overturned sex as a concern passed from one profession to the next: jurists, physicians, psychologists, geneticists. In 'Intersex', those judged and prodded return their twofold judgement. As host or chorus, hermaphrodites speak back.

History allowed intersex people to contest the harms done to those with physiologies regarded by the medical system as an error to be resolved. Back in the '90s, as an act of political expression, some openly declared themselves 'intersexuals'. This advocacy denaturalised the harm done by medics, and denuded professional claims to sovereignty over sex. Intersexuals wrenched their own history into view, demanding justification for what had become routine, by naming themselves rather accepting the term 'intersex conditions' as applied to a cluster of natural states. Not only defiant of the disciplinary moves against them, this moment was also *expressive*: showing the intuitive unity that came out of shared harms. The intersex movement also gave voice to emerging class forces that were less often understood. At the end of the twentieth century, the rise of tech industries meant that a new fraction of the intelligentsia was being birthed. Knowledge which had been siloed in professional training became more readily accessible to those with resolve and the unique motivation instilled by medical mistreatment.

So the picketing of the paediatricians delivered historical tidings: it revealed something beautiful and terrible. It showed a wit that had survived all the cutting and injections, and become cold. It played up the linkage between one group habitually shamed by heterosexual households, and the next. It drew into view centuries of efforts from professionals to cleanly integrate intersex people into juridical and clinical systems that demanded each physique be marked 'M' or 'F'.

At all points, the poem 'Intersex' works towards a judicious balancing, until finally asserting the angelic physique's primacy: 'THE PHALLIC/VOID DIVISION COLLAPSES. NOT AT THE LEVEL OF METAPHOR BUT IN FLESH'. Previously reigning partitions fall to pieces before angelic force. Huxtable's vision of sacred suspension of sex orders neither allows the divide that has been demanded, nor lets us escape it: 'WHAT BETTER WAY TO RE-ARTICULATE SPACE AND TIME THAN THROUGH A BODY LITERALLY BEYOND THE SCOPE OF, YET STILL WITHIN, THE WORLD OF MAN (AND WOMAN).'

Huxtable's 'Intersex' was originally written for the art show *Gender Talents*, and later rendered as its own artwork, in a narrow white font embedded into green latex. The Spanish translation (by Pilar Córdoba) was a bolder roman font embossed into a translucent tablet, intended to be equal parts 'stone tablet and mural slime'. Huxtable's caps lock throughout 'Intersex' suggests ancient scripts and web 1.0 rants at once: wisdom-writing that churns through contexts and generates new ones. In this case, it is reminiscent of the late HIV activist Bryn Kelly's writing in her guise as Party Bottom, which merged affirmations shared between those living with HIV with the dizzying abjections of queer theory:

YOU HAVE TIGER BLOOD AND ADONIS DNA – YOU HAVE BECOME A CYBORG GOD/DESS – YOU ARE EVOLVED BEYOND THE GRASP OF A MERE VIRUS THAT HAS CLAIMED THE LIVES OF 39 MILLION PEOPLE – YOU ARE THE BASTARD STEP DAUGHTER OF STATE SOCIALISM AND GLOBAL CAPITALISM – YOU ARE A NEW PHARMA-COPORNOGRAPHIC REGIME.

To the same end, Huxtable's 'Intersex' ends with clinical jargon stitched into a mocking list, partitions immediately lined up to be overcome: 'HYPERTROPHY, HYPOSPADIA, TRUE AND PSEUDO, MALE AND FEMALE'. Intersex advocates' mocking appropriation of medical terms sees them rinsed and reclaimed. This sign-off channels the attitude of 'The Murk Manual: How to Understand Medical Writing on Intersex'. Raphael Carter's satirical glossary grasped onto clinical harms through mockery, lifting jargon from the context of domination to undo its capacity for command. Fluency by the subjugated provides a challenge the poem calls angelic (otherwise known as the political).

Hermaphroditism is an abiding fascination that the professions evoked, and tried to tame. 'Intersex' celebrates the obvious disintegration of these efforts: contradictory motion made to look easy, wounds and rust not enough to halt the angel's ascent. Huxtable's fragment offers an *apocalyptic moment:* the hidden revealed and an old world torn through by this disorder, a mingling not of M/F but old, overly familiar wounds and new apprehensions that arise once we question whether any of it was necessary.

Meanwhile, Aaron Apps takes us from the heavens to the public toilet. *Intersex* provides an unsparing account of a childhood shaped around unnecessary medical interventions. Not much research is needed for the reader to know what they're in for. On the cover of this small grey chapbook, a pair of shears stands in for the *x* in 'intersex'.

Apps begins with animal flesh and function: 'twenty hacked and butterflied pigs' are roasted. Having feasted, Aaron then continues with a companion (perhaps a lover, perhaps you) to a department store. The sequence ('Barbeque Catharsis') continues with an extensive account of his explosive bowel movements and struggles with wiping. As Aaron finally finishes up, he realises his mistake as a small girl 'squeals' and is replied to by her concerned mother. Trying to avoid them, Apps fails and ends up face-to-face with the midwestern Karen ('Her eyebrows grimace').

During this lavatory encounter, Apps can still offer this mother no excuse, provide her no account that would either place him, or exonerate his presence. This mute entry point sets the tone for the rest of *Intersex*. Silenced by the disapproval of the parent, he recounts precisely this moment of being 'gender non-conforming' after all, despite the brutal best practices of the medical profession, with determined assistance by his parents.

This memoir recounts how desperate motion continues while held in place, offering writing that punctures so many years being held down:

> And I say I am the same as many images and bodies that move and shudder the way the captured genitals move frantically in the same place – the way everything does – while stilled in a grip like slim minnows in a net.

Intersex reveals to us the monstrous process by which Aaron finds himself human. Apps recalls a moment when he unexpectedly met an alligator, while aged eighteen ('almost a man'). After they struggle over a red broom, Apps finally begins to bludgeon the reptile to death, continuing long after the need for self-preservation has passed. The gator slaying is described as a transformative act of penetration and merger:

> All the muscles in my limbs, hands, lips, tongue and jaw become static. All of the muscles down into the peristaltic pulsing of my lava lamp guts stilled for a moment as we both became animal, as we both flooded outwards, mixed, and coagulated together.

Apps regards the dead alligator and ponders especially over a potential hatchling, picturing nursing out of the bloodshed the next generation of sexed (or sexless) animals: 'Lukewarm and asexual like a menstruating penis, always there becoming against threatening omnivorous teeth.'

These lingering descriptions introduce Apps's bleak and resigned view of manhood as an imposition, which he could only comply with through acts of grotesquery. ('When I was a child I was pushed down a masculine sludge stream.') But equally, they demonstrate how even while giving way to this brutality, he finds moments of recognition with animal androgyny.

Between these narrative sequences, untitled bursts of intensive reflections run for a few paragraphs. Epigraphs by thinkers especially concerned with bodily motions and predicaments, including Maurice Merleau-Ponty, Simone de Beauvoir and Sara Ahmed, appear. A quote from French pornographic philosopher Georges Bataille appears on two otherwise empty pages, summarising the poem's method: 'Only with the human does there appear transcendence of consciousness . . . The animal is in the world like water in water.'

Intersex tells us that Apps's *medicalisation* took place across the 1980s. Beginning with a hospital-room encounter between his parents and their OB-GYN, Apps provides fine-grain details from the experience of his mother ('a slow good hurt. Things stretch, fail, are cut . . .) to the medic's patter as his intersex variation is assessed ('the doctor talks diligently about *ethics* and *sociability* and *proper action* . . . *Strictly cosmetic. Necessary.* A strange knot in the conflict between those two statements'), through to detailed descriptions of the physician and his father's matching Adam's apples. Moving into his own memories, Apps relates having silicon faux gonads fitted, and being held down by nurses and his parents for testosterone injections (starting at six years old). Both the struggles and agonies of these moments linger: from being fed ice cream to mollify him, to the interchangeability of a nurse and his parents pinning him down for injections. Apps presents himself as undergoing a transformation in which he is at once hapless and complicit, passive and immersed: 'I, a violence done, doing violence; I, a boy boying it, it a thing.'

Apps refuses innocence, showing violent exchanges that follow on directly from those he endured. His personal brutality and its originating subjugation appear as an alternation between dominating and pathetic terms: 'My little dick is a needle.' These moments of symmetrical self-awareness seem to undercut themselves: we see again an acute sensitivity to quite how numbed up these developmental injuries left him. *Intersex* attempts to *express* the resulting *non-responsiveness* following medical harms found throughout intersex movement writings. The viciousness Apps describes himself performing (or at least imagining in precise detail) is an attempt to feel anything, despite it all.

Intersex is uncompromising while describing parental involvement in the normalising force of medical interventions: 'The pattern of the crochet embedded in my forehead. Such force. Into my ass my mother sticks the needle as I fight against my father's arms and weight.' Yet Apps continuously doubles back after describing the worst moments of this abuse, deflating the tension by observing how they'd have treated him better if he was a gorilla rather than a six-year-old, or providing wry remarks: 'It's not that they shouldn't have done it. It's that the dynamic is strange.' Is this a parody of calls for nuance, or just the reality of an upbringing spent beneath a veil?

Throughout *Intersex*, Apps swings between depicting himself at his most vulnerable and his least flattering, with layers of self-deprecation to leave even the sharpest reader wrongfooted: 'Lines that hidden are as tangled and intersecting as the hole is in my weaving above. Hole or hole? Whole or hole? Hole or line? Prick or slit? Cock or cunt? Excuse my language.'

Threaded through Apps's memoir of medical trauma we find the most troubling feature of the little book: an extreme close-up of genitals held firmly in place by pale fingers. Apps implies the photo is from his childhood ('and I am words seeping into images'), then confronts the reader in the caption beneath the photo: 'and I wonder if that makes you comfortable as you slide with your tearing eye-lube', before becoming warmer: 'Welcome to the intersection of my intersex, my fellow animals, I will point you to the appearances of shuddering and violence that I trace as I finger the wire lines of a grotesque harp.'

Finally, the image is revealed as an 1888 photograph entitled 'living specimen of a hermaphrodite', taken by Dr. Ernest Muirhead Little (name of the subject and medical examiner unknown). As explained by Anna Blume in her 'Mesh: The Tale of the Hermaphrodite', this image is a cruder and crueller rendition of Nadar's 1861 composition, *Examination of a Hermaphrodite*. We're exposed to a captured anatomy, and to an example of how quickly the history of intersex surveillance became wrapped up with the practice of photography. This new technology merged swiftly with ancient fascinations, and flesh that would otherwise have perhaps been kept veiled and concealed was drawn into full view for a new mode of capture, preservation, and display.

The revelation also somewhat lets the reader off the hook. While it's unclear how willing the subject was (their blurred face either in a deep slumber, or horrified rictus), it seems sound to assume the worst. Yet the displayed subject is surely long since dead. The picture is then repeated across page after page of Apps's book, manipulated until genitals and face merge. This act of compulsive return seems both harsh and measured. Apps unmistakably demonstrates the damage done by what Katrina Karkazis's study calls 'the medical gaze' that defines intersex, while mitigating any further injury that would have ensued if he had deployed an image from a living party (including himself).

Intersex displays a refusal to flinch from the injuries done, nor use them as a pretext for abandoning reason. Apps reassures us he is not a positivist (an unlikely accusation for most poets). Instead, he explains that his process of merging animal, human, and more gathers debris for an expressive purpose:

> The body is concerned with the interactions that happen between living machines . . . This is a collection of stones, wires, animals,

hinges, oranges, motors, organs, digested peas, stamen, figs, hemoglobin, plasticmedia, bubbles, ovules, and nebulas. I write about gender the way I eat straight from the plasma that runs through the blood-pink placenta – there is a genealogy to be teased out of the flesh. I am a humanist and positivist only so much as I acknowledge that these stances are catastrophic.

This vision toys with both literal and philosophical plastic: beginning in sex's ruins without denial. Apps recounts the way his parents brought him up to be the master of things, and replies by juxtaposing himself alongside debris – defined by reptiles and scoops of sickly sweet soft-serve, devouring and devoured by them, mastering, hapless.

Do Huxtable's and Apps's works serve as perfect counterpoint: transcendent exuberance against suffering flesh, the popped hip against the flat chest? No. Both hopes of tearing free of sedimented weight of bygone concepts and the full scope of damage done to existing intersex lives were revealed by the same historical moment. The intersex liberation movement sketched another world exactly as the atrocities required to sustain the present were brought into view. Together, both Huxtable's 'Intersex' and Apps's *Intersex* are testament to a new reconnection with ancient forms and animal affinities. Together they move us beyond the breakthrough of 'experience', the desiccation of 'bioethics', and any claim to one identity – reconnecting us with the animal and angelic, recovery and revelation.

In 'The Marks on Our Bodies', Mauro Cabral denounces the reliance of the intersex movement on both Anglophone discussions and reductions of intersex struggles to medical accounts:

> The construction of an international intersex movement not only has depended – and still depends – on that hegemony, but has also considerably restricted the possibilities of other ways of communicating, including those of poetry, fiction, erotic, and other manifestations of 'inefficient' speech.

Even against this double suture, the word 'intersex' still designates a persistent question, a scarred question that lies from tongue to language, a scar never fully healed, constantly reopened.

It's one thing to say that intersex variations *shouldn't* be reduced to a pathological malady, to be clinically overseen as an emergency or a cluster of undesirable traits (to be eliminated where possible). But it was another to *know* it. The place of poems, memoir, fiction, and 'inefficient' texts was filling lives, in the way medical records and clinical encounters never could.

It's for that reason that we can't take terms such as 'intersexual' or 'hermaphrodites' to be mere vestiges, to be forgotten whenever possible. Hermaphroditism is a living legacy. Intersex variations can never be fully grasped by anatomists or geneticists, lawyers or doctors. There will always be a need for tongues that do not belong to the clinic, or courtroom.

Back to the '90s

Since the public emergence of intersex advocacy in 1996, a continuous challenge has been posed to sex and science. The sacrifices required for the twentieth century's clinical regime to set male and female apart were brought into harsh view. What were taken to be quirks of nature, anatomical oddities that demanded the vice grip of 'gender' (and its clinical oversight), came to be seen as a set of historical interventions. Medical deliberations that masked their routinised butchery with the veneer of the technical, and became contested before the press and broader public opinion, were now required to justify themselves in terms that led beyond medical assessments.

This political struggle left the norming of bodies still not reliably prevented, yet increasingly beyond justification. For the past thirty or so years, intersex advocacy has attempted to achieve humane treatment for those at the sharp end of human sexual lability. And how far have we come?

What had been hidden away became noisily revealed by advocates who had borrowed and bent clinical terminology. This movement sprawled across national borders, yet operated within the confines of a uniquely inhospitable era for internationalist struggles. The rich exchanges of information (personal, terminological, self-referential) opened up by novel channels of communication permitted the spilling of what had been hidden, and the freakish became nothing but an alternative set of conventions. 'Lost cases' came to name themselves and relate the harms they'd received. Today, in the wake of that struggle, we address sex with terms both novel and ancient.

This book has followed the intersex coming to know themselves, through seeing how they're known. Resisting those who've tried to hide them away, at whatever cost. Spinning the last gasp of counterculture into a new hermaphrodite underground. Turning clinical tongues to their own purposes, and developing their own. Edgy while holding those we've saved close to us.

What is needed now is not reform, but rupture.[2] Sex is being reshaped, and a new natural order is emerging. The tangle of sex can make those confined by it feel monstrous, or angelic. We grow out of clinic and colony, and will overcome them both:

> She wraps him round with her embrace, as a serpent, when the king of birds has caught her and is bearing her on high: which, hanging from his claws, wraps her folds around his head and feet and entangles his flapping wings with her tail; or as the ivy ofttimes embraces great trunks of trees, or as the sea-polyp holds its enemy caught beneath the sea, its tentacles embracing him on every side.

Another view of what's human and a new science of sex, expressed through dialogue between the dehumanised. Back with an attitude – after thirty years in motion – their awakening is still only beginning.

Acknowledgements

Thanks are due to:

Both my sisters and late brother, who taught me how to read.

My patient editors Rosie Warren, Leo Hollis, Jeanne Tao, and the Verso Books Union.

Among other favours they've offered: Alex Adamson, Alexandra Vukovich, Alexis Davin, Jose Sarvis, Lydia MacKinnon, and Aurelio Giardini each read drafts of these chapters. This book is a dialogue with them.

Austria's Platform for Intersex People (VIMÖ) first introduced me to this political struggle – through rooms filled with intersex *people*. From community hangouts to book launches, a stage show and censored comedy set, to global gatherings in Vienna's grandiose city hall – a world was opened to me. To Hida Viloria, for welcoming me. Valerie for giving me hope for a gentler future (with no colonies). Sophie for the afterwardness. Anja and Nicole – despite it all. Iain Morland and Morgan Holmes – both I've yet to meet – whose work made this book feel like catch-up. Back in 2017, Christopher Breu shared an early version of *In Defense of Sex* that permanently altered my approach (citation now feels insufficient). Meeting Pidge Pagonis after they spoke in Vienna sharpened this book's internationalist political vision. Erin Vlahović went out of his way to introduce me to intersex advocates in Zagreb. Ins A Kromminga (with OII Germany) taught me how to use a button press. Morgan Carpenter was generous in conversation, while open to this book's thrust. Kitty Anderson offered guidance I still follow closely. And Betsy Driver was tough when I needed it.

Acknowledgements

My friends:

Jason Walter supported my early career with persistent encouragement, and money. Aaron Jaffe for so many conversations that helped join dots as I mapped this manuscript out. Nathan Tankus for keeping it locked and heterodox. Damon, my oldest living friend. Min and Max for hanging out. Rose-Anne for the book club. Rebeka Pushkar for the laughs. Liola and Thekla, for warmth and rigour. Dylan, Robyn, Nick, and Calvin for coming through. Jolene Zubrow chewed over plasticity with me. Everyone who brought me to Zagreb, Graz, Bielefeld, and Bochum. Jamilah, Joana, Kerstin, Lain, SharPuta, Bruno, Jack, Jackie, Bernard, Ira, Mia, and Lina Gonan, and Jordy Rosenberg all championed my work in ways I'd never have expected. Mati Klitgård hired me to deliver an early version of the arguments found here (and not found). David Shulman offered sound advice when most needed. Mariana Silva and Joss graciously hosted in Lisbon and Leytonstone. Barno for our jaunt to Torquay. Nat for all the nursing chat. Syd for recognising me. Linda for always asking. Wanda Vrasti cleared the final bureaucratic hurdle to include the entangled herm. Rooz and everyone else who listened to all this at x2, one New Year's. Everyone who made Leftovers what it was, and QTHOMO what it's becoming. Lecken for the disintegration. My Warschauer weightlifting crew for building up my bones, Sunday by Sunday. And the Communist Pharmacy, IYKYK.

Milinda Bannerjee for introducing me to the *Tribhanga* hip position.

Eliana Leztzer, whose memory could only be a blessing.

Zori for everything.

The City of Vienna's artist lockdown scheme, and the ÖH Queer-Fem Fund gave me one-off payments that helped me get through 2020. Berlin's InterTransBeratung Leben team went above and beyond helping me settle here.

Nina Kosmonin, who did more than anyone to prevent my arrival in Berlin becoming a crash landing. A warm meal when I needed one.

Flora – only I say Flo – for hours listening to this book's big ideas and fussy details, while freely sharing her knowledge of biochemistry, endocrinology, and skincare (... Not pharmacology!)

My late Linzer love Martina Salakova was the first to hear of *Hermaphrodite Logic*. Not easily wowed, she pressed me on the book's scope and focus with her usual cute intensity. Hope I've done her proud.

My calico Kiyfa curled up next to my writing desk throughout the balmy summer I wrote my first draft – a faithful distraction.

This book is dedicated to Fayoza. We met as I first began writing it, then migrated as wives while I redrafted. She saw this through in more ways than I could count, or list. Thank you.

The conclusion quotes from Aristophanes' Speech in Plato's *Symposium* (amended English translation from *Plato in Twelve Volumes*, vol. 9, by Harold N. Fowler), and the birth of Hermaphroditus in Ovid's *Metamorphoses* (English translation from Loeb Classical Library's Ovid, *Metamorphoses*, vol. 1, by Frank Justus Miller, revised by G. P. Goeld).

In truth, since a burning passion caused me to forsake this flesh . . .
You now will hear what – at first – was hidden, through my voice.

Notes

Preface

1. GLAAD and interACT, 'Fact Sheet: Olympic Boxers and Accurate Information about Participation and Eligibility', press release, 2 August 2024, glaad.org.

Introduction

1. The American Academy of Pediatrics, 'Evaluation of the Newborn with Developmental Anomalies of the External Genitalia', *Pediatrics* 106, no. 1 (2000).
2. David Andrew Griffiths, 'Shifting Syndromes: Sex Chromosome Variations and Intersex Classifications', *Social Studies of Science* 48, no. 1 (2018); Sarah S. Richardson, *Sex Itself: The Search for Male and Female in the Human Genome* (Chicago, IL: University of Chicago Press, 2013).
3. M. L. Barr and E. G. Bertram, 'A Morphological Distinction between Neurones of the Male and Female, and the Behaviour of the Nucleolar Satellite during Accelerated Nucleoprotein Synthesis', *Nature* 163, no. 4148 (1949): 676–7.

1. The Boston Revelation

1. AAP Division of Public Relations, 'Academy Leaders Attract Nationwide Press Coverage', *AAP News* 12, no. 12 (1996): 15.
2. Max Beck, 'Hermaphrodites with Attitude Take to the Streets', in 'Intersex Awakening', special issue, *Chrysalis* 2, no. 5 (Fall 1997): 45–6, 50. Throughout this chapter I'll also refer to Morgan Holmes's recollection of the events, around twenty years later: 'When Max Beck

and Morgan Holmes Went to Boston', Intersex Day, 17 October 2015, intersexday.org.

3. Anne Fausto-Sterling, 'The Five Sexes, Revisited', *Sciences* 40, no. 4 (July–August 2000).

4. Beyond Money's most obvious role as an author of manuals concerning intersex 'management', he also served as a prolific co-author of influential papers by specialists researching childhood hormonal development. For a thoroughgoing investigation of Money's most influential notions, including his account of 'hermaphroditism', check out Iain Morland, Lisa Downing, and Nikki Sullivan, *Fuckology: Critical Essays on John Money's Diagnostic Concepts* (Chicago: University of Chicago Press, 2014).

5. Several copies have been uploaded to YouTube, including through OII France's official account, and by intersex writer and performer Carta Monir.

6. 'Morgan Awarded M.A.!', *Hermaphrodites with Attitudes* 1, no. 1 (Winter 1994): 4.

7. David A. Rubin, '"An Unnamed Blank That Craved a Name": A Genealogy of Intersex as Gender', *Signs: Journal of Women in Culture and Society* 37, no. 4 (Summer 2012): 883–908.

8. Iain Morland, 'Cybernetic Sexology', in Downing, Morland, and Sullivan, *Fuckology*.

9. Beck, 'Hermaphrodites with Attitude Take to the Streets'.

10. Cheryl Chase, 'Cultural Practice or Reconstructive Surgery? US Genital Cutting, the Intersex Movement, and Medical Double Standards', in Stanlie M. James and Claire C. Robertson, eds, *Genital Cutting and Transnational Sisterhood: Disputing US Polemics* (Urbana: University of Illinois Press, 2002).

11. Beck, 'Hermaphrodites with Attitude Take to the Streets'.

12. For a comprehensive history of this divide between 'drugs in bodies' oriented activists and those who saw HIV/AIDS healthcare struggles as one front in a broader worldwide social struggle, see the opening chapters of Michelle O'Brien, 'Queer Movements and Class Politics in New York City' (PhD diss., New York University, 2021).

2. The Clinic Strikes Back

1. David Andrew Griffiths, 'Diagnosing Sex: Intersex Surgery and "Sex Change" in Britain 1930–1955', *Sexualities* 21, no. 3 (2018).

2. Throughout, my criticisms of the Chicago 'Consensus' are informed

by Paula Sandrine Machado, 'Intersexuality and the "Chicago Consensus": The Vicissitudes of Nomenclature and Their Regulatory Implications', trans. Eduardo Marques, *Revista Brasileira de Ciências Sociais* 4 (2008).

3. Here, I am echoing the arguments of feminist philosopher Catherine Clune-Taylor in her essay 'Securing Cisgendered Futures: Intersex Management under the "Disorders of Sex Development" Treatment Model', *Hypatia* 34, no. 4 (Fall 2019).

4. Barbara Thomas, 'Report to AISSG on Chicago Consensus Conference' (October 2005), 2006, formerly available at aissg.org.

5. Lih-Mei Liao, 'Western Management of Intersex and the Myth of Patient-Centred Care', in Megan Walker, ed., *Interdisciplinary and Global Perspectives on Intersex* (Cham: Palgrave Macmillan, 2022).

6. Machado, 'Intersexuality and the "Chicago Consensus"'.

7. How far Money was truly innovative in his formulation of 'original gender of rearing' is still up for discussion. Clearly, in referencing 'hermaphroditism' in humans, he was fully in continuity with the sexology of his era.

8. Peter A. Lee et al., 'Consensus Statement on Management of Intersex Disorders', *Pediatrics* 118, no. 2 (August 2006).

9. Emi Koyama, 'Questions and Answers about Intersex/DSD: Difficulty Goes beyond Simply Finding the Right Terminology', mailing list commentary, *Eminism* (blog), 5 February 2011, eminism.org.

10. Liao, 'Western Management of Intersex'.

11. Ricardo González and Barbara M. Ludwikowski, 'Should CAH in Females Be Classified as DSD?', *Frontiers in Pediatrics* 40 (2016).

12. Machado, 'Intersexuality and the "Chicago Consensus"'.

13. E. Eroğlu et al., 'Feminizing Surgical Management of Intersex Patients', *Pediatric Surgery International* 20 (2004).

14. González and Ludwikowski, 'Should CAH in Females Be Classified as DSD?'. Having read this paper several times, I would like to urgently call for more research into the brain composition of those who've passed through med school.

15. Elizabeth Reis, 'Who Stands under the Umbrella? The Politics of Naming and Categorizing Intersex', in *Bodies in Doubt: An American History of Intersex*, 2nd ed. (Baltimore: Johns Hopkins University Press, 2019).

16. Morgan Carpenter, 'The Human Rights of Intersex People: Addressing Harmful Practices and Rhetoric of Change', *Reproductive Health Matters* 24, no. 47 (2016).

17. Hida Viloria, 'What's in a Name: Intersex and Identity', op-ed, *Advocate*, 14 May 2014.

18. Nora Caplan-Bricker, 'Their Time: After Generations in the Shadows, the Intersex Movement Has a Message for This World: We Aren't Disordered and We Aren't Ashamed', *Washington Post*, 5 October 2017.

19. Morgan Holmes, 'Rethinking the Meaning and Management of Intersexuality', *Sexualities* 5, no. 2 (2002).

3. Bringing in the Intersex

1. The same year, the International Lesbian and Gay Human Rights Association awarded ISNA their annual Felipa de Souza Award following the success of their amicus brief to the Colombian high court in winning protections for local children. Laurent once again accepted.

2. Sandra Eder, 'From "Following the Push of Nature" to "Restoring One's Proper Sex": Cortisone and Sex at Johns Hopkins's Pediatric Endocrinology Clinic', *Endeavour* 36, no. 2 (June 2012).

3. In an interview with another intersex scholar and advocate, Georgiann Davis, historian of intersexuality in America Elizabeth Reis offered the following relevant reflection on this mismatch of epistemic approaches: 'The first thing that comes to my mind is the nature of different kinds of evidence. In history we don't call our evidence "data", and in science writing they do, but it's basically the same thing: it's the information – the facts or articulated claims – that you're pulling together as the basis for your arguments. As a historian, I found countless intersex adults saying that these surgeries performed on infants and children without their consent were misguided and wrong, human rights abuses, etc. That to me constitutes an abundance of evidence. But scientists looking for double-blind studies as their data see my kind of historical evidence as insufficient, just disgruntled, anecdotal stories from people who have been wronged. To me, this is a lesson that we can learn: there are varying kinds of evidence, and a first-hand account from a person who experienced something is a historian's goldmine. As a historian, listening to people's voices is key, and I would love it if scientists honored first-person accounts because it might give them a different perspective about the way they interpret their data.' Georgiann Davis, '*Bodies in Doubt*: A New and Expanded Edition: An Interview with Elizabeth Reis', *Nursing Clio* (blog), 26 October 2021, nursingclio.org.

4. Alice Dreger, 'Twenty Years of Working toward Intersex Rights', in Françoise Baylis and Alice Dreger, eds, *Bioethics in Action* (Cambridge: Cambridge University Press, 2018), 55–73

5. While Hausman's account of intersex surgeries as a key *technological* breakthrough remains influential in a sublimated way, the book's reception was limited by its historical narrative building towards an eccentric critique of 'transsexualism' (delivered in a 'love the sinner, hate the sin' style). For both of these reasons, Dreger's account proved more popular with the young feminists who propelled the next two decades' spiking interest in intersex.

6. Geertje Mak, '"So We Must Go behind Even What the Microscope Can Reveal": The Hermaphrodite's "Self" in Medical Discourse at the Start of the Twentieth Century', *GLQ* 11, no. 1 (2005).

7. John Money claimed he had originally preferred to think of sexology as 'fuckology', and the same trollish spirit was certainly retained in those who followed in his wake. This matter is best discussed in detail in another book, written by another author.

8. Much of this debate (but by no means all) is preserved on the original Organisation Intersex International – USA blog, oii-usa.blogspot.com. Among other articles: 'Cheryl Chase and Disorders of Sex Development (DSD)', 2 October 2006; 'Alice Dreger: DSD – Update and Response from the OII-UK', 2 October 2006; and a compendium: 'The DSD Chronicles', 6 October 2006.

9. Curtis Hinkle, 'Handbook for Parents Is Transphobic and Homophobic', Organisation Intersex International – USA blog, 21 September 2006, oii-usa.blogspot.com.

10. Ibid.

11. Emi Koyama, 'A Letter to Intersex Society of North America' and 'Statement on ISNA/BDRC Research Collaboration', *Intersex Critiques: Notes on Intersex, Disability and Biomedical Ethics* (Portland, OR: Confluere, 2003).

12. Ellen K. Feder, *Making Sense of Intersex: Changing Ethical Perspectives in Biomedicine* (Bloomington: Indiana University Press, 2014), 21.

13. Emi Koyama, 'Questions and Answers about Intersex/DSD: Difficulty Goes beyond Simply Finding the Right Terminology', mailing list commentary, *Eminism* (blog), 5 February 2011, eminism.org.

14. Danielle Chiriguayo, 'LA Has Zero Lesbian Bars. A New Wave of Queer Women Are Changing That', *Greater LA*, podcast, 17 June 2021, kcrw.com.

15. 'Evaluation of the Newborn with Developmental Anomalies of the External Genitalia', *Pediatrics* 106, no. 1 (2000): 138–42.

16. Robert Brandom, *Articulating Reasons: An Introduction to Inferentialism* (Cambridge, MA: Harvard University Press, 2000).

17. See three papers on shame as *recalcitrant*, in other words a persistent response to stigmatisation: Phil Hutchinson and Rageshri Dhairyawan, 'Shame, Stigma, HIV: Philosophical Reflections', *Medical Humanities* 43, no. 4 (December 2017): 225–30; Phil Hutchinson and Rageshri Dhairyawan, 'Shame and HIV: Strategies for Addressing the Negative Impact Shame Has on Public Health and Diagnosis and Treatment of HIV', *Bioethics* 32, no. 1 (January 2018): 68–76; Phil Hutchinson, 'Stigma Respecified: Investigating HIV Stigma as an Interactional Phenomenon', *Journal of Evaluation in Clinical Practice* 28, no. 5 (2022): 861–6.

18. Tony Kirby, 'PrEP Finally Approved on NHS in England', *Lancet*, 28 March 2020.

19. Jeremy W. Peters, 'The Decline and Fall of the "H" Word', *New York Times*, 21 March 2014.

20. Philosopher Charles Taylor's work on identity sets up a distinction between what he calls 'moral intuitions' and mere reactions on the basis of whether wider implications can be articulated or assessed on grounds that 'involve claims, implicit or explicit, about the nature and status of human beings'. In calling the sense of solidarity that the '90s gay/lesbian movement clearly felt for intersex people 'visceral', Feder's clear implication is that the perceived commonality was *not* one of fully-fledged moral intuition. She is wrong. Did the gay/lesbian and intersex movement have a shared 'ontology of the human', in Taylor's sense? Whether or not they did, it seems reasonable to conclude that the alliance was a morally intuitive one: not a knee-jerk or turning of the stomach, but a basic sense that 'homosexual' and 'intersexual' had passed through a comparable struggle in light of society's overarching domination by mandatory heterosexuality. It was for that reason the term 'heterosexism' appeared seamlessly in Kessler's assessment of intersex 'management' in the 1980s. That both terms (intersexual and homosexual) have since faded from use is beside the point: the sense of solidarity was real in the 1990s, and has continued since in other forms and with other idioms. Charles Taylor, *Sources of the Self: The Making of the Modern Identity* (Cambridge, MA: Harvard University Press, 1989), 5.

21. David Rubin, *Intersex Matters: Biomedical Embodiment, Gender Regulation, and Transnational Activism* (Albany: State University of New York Press, 2017), 143.

22. Catherine Clune-Taylor, 'From Intersex to DSD: The Disciplining of Sex Development' *PhænEx* 5, no. 2 (2010).

23. Morgan Holmes, *Intersex: A Perilous Difference* (Selinsgrove, PA: Susquehanna University Press, 2008), 44.

24. Emi Koyama, '"Five Sexes": In Response to Inquiry', forum commentary, *Eminism* (blog), 9 September 2000, eminism.org.

25. This example is an off note in an otherwise excellent and groundbreaking collection of scholarship. To her credit, Stryker does cite the books of Dreger, Fausto-Sterling, and Kessler, hopefully directing many readers towards a meatier view.

26. Georgiann Davis, 'The Transformation of Intersex Advocacy', in *Contesting Intersex: The Dubious Diagnosis* (New York: New York University Press, 2015).

27. Emi Koyama, 'Frequently Asked Questions about the "DSD" Controversy', Intersex Initiative, 29 June 2008, ipdx.org.

28. Julia Serano, *Whipping Girl: A Transsexual Woman on Sexism and the Scapegoating of Femininity* (Emeryville, CA: Seal Press, 2016), 210–11.

29. Alice Dreger, 'The Dex Diaries, Part 1: Changed in the Womb', *Psychology Today*, 15 August 2012, psychologytoday.com.

30. Dreger's own account of this affair is found on her website: 'The Cutting and the Vibrators Continue', 11 November 2015, alicedreger. com, following from a co-written piece: Alice Dreger and Ellen K. Feder, 'Bad Vibrations', Hastings Center, Bioethics Forum Essay, 16 June 2010, thehastingscenter.org.

31. 'Update: Cornell Responds to Criticism of "Genital Sensitivity" Testing; Federal Agency Continues Inquiry', Advocates for Informed Choice, aiclegal.wordpress.com.

32. Jennifer Yang, Diane Felsen, and Dix P. Poppas, 'Nerve Sparing Ventral Clitoroplasty: Analysis of Clitoral Sensitivity and Viability', *Journal of Urology* 178, no. 4 (October 2007).

33. 'Weill Medical College Says Poppas' Surgical Procedure Is Standard', *Cornell Daily Sun*, 4 October 2020, cornellsun.com.

34. Casey Orozco-Poore and Alex S. Keuroghlian, 'Neurological Considerations for "Nerve-Sparing" Cosmetic Genital Surgeries Performed on Children with XX Chromosomes Diagnosed with 21-Hydroxylase

Congenital Adrenal Hyperplasia and Clitoromegaly', *LGBT Health* 10, no. 8 (November–December 2023): 567–75.

35. Cynthia Kraus et al., 'Démédicaliser les corps, politiser les identités: convergences des luttes féministes et intersexes', *Nouvelles Questions Féministes* 27, no. 1 (2008): 4–15.

36. Morgan Holmes, 'Deciding the Fate or Protecting a Developing Autonomy? Intersex Children and the Colombian Constitutional Court', in Paisley Currah, Richard M. Juang, and Shannon Price Minter, eds, *Transgender Rights* (Minneapolis: University of Minnesota Press, 2006); Julia Sandra Bernal Crespo, 'Estados intersexuales en menores de edad: Los principios de autonomía y beneficencia', *Revista de Derecho* 36 (July/December 2011); and David A. Rubin, 'Provincializing Intersex: US Intersex Activism, Human Rights, and Transnational Body Politics', *Frontiers: A Journal of Women Studies* 36, no. 3 (2015): 51–83.

37. Ulrike Klöppel, 'Wer hat das Recht zum Geschlechtswechsel? Juristische und medizinische Grenzziehungen zwischen Inter- und Transsexualität, 1945 bis 1980', in *XXoXY ungelöst: Hermaphroditismus, Sex und Gender in der deutschen Medizin. Eine historische Studie zur Intersexualität* (Bielefeld: Transcript, 2010), also published in English a year earlier as 'Who Has the Right to Change Gender Status? Drawing Boundaries between Inter- and Transsexuality', in Morgan Holmes, ed., *Critical Intersex* (London: Routledge, 2016).

38. Leon L. Solomon, 'Hermaphroditism: Report of a Case of Apparently True Hermaphroditism with Photographs of the "Woman"', *Medical Record* 35 (1929), quoted in Elizabeth Reis, *Bodies In Doubt: An American History of Intersex*, 2nd ed. (Baltimore: Johns Hopkins University Press, 2019), 83–4.

39. 'The first is sort of semantic, but very real. My ten years of work on medical reform in intersex care had taught me that you just can't get doctors and patient advocates to agree on what you're talking about when you use the term "intersex". Even the most sane, smart, pro-intersex-rights docs and patient advocates can't seem to agree on which conditions count. To state the obvious, if you can't get people to agree on what you're talking about, you can't get anywhere. I was spending so much energy playing the "Is CAH intersex? Is AIS intersex? Is hypospadias intersex? Is Klinefelter Syndrome intersex?" name game that I couldn't get people to talk about the (problematic) clinical practices that all these conditions had in common.

As I work on the handbooks, I know that affected individuals, their families, and their clinicians will all be better off if we can get them to see that a multi-disciplinary team approach that focuses on long-term psychosocial well-being is the way to go for all of these conditions. But first we have to get them to see them as alike – as fitting under some logical umbrella term. And "intersex" isn't going to be the one. It doesn't work.'

40. Dani Coyle, 'Anick Soni', *Inter_View: An Intersex Podcast*, 31 January 2022.

41. Curtis Hinkle, 'Why We Do Not Use "Disorder of Sex Development"', OII-UK, Intersex in the UK, 12 February 2014, oiiuk.org.

42. Mauro Cabral Grinspan, 'The Marks on Our Bodies', Intersex Day, 25 October 2015, intersexday.org.

4. Herms as Humans

1. Ashutosh Pandey, 'A Timeline of IAAF Doping Scandal', dw.com, 11 September 2015.

2. Donald McRae, 'The Return of Caster Semenya: Olympic Favourite and Ticking Timebomb', *Guardian*, 29 July 2016.

3. Ockert de Villiers, 'South Africa: Caster Semenya – "I Try to Do Crazy Stuff"', New Frame, 15 February 2020.

4. Robyn Dixon, 'Gender Issue Has Always Chased Her', *Los Angeles Times*, 21 August 2009, quoted in the introduction to Lena Eckert, *Intersexualization: The Clinic and the Colony* (New York: Routledge, 2017).

5. Hans Lindahl, 'Intersex Youth React to the Discriminatory Ruling against Caster Semenya', *them*, 2 May 2019, them.us.

6. While Zine Magubane's analysis of the particular valences of this discussion in South Africa and assessment of intersex-phobic feminist reactions are invaluable, this account relies overly on Dreger and Herndon's *GLQ* piece for its summation of existing scholarship. Zine Magubane, 'Spectacles and Scholarship: Caster Semenya, Intersex Studies, and the Problem of Race in Feminist Theory', *Signs: Journal of Women in Culture and Society* 39, no. 3 (Spring 2014).

7. Amanda Shalala, 'Intersex Runner Annet Negesa Fighting for Everyone's Right to Compete in Sport', ABC News, 11 March 2023.

8. Laine Higgins, 'The Study That Blocked Caster Semenya from the Tokyo Olympics Has Been Corrected by Its Publishers', *Wall Street Journal*, 19 August 2021.

9. Ruth Padawer, 'The Humiliating Practice of Sex-Testing Female Athletes', *New York Times*, 28 June 2016.

10. Aisha Salaudeen, 'Growing Up Intersex in a Country Where It Is Believed to Be Bad Luck', *Inside Africa*, CNN, 22 September 2019.

11. Nthabiseng Mokoena, Interface Project video transcript, Stockholm, Sweden, 10 December 2012, interfaceproject.org.

12. 'CHR Commends African Commission on Adoption of First Resolution on Intersex Persons in Africa', Centre for Human Rights, University of Pretoria, 22 March 2023, chr.up.ac.za.

13. Helen Grady and Anne Soy, 'The Midwife Who Saved Intersex Babies', BBC News, 4 May 2017.

14. Alex Adamson, 'Beyond the Coloniality of Gender: María Lugones, Sylvia Wynter, Decolonial Feminism, and Trans and Intersex Liberation', *Philosophy and Global Affairs* 2, no. 2 (2022).

15. Tellingly, they used the word 'clinical' as a pretext for sidestepping the ethical considerations and sincere engagement with legacies of imperialism that had preoccupied much of cultural anthropology.

5. A Struggle without a Centre

1. Andreas Kyriakou et al., 'Current Models of Care for Disorders of Sex Development – Results from an International Survey of Specialist Centres', *Orphanet Journal of Rare Diseases* 11 (2016).

2. Georgiann Davis, 'What's Marriage Equality Got to Do with Intersex?', *Contexts* blog, 7 July 2015, contexts.org.

3. Intersex Greece, 'Words Hurt: Hate Speech against Intersex People in Greece', YouTube, 26 October 2022.

4. 'Victory for Greece – Intersex Genital Mutilation Has Been Banned!', interACT, 20 July 2022, interactadvocates.org.

5. 'How Activism Led the Way Forward to Protect Intersex Children in Greece', ILGA-Europe, 10 November 2022, ilga-europe.org.

6. Meiwita Budiharsana, 'Female Genital Cutting Common in Indonesia, Offered as Part of Child Delivery by Birth Clinics', *Conversation*, 16 February 2016, theconversation.com.

7. Ino Kehrer, 'Towards an Inclusive Approach to Harmful Practices: The Case of Western Elective Surgeries on Intersex Children', in Megan Walker, ed., *Interdisciplinary and Global Perspectives on Intersex* (Cham: Palgrave Macmillan, 2022); Fae Garland and Mitchell Travis, 'Legislating Intersex Equality: Building the Resilience of Intersex People through Law', *Legal Studies* 38, no. 4 (2018).

8. IGLYO, OII Europe, and EPA, *Supporting Your Intersex Child: A Parents' Toolkit* (Brussels: IGLYO, 2018).

9. Enrique Anarte, 'Germany Bans Surgeries on Intersex Babies, but Loopholes Feared', Reuters, 26 March 2021.

10. Bhakti Ananda Goswami, 'About the Term Intersex Versus the Term DSD', OII Intersex Network, 18 January 2010, oiiinternational.com.

11. Ina Linge, 'The Potency of the Butterfly: The Reception of Richard B. Goldschmidt's Animal Experiments in German Sexology around 1920', *History of the Human Sciences* 34, no. 1 (2021): 40–70.

12. It later was confirmed that freemartin fetuses were exposed to androgens and anti-Müllerian hormone through shared blood pathways, before absorbing XY genetics *in utero,* resulting in a calf chimera.

13. Richard Goldschmidt, 'Intersexuality and the Endocrine Aspect of Sex', *Endocrinology* 1, no. 4 (October 1917): 433–56. This paper has been made freely available with an introduction by Intersex Human Rights Australia, 13 November 2009, ihra.org.au.

14. Nathan Q. Ha, 'Diagnosing Sex Chromatin: A Binary for Every Cell', *Historical Studies in the Natural Sciences* 45, no. 1 (2015).

15. Alisa L. Rich et al., 'The Increasing Prevalence in Intersex Variation from Toxicological Dysregulation in Fetal Reproductive Tissue Differentiation and Development by Endocrine-Disrupting Chemicals', *Environmental Health Insights* 10 (2016): 163–71.

16. Sara Reardon, 'The Spectrum of Sex Development: Eric Vilain and the Intersex Controversy', *Nature* 533 (May 2016).

17. Jenny Kleeman, '"We Don't Know If Your Baby's a Boy or a Girl": Growing Up Intersex', *Guardian*, 2 July 2016.

18. Linda A. Hatfield, 'Neonatal Pain: What's Age Got to Do with It?', *Surgical Neurology International* 5 (2014): S479–89.

19. Human Rights Watch and interACT, *A Changing Paradigm: US Medical Provider Discomfort with Intersex Care Practices* (Washington, DC: Human Rights Watch, 2017).

20. 'US: Harmful Surgery on Intersex Children: Medically Unnecessary Operations Risk Lifelong Suffering', Human Rights Watch, 25 July 2017, hrw.org.

21. Hida Viloria was the first intersex person to appear on Oprah after the movement started, in 2007.

22. Mish O'Brien, 'Holistic Medicine without Autonomy!', OII Intersex Network, 13 November 2013, oiiinternational.com.

23. Morgan Carpenter, 'Bioethicists and Paediatric Surgeons Debate Intersex Medical Interventions', Intersex Human Rights Australia, 6 July 2020, ihra.org.au.

24. 'AAP Recognizes Intersex Awareness Day', American Academy of Pediatrics, available at intersexday.org, 29 October 2017.

25. Pidgeon Pagonis, 'How Pidgeon Pagonis Helped End Intersex Surgeries at Lurie', interview by Lauren Williamson, *Chicago*, 21 September 2020, chicagomag.com.

26. Nico Lang, 'Activists Got a Chicago Children's Hospital to End Intersex Surgeries. For Them, It's Just the Beginning', Buzzfeed, 4 August 2020.

27. Wall describes his experiences in 'Intersex', in Keywords Feminist Editorial Collective, eds, *Keywords for Gender and Sexuality Studies* (New York: New York University Press, 2021). Kyle Knight, 'Protest Demands End to Harmful Surgeries on Intersex Children; Hospital Should Halt Medically Unnecessary Surgeries', Human Rights Watch, 2 September 2021, hrw.org.

28. Elizabeth Reis, '*Bodies in Doubt: An American History of Intersex*', interview, *Notches* (blog), 3 March 2022, notchesblog.com.

29. The border between intersex advocacy and research has always been porous: At the start of the 2020s, Wall moved to Britain to begin a PhD exploring intersex issues in public policy.

30. By this point, the intersex movement had mostly come to avoid using the term 'mutilation', deeming it re-traumatising for those who'd been through the worst of this cutting. Today 'non-consensual genital cutting' is mostly used instead, although of course personal self-understandings may be considerably less erudite.

31. Kiara Alfonseca and Mary Kekatos, 'Amid Transgender Care Bans, Exceptions Made for Surgery on Intersex Children', ABC News, 18 July 2023.

32. Vasilis Sotiropoulos, 'The Rights of Intersex Persons in Greece', Heinrich Böll Stiftung, Thessaloniki, 2 August 2022, gr.boell.org.

33. This reading follows from Malcolm Bull's gloss of Du Bois from 'Coming into Hiding: Master–Slave Dialectic', in *Seeing Things Hidden: Apocalypse, Vision and Totality* (London: Verso, 1999). I'm also grateful for Bull's reading of Charles Taylor. I have avoided working through Bull's distinction of hidden/apocalypse explicitly, in favour of hidden/revealed throughout this book, mostly to avoid upsetting delicate sensibilities.

34. Whether Fanon drew this from Du Bois or directly from his own

reading of Hegel is unclear to their scholars, and not especially relevant for our purposes.

6. Sex in the Wreckage

1. Iain Morland, '"The Glans Opens Like a Book": Writing and Reading the Intersexed Body', *Continuum* 19, no. 3 (2005): 339.

2. Christopher Breu, '*Middlesex* Meditations: Understanding and Teaching Intersex', *English Journal* 98, no. 4 (March 2009): 102–8; Rachel Carroll, 'Retrospective Sex: Rewriting Intersexuality in Jeffrey Eugenides's *Middlesex*', *Journal of American Studies* 44, no. 1 (February 2010): 187–201.

3. Christopher Breu, *In Defense of Sex: Nonbinary Embodiment and Desire* (New York: Fordham University Press, 2024).

4. As then OII Europe co-chair Miriam Van der Have puts it in her 'post-medical definition', intersex describes 'the lived experience of the socio-cultural consequences of being born with a body that does not fit with normative social constructions of male and female'. See in full: 'Intersex issues in the International Classification of Diseases (ICD)' (2016).

5. Alex Jürgen, Interface Project video transcript, Neumarkt, Austria, 2 May 2013, interfaceproject.org.

6. Enrique Anarte and Rachel Savage, 'Austria Issues First Intersex Birth Certificate after Four-Year Battle', Reuters, 16 July 2020.

7. Katrina Karkazis, *Fixing Sex: Intersex, Medical Authority, and Lived Experience* (Durham, NC: Duke University Press, 2008), 222–3.

8. Pidgeon Pagonis, 'The Son They Never Had', *Narrative Inquiry in Bioethics* 5, no. 2 (Summer 2015): 103–6.

9. Sydneykidneybean, 'Finding Out I Was Intersex', TikTok, October 2022. Sydney was later interviewed by advocate Blume for the *Interesting & SeXY* podcast in the video 'SYDNEY: Intersex TikTok Star', YouTube, 15 September 2023.

10. Emily Quinn, 'Stand Up', *Narrative Inquiry in Bioethics* 5, no. 2 (2015).

11. Sean Saifa Wall, 'Navigating Life as a Black Intersex Man', *Narrative Inquiry in Bioethics* 5, no. 2 (2015).

12. John L. Delk, R. Burt Madden, Mary Livingston, and Timothy T. Ryan, 'Adult Perceptions of the Infant as a Function of Gender Labeling and Observer Gender', *Sex Roles* 15 (1986). Discussed by Rebecca Jordan-Young in 'Taking Context Seriously'.

13. In other words, if you're keeping score of the sexology jargon, not reducible to John Money's cybernetics terminology of 'feedback' (as

invoked by Max Beck in 1996), nor the preferred 'cascade' mechanism of brain organisation theory.

14. Anne Fausto-Sterling, 'A Dynamic Systems Framework for Gender/ Sex Development: From Sensory Input in Infancy to Subjective Certainty in Toddlerhood', *Frontiers in Human Neuroscience* 15 (April 2021).

15. 'If she's helping other doctors to learn about it, that's fine. But when she gets older I don't want everyone poking and prodding her, and every doctor experience to be, "I've got to look between your legs."'

Conclusion

1. Cary Gabrielle Costello, 'Intersex and Trans* Communities: Commonalities and Tensions', in Stefan Horlacher, ed., *Transgender and Intersex: Theoretical, Practical, and Artistic Perspectives* (New York: Palgrave Macmillan, 2016).

2. Alex Adamson, 'Beyond the Coloniality of Gender: María Lugones, Sylvia Wynter, Decolonial Feminism, and Trans and Intersex Liberation', *Philosophy and Global Affairs* 2, no. 2 (2022).

Index